Resurrection

Table of Contents

Chapter 1

    It's Over...1

    The Joke was On Me..10

Chapter 2

    Learning to Jail..13

    F Ward..18

    The Ranch..22

    Meet the Boss..30

Chapter 3

    Growing up/The Irish Riviera..38

    Giro's Café...43

    Blast from the Past...49

Chapter 4

    Body Shop Blues..51

    Flying...53

    Marty's Boys..57

    No One Gives a Shit..60

Chapter 5

    Quincy Junior College..64

    The Combat Zone...66

    Kenmore Square...74

    Bank Robbery and Other Job Opportunities................................78

    Flix...80

    Quincy District Court...83

    The Rat..87

Chapter 6

    Okinawa...89

    MSP..95

    East Bum Fuck...98

Reckoning..108

Chapter 7

Cool Cash..112

Pain Spotting..121

Chapter 8

Bump and Run..125

Cold Feet..127

Chinatown..129

Chapter 9

Nuts and Bolts..142

Billy the Greek..146

Club Soda..151

Chapter 10

Tale of Two Banks..158

Badger and Flashlight..163

Be Prepared..165

    Killing Field..169

    Dead End...171

    Hard Ball...177

    Shit Storm...180

    Red Head Ginger Bread..182

Chapter 11

    Mind Field..185

    Bottoming Out..191

    Edgehill Newport..197

Chapter 12

    Re-Entry...202

    Berkshire County..203

    Westward Ho..206

    Berkshire Follies...209

    The Rat from the Rat..210

Chapter 13

Babbling Bean..214

Chapter 14

Concord Prison..220

MCI Norfolk..226

BU Prison School..234

Bad Moon Rising..237

Big House Bug House..242

Future Tense..250

MCI Shithole..254

Second Thoughts..258

Chapter 15

Old World..266

Job Fair..271

Chapter 16

Sandhog..277

Tunnel Nuts..282

Chapter 17

    All Lies..285

    Reunion...289

Chapter 18

    Boyos...293

    Out of Work but Not Out of Luck..297

    In For a Pound..299

Chapter 19

    NCSO...302

    Jail Do..305

Chapter 20

    Bouncing back and Back Bouncing..312

Page

It's Over

April 1986

It was supposed to be my last score, an armored car robbery that would yield a million dollars or more. I had been involved in successful bank jobs before, but no score delivered what armored trucks did after they dropped off or picked up from a bank.

I had a crew from prior jobs, plus one new guy. The heist had been planned meticulously. Once a week for almost two months, I'd driven from Boston to Williamstown always coming at the town from a different direction, and always dressed in a suit with a briefcase and wearing glasses. Already parked in the bank's lot when the Berkshire Armored Carrier (BAC) arrived, I'd get out when the guards got out and walk past the truck slow enough to get a good look at the cargo. It always transported between ten and fourteen bags of cash. I guessed there was at least a million there, probably more.

The Williamstown score had one big problem. The small town, located in a valley in the northwestern corner of Massachusetts, had only one way in and one way out. It was a given that we'd hit the BAC cleanly. Escaping after was another story. There would be roadblocks, and unlike after an earlier bank job in Pittsfield, no house to hole up in later.

Giving him a fifty thousand dollar cut I brought in an old friend, the Greek. We'd done a lot of work together in the past, and I knew I could trust him. We did a hit in Rhode Island once at a big discount store specializing in overstock and manufacturers' closeout merchandise. They had an armored truck cash delivery every Tuesday morning. The guard got out and carried a satchel into the place.

The store was huge, and the Greek and I were waiting for him in the sporting goods section, some eighty yards inside, me on one side of the aisle the Greek on the other. When the guard came between us we had him, like in a vise, with guns to his head. He dropped the bag and we took his weapon, made him lie on the floor, and we were gone.

A couple of aisles over, a double door led into to the warehouse area of the building. We walked through them nice and calm, made it to the side door, and went out the opposite end of the building from where the truck was parked. Another trusted friend, Tank, was out there in a burner (stolen car), listening to a Madonna tape. We left the lot and switched to another burner a half-mile down the road behind a half empty strip mall. It was as slick as it was supposed to be. The bad news? The score netted only a disappointing $35,000.00.

Two months later we hit another armored truck guard inside a shopping mall in Massachusetts. We nailed him inside the door of a department store, but once again the take, a lousy $28,000.00, was lousy. Frustrated I said, "No more of this shit risking our lives. Next time we take the whole truck."

The plan for Williamstown called for the Greek to transport the money back to Boston. Following the robbery, miles from the bank, we would rendezvous with the Greek, his girlfriend and grandchild in a North Adams parking lot, not far from Williamstown. Accompanying him would be Tommy H., a South End hoodlum, and a mutual friend from the Franklin Café. Tommy would bring his wife along also, and two of their grandchildren. The money and guns, already packed into two large hockey equipment bags, would go into their station wagon, and they would take a lazy route home. If they ran into a police roadblock, they were just tourists with their grandkids out for a spring drive in western MA, and be waved right through.

I never doubted that if we got to North Adams we'd be home free. Along with the Greek and his station wagon, two other cars would also be waiting. Bean and I would take one into Vermont, drive across New Hampshire then down into Boston. Sean and Danny would drive the other to Pittsfield and take the Mass Pike home.

On April 2nd just before noon, in a parking lot across the street from the Bank of New England, three of us huddled in the back of the van with Bean at the wheel. I had stolen the van a week earlier from a South Shore car dealership. Back in Southie, I had lettered its sides with the name of a fictitious company, *Kyle's Expert Carpentry*, and beneath it a real Pittsfield address and phone exchange. If someone happened to notice the van in the lot, Bean was probably just a carpenter eating his lunch.

To further protect us from prying eyes, I had spray-painted the rear windows black. If someone with X-ray vision could have looked inside the van though they would have seen three men in ski masks wearing bulletproof vests outside their jackets. See, the thinking was wearing the vests in plain view would be a clear deterrent. When the BAC guards saw them they would realize they'd need a head shot to stop us, hopefully compromising their willingness to fight.

Sean had a pistol on his hip and carried an Uzi Model 8, 9mm rifle with a thirty-round clip. I had a Mossberg twelve gauge with extra rounds. Danny carried two pistols. Because Bean was a nervous wreck, we didn't trust him with a weapon.

The Bank of New England West had a driveway on either side of the building. The BAC would approach the bank, traveling east on Main Street, then turn right into the second driveway, follow it around the back of the building and end up on the other side facing the street.

The first guard would get out, walk to the back and rap on the rear door. After the driver hit the button that released the rear door lock, he'd get out himself, head to the rear, and help his partner unload. That's when we'd hit them.

When Bean saw the rear door swing open, he'd drive across Main Street and follow the same route the truck had around the building. Timed perfectly, the BAC driver would be just about to the rear while, in the approaching van, I'd open the side door and hit the ground running, catching both guards by surprise.

We would hit them fast and hard and, like a cloudburst, be gone. It all depended on the driver remaining cool, not moving too slowly or quickly. Bean could make up for his past mistakes by getting this right.

A few minutes before the BAC was due a citizen walked by the front of the van, and for some reason, paused and looked in at Bean. From where I sat, I could see the top of the guy's head. I watched Bean give him a nod, and continue to drink his coffee.

I whispered, "What the fuck's he doing?"

"I dunno," Bean said. He nodded again as the guy walked away. "It was like he recognized me or something."

It had to be Bean's beard. He looked like every other yokel up there.

What the hell was I thinking asking this guy in?

I swore if we pulled this off, I'd never work with Bean again.

The BAC showed up late, at 12:15. I watched it make the loop, then come to a stop on the other side facing the street. The guard stepped out and went to the rear. I tapped Bean's shoulder, "Go," I said, "nice and fucking slow."

But as we drove around the back of the bank, Bean was picking up speed. The driver wasn't out yet. I said to Bean, "Slow down, slow down."

Then the driver's door popped and his boots hit the ground, but Bean had us moving too quickly. I had no choice but to throw open the side door, leap out, and run. All the months of high impact aerobics paid off as I shouldered the shotgun and screamed at the guards, "Hands up, hands up!"

But once again the unexpected happened. The driver, caught between his own open compartment and the rear of the truck, bolted back and climbed inside, slamming the door.

I was caught now between the armed guard behind me and the driver. The van screeched to a stop and Sean jumped out with the Uzi.

It was like an earlier robbery where things went so wrong one of us was killed. I was not going to allow this to happen again.

I rammed the shotgun barrel into the driver's side window and screamed, "Get out, get the fuck out!" I stepped back and aimed at his face. This time no one would to shoot us from inside the truck. "Get out, now!" I roared.

The driver threw his hands up and I heard a muffled, "Don't shoot. Don't shoot."

He opened the door and started to slide out, but furious and pumped with adrenalin, I reached in and ripped him out. He felt like a rag doll as I shoved him ahead of me, disarmed him and then used him as a shield as we moved toward the back of the truck.

What was out of control was under again, just like that.

When I initially jumped from the van the first guard had bolted to the opposite side of the truck. I shouted now for him to come out and he did, both hands reaching for sky. He nervously lowered one hand, his fingers searching, finding, then tugging a string on the holster that allowed his gun belt to drop to the ground.

Both guards lying face down, with me standing over them, Sean jumped into the back of the truck and started tossing bags to Danny, who lobbed them into the van. I knew we had this. I said, "This is fucking beautiful."

Just before a voice behind me shouted, "Freeze, Williamstown Police!"

I looked over my shoulder. Fifty feet from where I stood, on a side road that ran parallel to the parking lot, a cop aimed his gun at me over the roof of his patrol car.

When he shouted, "I said freeze, Williamstown police!" I heard Sean's maniacal laugher coming from inside the truck.

Pivoting, I aimed the shotgun at the cop's head, and he quickly dropped behind the patrol car. I wouldn't shoot unless he shot at me first.

The van loaded with money, we raced out of the parking lot with the cruiser right behind us, siren blaring. By now every cop in the valley had to have been alerted. As we sped down

Main Street I was standing up in back of the van, struggling to maintain my balance and unable to see out the rear windows. I expected bullets to riddle the rear doors any moment.

A quarter mile down the road Bean almost lost control turning into the Colonial Shopping Center. He drove in behind a building where, half an hour earlier, we'd stashed a Toyota truck with a camper on its back. On the rear bumper a yellow sticker read: *The One Who Dies with The Most 'Toys' Wins.*

The money was already packed into a huge hockey equipment bag by the time we skidded up next to the truck. While the others climbed into the camper Sean and I yanked the heavy bag out and tossed it in behind them.

Assuming the role of driver, I jumped behind the Toyota's wheel and punched the accelerator, shouting "Everyone down." Ducking under the dash myself as we came out from behind the building, I expected a fusillade of bullets, but nothing happened. Danny was screaming through the tiny window in back of my head, "Rick, sit up, there aren't any cops. You're going to fucking kill us."

He was right. When we had turned into the strip mall, the cop behind us had apparently kept going. He reported later that he had lost us—a white van three hundred feet in front of him with nothing in between—after we made the turn. It didn't matter why, I was ecstatic and thought we were home safe.

The escape route took us up the side of Mount Greylock, the tallest mountain in Massachusetts, then onto some old logging roads that, on at least a dozen occasions, we had practiced driving over at high speeds. Once we were on the other side of the mountain a series of back roads would take us to North Adams Center, where the disposal team waited.

But things aren't meant to be sometimes.

The day after the robbery a headline in the local newspaper, *Berkshire Eagle*, read: *Residents puzzled by 'escape route.'* Apparently, many locals questioned why we'd chosen the route we did. The consensus being, we could have never escaped on those narrow roads.

I have no doubt though that we would have escaped if two things hadn't happened. An ambulance attendant eating lunch in the parking lot of the Colonial Shopping Center was listening to the chase on his scanner. He saw a white van, watched it drive in back of the building, and then watched a Toyota truck with a camper roar out immediately after. He reported this to police.

In the end the thing that finished us was something that I had considered a possibility, yet was willing to ignore. Somewhere up on the mountain there was a guy inside a house listening to the pursuit on a scanner as we passed. He contacted authorities and told them that a truck and camper had passed by, "Going like hell."

At the bottom of the mountain, a half-mile from North Adams Center, we ran into a roadblock manned by a half dozen cops with long guns. I rolled to a stop one hundred feet away and, in an attempt to buy us some time, waved at them over the steering wheel. It had the desired effect. Police heads popped up and they lowered their guns. Maybe they'd made a mistake?

I heard sirens approaching in the mountain behind us then the sound of a shotgun being racked and someone tugging back on the Uzi's receiver. Danny stuck his big head through the opening behind me and said. "Rick, what do you want to do? Up to you man."

I thought about throwing the truck into reverse, grabbing the weapons, and hitting the woods. Hadn't we shot our way out of trouble before? But it was at that exact moment that I heard the voice, loud as hell, a command in my head. *"It's over."*

In all the years that have passed since the Williamstown robbery, and as often as I have told this story, I have no doubt, none, that it was God telling me it was over that day.

Dumbstruck, I repeated His words, "It's over," I said.

"What?"

I repeated it louder, "It's over. No one's been shot and we're not getting out of here. Put the guns down."

The Joke Was On Me

Later, alone in a cell, I thought about the voice I heard, and I guess I wasn't surprised. That morning, after I left my apartment, I had gone out to the parking lot to find one of my recently bought tires completely flat. It was a bad omen, seriously bad, but what could I do? There were others, solid Southie men, depending on me to be there today.

Then I got another bad sign. When I arrived at the rendezvous point, Kelly's Landing in South Boston, everyone else arrived late. They're treating this like a game I thought, and then I thought I'm dying today.

But I was in now, part of it, so I couldn't back out.

So, there I was face down on the street with a shotgun pinning my head, and two things became remarkably clear: I wasn't dying today, and my bank-robbing career was over. I looked at Brian Bean laying next me. Tears were streaming down his face.

I tried to calm him. "It's okay, Brian, relax," I said. In his eyes the fear was evident. And it wasn't just fear. Bean was terrified.

He was taken off the street first and led to a cruiser. I learned later that he began giving me up then, telling the cops everything that he knew about me. At the North Adams police station, Bean was locked up in a separate block and I had been in my cell for less than ten minutes when a cop approached the bars and asked if I'd been a state trooper? I didn't respond but wondered how the hell he knew?

Over the course of the next five hours every cop in North Adams, even some firemen, came in to inspect us like we were caged tigers.

Curious about the take, how much we had actually got—the tag on one of the bags said $250,000.00—I asked a cop if they had made a tally. When he returned and told me the take was just over eight hundred thousand. I was shocked because I expected a lot more.

When Sean, Danny and Bean were arraigned the next day, in Northern Berkshire District Court, the DA announced to the packed courtroom that the take was six hundred and sixty-thousand dollars. Wait, something was wrong. We had taken every bag a total of seven. Where did all the money go?

Then it got crazier. By the time my lawyer arrived from Boston and accompanied me to my own arraignment, they had a new tally the take now was $435,000.00. Baffled, I decided one of two things happened. Either the cops themselves had stolen the money, which I didn't believe, or the Berkshire Armored Transport Service had purposely kept the total low, so no one would get any ideas. Years later, after Watson nailed the BAC depository in Pittsfield[1], I would learn that this was SOP for the company.

Bail was set at five hundred thousand cash, no surety, for each of us. The first tangible proof that something was up with my former friend, Bean, came the morning after our first night in jail. I woke up to him singing, in the cell below mine, the Police song, *Roxanne*, the same song the Eddie Murphy character sang in the movie *48 Hours*, after he was locked up. Bean was acting like this was a joke.

It didn't take long to realize the joke was on me.

Within days, Bean's bail was mysteriously reduced to fifty thousand cash, which his family put up and Bean was gone. Soon after his release, I got word from the street that Bean not only was ratting the crew out but telling anyone who would listen that I was the one cooperating with police. Unfortunately, that's how it works. Someone flips and the first thing they do is point their finger at somebody else.

I admit there were probably believers because, out of everyone, I had the most to lose. I would be entering the prison system not just an ex-cop, but as a former state trooper. Convicts despise them because when prisons erupt and riot-trained guards lose control, it's the state police, known for their heavy handedness, who are called in.

That I had left the MSP after only a short time on the job didn't matter. I had no delusions about the type of pressure I would be under, but my attitude was straightforward: I did the crime, I'd do the time, and fuck *anyone* who had something to say.

Extra angst came from some of my former friends, like a bouncer I had hired at the Rat, Tom P, believing Bean, the only guy whose bail was reduced. He might not have taken Bean at his word if he had known that Bean was banging his ex-wife.

Fortunately, I still had friends on the street. In the wee hours of a weekend morning in Chinatown's *Four Seas* restaurant a friend, Eric Joseph, confronted Tom, and his accusations, and broke his nose and cheekbone.

2.

Learning to Jail

I spent the next six months in the Berkshire County House of Correction. Danny had served time before, so I used him as a coach. I quickly learned that CO's, correction officers commonly called "screws", took head counts throughout the day, and every hour on the hour at night.

In the morning, there's an etiquette followed at the communal sink where everyone shaves and prepares for breakfast. The first rule? Wait your turn. If there's a queue, don't cut it, or you risk real violence.

The violent nature of our crime put us at the top of the jail's criminal hierarchy. Even so, it paid to be decent to others because even the smallest things, like nail clippers, were in very short supply. I learned quickly that jails, and later prisons, stunk all the time from backed up toilets, poor ventilation, and men who refused to shower. Also the incessant cigarette smoke and constant noise would drive anyone crazy. TV's blared most of the day, inmates shouted back and forth in different languages, and there was the constant slamming of dominoes on tables.

In jail even the smallest thing becomes a major project. Want a haircut? Sign up early. Haircuts were given once a week, with a screw (corrections officer) near-by keeping an eye on the guy with the scissors. The haircut list too long? You're out of luck, or if the barber gets lugged (thrown in the hole) for some offense, then *everyone's* out of luck. Sometimes, for months, there is no barber, and inmates have to cut each other's hair with cheap, canteen razors.

In the Berkshire County House, every six-by-seven-foot cell had a steel bunk, cold-water sink, and toilet. Food is an important part of every convict's life, and the quality of jail food is generally poor. I didn't realize it then, but the chow that I got in Berkshire County would be some of the best I'd receive in the ten years I was down. And chow halls have rules.

You lined up to eat and didn't cut. At the table, you always said please and thank you when requesting salt or pepper, and you never reached in front of anyone for it. The first time I did, I almost wound up in a fight. In jail, then later prison, I learned how to be polite if for only one reason, disrespect could get you injured, add time to your sentence, or even cost you your life.

Years later, while I was serving time in Norfolk State Prison a good friend, Ron MacDonald from South Boston, told me, "When you hit the streets again, Rick, you'll have to watch your temper because people on the street are rude motherfuckers. Before you'd kick the shit out of them for it, now, after years behind the walls, you're going to want to kill them, and that will bring you back."

I laid low the first two weeks before I finally reached out to the Greek. All phone conversations at the jail were recorded and monitored by security, but, speaking in code, I was able to determine that after the heist the Greek and the others had waited for us for over an hour in the North Adams lot. The Greek said that he knew it went bad when the "valley came alive with the sound of sirens". It was a good thing Brian Bean had never met him or any other member of the disposal team. He couldn't rat them out.

The Greek and I trusted each other. Hell, we'd been through a lot together, but there's always concern when someone's part of a crime but not apprehended, and the rest of the crew is looking at "phone numbers" (years of incarceration). To calm any fears he may have had and speaking for Sean and Danny too, I told him, "When you see that other guy, tell him to relax, there won't be a problem." And that was the end of it. I never saw the Greek again. He died, years later, while I was still in prison.

Sean and Danny settled for a public defender, but I was dumb enough to talk my father into hiring an attorney. In hindsight, it was a huge waste of money and time because the

Berkshire County DA had made us an initial, and final, offer. Plead guilty to the robbery, and he would ask for 18-20 years in state prison. If we took it to trial, he would request life.

Even with statutory good time taken off the proposed 18-20 year sentence, I'd still have to serve eleven years, eight months. The sentence was devoid of parole opportunities, so I'd be required to "wrap it up", or do the sentence day-for-day, minus the deduction for statutory good time.

But the news wasn't all bad. By utilizing something called "earned good time" I could cut the sentence down further. Good time could be earned by working a prison job, attending school, and regularly attending so called self-help programs, such as Alcoholics Anonymous or Narcotics Anonymous. I could earn up to another seven and half days a month off my sentence. But even with earned good time deductions, I would still be incarcerated for at least the next decade, a lot of time for a guy who hadn't done any.

My attorney came up with a possible defense, something he called "Diminished Capacity." Since I had been previously diagnosed with having a Bi Polar Disorder, it meant that I wasn't insane when I committed the crime, but due to my mood swings, I wasn't in full control either. If the court determined that I suffered from diminished capacity, there was a good chance I would get a lower sentence.

Sean and Danny were not only younger than me, but smarter too. Resigned to their fate, they both pleaded guilty to the crime. But if I took the DA's "deal," at the age of thirty-five, the old man of the crew, I wouldn't see the streets again until I was forty-six.

I recall pacing the "Flats" (the first tier) of the cellblock with them. It's what you do a lot of in jail, pace, from one point to another, back and forth, over and over. What did they think about me not pleading out? Did either one have a problem with it?

"What's it involve?" Danny asked.

"They'll ship me to the Ranch," I said. The Ranch was the nickname for Bridgewater State Hospital for the Criminally Insane, a medium security prison.

Sean stopped in his tracks. "The fucking nuthouse?"

"They'll commit me for up to a year while the doctors work their magic," I said. "Then when sentencing time comes, one of the doctors will testify in court for me. See, I'm not actually crazy, but my capacity to understand everything I did, due to my mental illness, was diminished, so he'll recommend a lighter sentence to the judge. Everything goes well, I could be out on parole in six years."

Danny shook his head. "I dunno, it's a bad joint, Rick. Real bad. Everyone's medded out down there." He was talking about the reality of a crazy kingdom. Patients at Bridgewater State Hospital were doped up to the gills with mind-melting, psychotropic drugs inmates referred to as "chemical handcuffs." "You'll have to take 'em like everyone else," he said.

It was a legitimate concern, but what I couldn't divulge to my partners, or even to my own attorney, was that I had an *in* at Bridgewater State Hospital. Years before, a South End friend had told me about a connection he had in the Bridgewater facility. He said for the right amount, paid up front, this doctor could be a "go to" guy.

This doctor would treat you, document your progress, and then, when time came for sentencing, present his favorable report to the judge. It sounded like a slam dunk. If I could shave three or four years off the sentence, it would be well worth the risk.

And there were certainly risks.

At the time BSH was arguably the most dangerous joint in the system. People were murdered and/or committed suicide in the facility all the time. Its inmates, whether they were drugged up or not, were some of the most dangerous in the state: serial killers, men who had slaughtered entire families, who attacked others without provocation. I had a lot to think about. Should I roll the dice and go to Bridgewater, or pass on a chance to make an end-run around spending the next decade in prison?

In September, Sean and Danny pleaded guilty to the Williamstown robbery and were sentenced to 15-20 years at MCI Walpole, but the DA remained adamant that I receive the original deal of eighteen to twenty years. The difference between the two sentences was minimal, but on paper, mine appeared harsher.

Okay, I admit that I had screwed up for almost a decade. I was going to get hammered. But I still wasn't ready to throw in the towel.

F Ward

I had heard horror stories about The Ranch, what people called Bridgewater. In the sixties, they had filmed a documentary there, *Titicut Follies*, depicting conditions so brutal that a judge later banned it. I thought I knew what I was getting into, but when the Berkshire transport van turned in at the sign that said Bridgewater State Hospital, a cork popped in my gut and something bubbled inside.

The intake screw barely looked up from the paperwork on his desk as the Berkshire screws removed my shackles, unlocked the padlock on my waist, pulled the chain through, and took off my cuffs.

Soon I would learn there are worse restraints.

The cop completed the paperwork, picked up the phone and said tiredly into it, "One for F Ward." Then ordered the Berkshire cops to back up.

A steel door in front of me swung open and three huge cops squeezed into the room and took up position around me, securing damp folded towels around my wrists and another around my neck. The neck towel tightened and I was picked up and carried, struggling, into the building, the door slamming behind me.

On my feet again, the towel on my neck loosened, and a screw whispered into my ear, "Just wanted to show you how easy it is. You gonna behave?"

My eyes watered, but at least I could breathe.

The towel tightened again. "You gonna?"

I nodded.

They raised my arms up until they were parallel to my shoulders, then walked me, like a glider coming in, down a long corridor and into the large room called F Ward.

In the center was a hodgepodge of metal tables, desks, and chairs. A doctor in a long white coat sat at one writing. Nearby, a chubby nurse, with bowl haircut, like Moe from the Three Stooges, scribbled notes on a clipboard. An inmate, chin pinned to his chest, mopped the floor behind her. Every cell in F Ward had a pink, steel door with a faded black number on it, a tiny window, and nickel-sized holes drilled into the bottom for air.

The nurse stopped writing and looked up when we entered. She approached, sliding the pen into the clipboard, and asked, "Any problems, gentlemen?"

The cops lowered my arms but maintained the grip. One handed my papers to her and said, "A little at first but now he knows better."

"Good. How are you today," she said, looking past me.

I lowered my eyes. "Fine."

"They're going to release you."

"Fine."

"Are you sure that you're fine?"

"Yes."

She nodded at my escorts and the towels fell away.

"Are you anxious? We have something for you if you are."

"No, just thirsty."

"Strip him," she said, "and put him in three."

"You heard her, strip."

The nurse stood there, making notes on the clipboard, as I stepped out of my underwear.

The inside of the cell was pink like the door. Pink was supposed to calm you, but did nothing for thirst. It was the heart of July, and it had to be a hundred degrees in that cell.

On the floor was a green plastic mattresswith had pencils of urine pooled in the creases, and excrement smeared on in finger paint designs. The cell had no toilet or sink, just a hole in the floor ringed by dark turds.

I looked out between the steel shutters that covered the only window on the outside. F Ward was perched on the top of a small hill that was covered with burnt grass. Ten feet away, on a bald plate of earth, a yellow jacket hovered over an old Reese's wrapper. At the bottom of the hill was a delta wing-shaped building where men, in gray uniforms, paced in a circle in front of.

At a rap on the door, I turned and caught the flash of a face past the Plexi-glass window. I shouted out, "Hey, hello?" And the inmate mopping the floor reappeared and, like a fish swimming backwards, stared in with one eye.

I said, "Could you tell them please to get me some water."

Like he was sending out Morse code the mop handle tapped the side of his face. He took a deep breath and said, "Marie, this—mmman-needs-WATER," and his face was replaced by the nurse with the clipboard.

"You need something, Richard?"

"I told you before I'm thirsty, need water."

She looked at me curiously. "You don't recall? I gave you some already." She sighed, like it was a game show and I had picked the wrong door. "Alright," she said, "I'll get you more." The feeding slot in the door dropped open. "And something with it to calm you, back away from the door, now."

She put a tiny cup, containing pills, on the ledge.

"Elavil. I want you to take them," she said.

I stared at her without blinking.

"Richard, take the pills." She set a full cup of water beside it. "We can make you."

Dizzy and thirsty, I didn't care anymore, and washed down the pills with the water. I said, "Could I have more water, please?"

She said something to someone and another cup appeared.

"Drink it and don't pace. You'll dehydrate," she said. The panel slammed shut.

I paced until the soles of my feet were covered in a black, sticky film and the muscles in my legs were dead from fatigue. I sat on the floor with my back to the wall and pondered the things that had delivered me there: early abuse had etched me like acid, summits of rage, cocaine addiction.

Capped by the violent crimes I had committed.

I thought about the bottoms I had hit in my life, but nothing compared to this. Naked in a nuthouse, I couldn't get any lower. Worse, I believed I belonged in this place as the floor opened and I fell into blackness.

The Ranch

After three days of pig slop on a plastic tray, and watching my own shit collect in the corner, the feeding slot in the door opened and a pair of state boxer shorts sailed through landed at my feet. The heavy locked twisted, the door swung out, and the screw said, "Put 'em on Marinick, you're movin'."

This time I wasn't nervous as the cops followed the same routine, towels around my wrists, another around my neck. But as they lifted my arms I heard a muffled voice behind me say, "Hey, you a fish? I'm a fish, a *real* fucking fish."

I was able to turn my head just enough to see the face of an ancient man, with ravines in his cheeks, pressed against the window of the cell next door. Between puffing them out he shouted, "Fish, fish, FIIIISH."

A cop said, "He knows where you're going."

Now I was nervous.

The Fishbowl was referred to as a step-down unit. A twenty-by-twenty-foot room designed for short-term, close observation. Surrounded by glass walls the lights in the Fishbowl were never shut off. Ever.

The first night, after I'd fallen into a restless sleep, a drumming noise startled me awake. In the outside corridor twenty recruits, a training class from the academy was rapping their knuckles on the glass the way people do on fish tanks to get a reaction. Finally, the captain ordered them to stop.

He unlocked the door, stepped into the room, and like some kind of lion tamer, strode to the end of my bed.

"Who the fuck do you think you are?" he said. He pointed at the wall lamp above my bed. "Unwrap it," he barked.

In addition to the overhead lamps, a fluorescent light, encased in a heavy, clear, plastic security shield, was mounted on the wall above each bed. Unable to sleep with the light in my face, I had spooled toilet paper around it. I unwrapped it.

The captain positioned himself, Captain America style, hands on his hips, feet spread and announced to the recruits, "This's an example of the crap you'll deal with here. But we run the facility, not assholes like this.

Within two days I was transferred from the Fishbowl to the Maximum-security end of the camp. The Max building, designed like a delta wing, held fifteen inmates or, *patients* as they're referred to in Bridgewater. In front was a yard, a tiny parcel of grass encircled by a cement walkway, where men paced around like zombies for hours.

I was issued an ill-fitted gray uniform and assigned to a single cell equipped with a bunk, the same type of plastic mattress, and a shit bucket that was emptied each morning. On the second day, on my way out to the yard, I was attacked without provocation.

I had had been warned about patients at the Ranch and told they had superhuman strength and couldn't be hurt. My attacker was six feet tall and built like a refrigerator. His shaved head was full of nicks, as if he used a chisel instead of a razor. As I headed through the main door to go outside he blew past me, shoving me into the frame hard enough that I saw stars. Then I saw red.

I ran up and viciously left-hooked him from behind. Stunned, the bug staggered a few steps, then turned around into a perfect right hand that crushed his nose and dropped him. Wow, they could be hurt I thought, seconds before I was smothered by a sea of blue uniforms and hauled back to F Ward.

They spin dried me for two days then returned me to the Max End. Two weeks later I was reclassified to the minimum-security end of the camp.

Although Bridgewater State Hospital was a prison, it was different from a regular prison. For example, in a generic state prison it doesn't matter who starts a fight, both cons get lugged to the hole. You could be standing there minding your own business and get sucker punched, and both you and your attacker will be sent to the hole. If you assault a screw, you'll likely be charged with a new crime, and years will be added to your sentence.

The Ranch was different because inmates were considered *patients*. If you got into a fight, or hit a cop, you would be lugged to F Ward and put in four point restraints, and maybe hit with heavier meds, but you could not be charged with a crime, especially if you were *committed*.

The Ranch had triple rows of security fence, rippling with concertina wire, and gun towers all around it. The Ranch was a dump, a human dump, where seagulls constantly circled in the sky overhead. After weeks of observation in the Maximum end, most inmates made it to minimum. Most. Those considered extremely violent, or who self-mutilated, remained in the Max End or F Ward permanently.

During my time there, one patient was notorious for self-mutilation, sticking everything from small springs to ink cartridges up his penis before eventually, utilizing a saw fashioned from a toothbrush handle, he cut the thing off.

Today when people ask if Bridgewater State Hospital was anything like the place in the movie *One Flew Over the Cuckoo's Nest*, I laugh because it's not even close. Comparing the two is like comparing *The Muppets Movie* to *The Dawn of the Dead*—and the Ranch was loaded with real zombies.

In my eleven months at the facility, seven men lost their lives by murder or suicide. In regard to the deaths, Philip W. Johnston, at the time State Secretary of Human Services, said, "I cannot remember such a large number of unexplained, unnatural deaths here."

But they died for many reasons.

The hospital was overcrowded and understaffed, and there was a huge disagreement over what should be done. In a *New York Times* article on the subject, Secretary Johnston said the problem was related to whether or not the Department of Corrections should run the facility, meaning mostly prison guards, or the Department of Mental Health.

In the same article, when asked to comment on how dangerous the place was, a lawyer, representing the family of a Bridgewater inmate who allegedly choked to death on a hot dog said, "Bridgewater is a secret tunnel that people drop into."

I was assigned to the second floor of B building, or simply B-2. At the top of the stairway was the bubble, the bullet resistant glass enclosed control booth that was always manned by two CO's. In front of it was the day room that contained a large TV, and a collection of plastic chairs with metal legs. Next to the Day Room was another room utilized mainly for group therapy sessions. The two rooms were separated by steel plate and wire-glass windows.

Off the Bubble, housing corridors ran east and west. In the west was the small, yellow-tiled room with six showerheads. There was also a tiny change room where twenty people would be stuffed into at once. The wing also contained five dormitory-style rooms.

Assigned to a dorm room, I had been there for two weeks when I awoke one night to the sensation of something soft and mushy splatting the blanket at my feet. I sat up and saw a cellmate, actually his flabby, bare ass-spraying shit, like from a fire hose, onto my bed. I screamed at him, "You son-of-a-bitch," and he yanked up his pants and bolted.

I jumped out of the bed and ran after him, but slipped in shit and hit the floor hard. Covered in it, I skidded sideways into the corridor in time to see him being tackled by screws in front of the Bubble.

I learned what his problem was the next day. My cellmate had purchased his first canteen in months then sat down and ate nearly twenty-five Hersey bars. At the end of the beds were draws for storage, and when he got up with the trots he decided to use mine as a toilet.

Welcome to Bridgewater.

Along with men awaiting evaluation, B-2 housed others that were *committed* to the institution. Commitments had to be ordered by the court and ranged from six months to a year.

Committed patients were assigned to the east wing with its single cells. In prison, singles are rare, and Bridgewater's singles were huge. Each contained a bed, a stainless steel toilet, sink, a polished steel mirror, and a locker.

The Ranch also held a small cadre of state prison inmates. Most in the cadre were decent men, the sanest in the institution. But occasionally state prison inmates were sent to the Ranch for PC, protective custody. One such, "Phil", been lugged out of Walpole for fighting. Heavily medicated when he arrived, Phil was still able to communicate clearly, and even exhibited a dry sense of humor. Then one day he disappeared, which wasn't uncommon, and I didn't see Phil again for weeks.

The next time I did, it blew me away. I was sitting on the lawn outside of B-2 when I spotted him coming toward me. Not only was it obvious that he had pissed his pants, but he was doing the Thorazine Shuffle, barely lifting his feet as he walked.

I approached and said, "Hey Jackie, what's up?" He didn't resist when I took an elbow and guided him to a bench. Sitting next to him I told him that the guys had been asking about him, but he didn't respond.

Then a voice behind us said, "He'll get worse, much worse."

When I turned it was Mark, one of the committed patients from my floor. I'd notice how he ignored just about everyone else, but always said hi to me.

Mark said, "That whopper dose of Thorazine? He's only supposed to be on it for a week, maybe two, but they'll keep him on it for months." He affected a southern drawl, "Shit's meltin' his brain like ice cubes in the rain."

I said, "They know this?"

"Yeah," he said, "they know but don't give two shits." He shook his head. "Look, what's done's done, can't be changed. C'mon, take a walk."

I said, "Thanks, I'll hang here."

Mark came around and stopped in front of me. He said, "You can't help him, man, nobody can." He walked away and motioned with his head for me to follow. "C'mon, take a walk and learn a little about Bridgewater."

Mark gave me the low-down on the place, as well himself. Arrested for the murder of a family member, then later diagnosed paranoid schizophrenic, he had been tried for murder, found NGI (i.e., not guilty by reason of insanity), and sentenced to Bridgewater for an indeterminate time. He had been in the facility fifteen years.

He also gave me the dope on Bridgewater's doctors. My doctor, a guy named Feld, was right at the top of his shit list. Mark said that Feld, a former cocaine addict, had once sought the same kind of treatment that I had at a facility much like the place where I had been, Edgehill Newport, in Rhode Island.

After a long leave of absence Feld had returned and was re-appointed to his former position. Mark went through a litany of other peculiar traits that the man allegedly had. But he ended up with something good. He hated Feld but admitted that the doctor was highly respected, and that he carried a lot of clout in the courts.

Next, he warned me about a more imminent danger, the screws. According to Mark, they were the worst in the system, many of them fuck-ups from other institutions and, facing termination, the Ranch was their last stop.

"Make no mistake, you attack and hurt one? They'll kill you," he said. "People are always dying around here. Seems like they can't stop hanging themselves. Later a bullshit investigation determines the cause of death to be *suicide*." He winked at me. "Know what I mean?"

The information was chilling, but I'd seen it for myself the place was dangerous. Fights between inmates were common. You could be sitting in the day room watching TV and the guy next to you, for no reason, suddenly leaps to his feet, grabs a chair and beats you or someone else over the head with it. The cops subdue and haul him away, the victim goes to the hospital, and everyone else goes back to watching TV. It happened twice my first week in B-2.

It paid to have an ace up your sleeve. On the streets, I carried a gun for protection. At the Ranch all I needed was a bank check—made out to a doctor employed there.

Meet the Boss

I had been in B-2 for over a month but had yet to meet *my* doctor. When I finally did the meeting was unusual—even for a place where everything was. It was eight-thirty in the evening and I was in bed reading when a screw unlocked the door and ordered me to "suit up" (dress in my state issued uniform).

The written pass that I received at the Bubble directed me to Doctor Feld's office in the Administration Building. I had been advised, through an earlier phone conversation with my connection on the street, that Feld had already taken delivery of an initial deposit of three thousand dollars, with three thousand still owed. I was about to learn what the money would buy.

As I crossed the prison yard, unescorted, the stars overhead amazed me. It was the first time I had been beneath them in over nine months.

In the Ad Building I handed the desk officer my pass, and without looking up, he pointed down the corridor and said, "Doctor Feld, office fourteen."

I followed the corridor and wondered about the kind of doctor that met his patients at night. How would he greet me? Was I the only patient in on his ruse?

It didn't take long to find out I wasn't alone. A few weeks later, I met a rich kid named Harvey who told me that he was involved in a similar scam, but paying Doctor Feld a hell of a lot more than I was.

I knocked on Feld's door and went in. Feld, middle-aged, overweight, and tired-looking, sat behind his desk, lit by the only light in the room, a small lamp on top. The knot in his tie loose, the top shirt button open, he directed me to sit in the wooden chair in front of him.

He started the interview with something easy. "How are we doing tonight?"

I owned him but was mindful to be respectful. "I'm okay, still getting used to the place," I said.

Feld knew exactly why I was there, but asked me anyways. When I finished relating what he already knew, he asked me about my prior diagnosis of a bi-polar disorder. At this point I was far from certain about whether I was actually bi-polar, or if my mood swings were the result of my former heavy cocaine use.

Feld said, "Tell me about the depression, and the times when you're elated."

He asked me about the types of behavior associated with each mood. How much did I sleep? Did I spend money like water? When depressed, were there certain tasks that I was unable to do? He also asked me simple things, like did I eat properly or have trouble with personal hygiene?

The more we talked, the more it became obvious that the symptoms of cocaine addiction ran a parallel path to those of manic depression. Hell, they were almost one and the same, which made it easy to answer his questions.

Warned by my new pal, Mark, I was prepared when, a half-hour into Feld's interview, things turned weird. Mark had mentioned that Feld was on the light side, and that his attraction to the same sex wasn't limited to simple romps on the street.

I wasn't surprised when Feld asked me about sex.

"How often do you have it?" he said.

"Whenever I can," I said, and his eyebrows shot up as he shifted his considerable bulk in his chair.

He said, "Does that statement also apply to a, uh, ... a penal environment?"

"No."

"Girlfriend?"

"No."

"Any reason?"

"On the street I didn't have the time for one. I was too busy trying to survive."

"But you said you had sex whenever you could. You found time for it somehow."

"The sex was just sex."

Feld made a notation, but still looked down when he said, "Homo-*sexual* tendencies?"

"None I'm aware of."

He glanced at me over the top of his glasses. "Then there may be—".

I felt my brow furrow. "Huh? What are you getting at?"

"Let's move on," Feld said.

The entire interview lasted less than an hour, and not once was there a mention of a pay-off, or the balance of money owed. The guy was slick.

At the end as I prepared to leave, he said, "We'll be putting you on medication for your disorder, and keeping close tabs on you. If you have any problems, you know how to reach me."

After the meeting with Feld, things settled down for me in the block. The unit manager, believing I was gaming him, had been busting my balls. But after Feld set him straight, the cop was on board.

As Feld promised I was put on meds, Lithium, a mood stabilizer. Although I was told that it was just a mineral, it still screwed up my head. My mood swings were so dramatic I felt as if I were saddled to a meteorite for the two months I was on it. One night while talking on the phone to my friend Elaine, I told her that I thought I was losing my mind.

Then somehow I was "protected" again when a routine electro-cardiogram detected an abnormality with my heartbeat, and a doctor ordered the treatment terminated.

With my head back on straight, Mark got me a job on Walks and Grounds. Walks and Grounds were responsible for maintaining the hospital's huge yard. We picked up trash and empty soda bottles littering the grounds, cut grass in summer beneath seagulls circling constantly overhead, and shoveled snow from the walkways in winter. The pay was a buck-fifty a day, but now I was also earning two and a half days a month "good time" off the end of my sentence.

The crew boss was a cop named Desmaris, a career corrections officer, who in the past had allegedly been a brutal one. He had been reassigned to the Ranch from MCI Walpole, the state's maximum-security facility, where allegedly he had messed with the wrong convict. Word around the camp was a contract had been put on his head, and he'd been sent to the Ranch for his own protection. I don't know if that story was true but will tell you this; Desmaris treated us decently and rewarded us for doing our jobs well.

Patients at the Ranch, due in part to the psych-medication they took, loved sugar and drank lots of soda, which meant tons of returnable bottles. The Grounds crew collected them and, every two or three weeks, Desmaris cashed them in and bought us food. Sometimes sub sandwiches; other times hotdogs, hamburgers, and chips. He even brought in a small Hibachi grill for us to cook on.

He was a decent cop in other ways too. He knew that shaving with lousy state razors had created a problem for me, in-grown neck hairs. One day at the end of the shift, Desmaris handed me a new pair of tweezers in a little plastic case (tweezers were considered "contraband"). All he said was, "You didn't get them from me."

For the next nine years, as I was transferred from prison to prison, I held onto those tweezers by concealing them inside the linings of sneakers. I still have them today.

The chow at the Ranch was pig slop, the absolute worst in the system. Maybe a lunatic couldn't taste the difference, but I sure as hell could. At chow time they would line us up outside the building then walk us in down formation. On the way, it wasn't unusual to see someone drop down to lick seagull shit off the sidewalk.

If you hope to do a decent bid, you better be able to hustle. Along with his grounds crew job Mark was also the block "houseman". A houseman's duties included washing, waxing, and stripping the floors at night, keeping the day rooms tidy, and passing out clean laundry. Mark got me a job as a houseman too.

A convict can't be paid for two jobs, so the screws allowed us the use a small electric frying pan, and Mark had a great connection with a con in the kitchen. He traded food for cigarettes and candy, so most nights we ate well. But eating well was only part of what it took to get through the Ranch.

You had to be able to handle the "bugs," what the patients were called.

Bridgewater was a psychedelic, through-the-looking glass, kingdom. Twenty-four-seven, I was surrounded by maniacs, guys who constantly babbled, laughed like hyenas, and threw punches in bunches at invisible adversaries. Daily, weather permitting, dozens would be passed-out on the lawn of the yard, strewn like boulders behind a psych-med glacier. Every few weeks, the DOC would hand out tobacco and rolling papers. The "bugs" would smoke it down then turn to grass clippings, rolled up in newspaper, and smoke that too.

The Ranch housed just over four hundred patients whose crimes ran the gamut from shoplifting to the slaughter of entire families. There were patients that killed siblings or parents. *The Vampire Slayer* took it a step further. When the police apprehended him at his home, he was cooking his mother in a collection of pots.

I had little interest in what a guy was in for. Why add to the negativity in my life already? But there were certain crimes so heinous that everyone in the "camp" (another term for prison) was aware. I got the dirt on the Vampire from a little guy who everyone, even the cops, called The Conductor, and his story was almost as gruesome.

A scorned lover, who happened to be an Orthodox Jew, he had murdered his girlfriend then taking the Biblical verse a bit too literally ("If thy right hand causes you to sin, cut it off and throw it away"), he hunkered down beside to a railroad track and allowed the train to cut off his arm.

But not everyone at the Ranch was a murderer.

One good example was Tiny. At six-five, four hundred plus pounds, Tiny was a twenty-five year old black man with a twelve-year-old mind. Committed for chronic shoplifting, he was convinced he could disappear at will. He would often lumber up to me and say, "Rick, ya know anytime I want, I'm outa this place."

And I would respond, "Yeah, then why the fuck aren't you?"

But a question like that was a curveball for Tiny. He'd shrug his huge shoulders, grin like the Joker and say, "Well, I-I don't kno-know, Rick." Then he'd hop around like his heels were on fire.

Of course, not everyone was as pleasant, and even Tiny could be testy at times. When he occasionally went off, he tossed inmates and cops around like Kachina dolls.

After nearly two months, my evaluation period completed, I was ready learn my fate. I had met with Doctor Feld on four occasions. During the final one, he explained what to expect in the courtroom.

The DA would argue for the eighteen to twenty years, my lawyer for less time. Feld would then testify that, in his professional opinion, my mental state at the time of the robbery diminished my capacity to understand what I was doing. Feld said he was confident that when the judge heard his argument, he would give me the ten to fifteen years sentence my lawyer requested.

When I went before Judge Cross, nicknamed "Hanging Cross," in Springfield Superior Court, Doctor Feld was impressive and convincing. Hell, by the time he was done, even I thought I was crazy. The judge listened politely to Feld for almost twenty minutes, and then he thanked him and promptly sentenced me to 18-20 years at MCI Walpole. I was disappointed, but I couldn't complain. Feld had done a great job, and there were no guarantees.

When I entered the gates of maximum security MCI Walpole, also known as "The Hill", it was with almost a sense of relief. At least now I could begin my bid in earnest, settle down, develop a good routine, and just do my time. But I never got the chance to get comfortable there.

Within a very short time two things happened: my lawyer filed an appeal with the Appellate Court, and Doctor Feld made arrangements to have me sent back to Bridgewater.

Soon after my arrival, I had another nighttime meeting with Doctor Feld. Visibly agitated when I entered the office, the first thing he said was, "I have no idea what that judge was thinking, but we're going to do something about it." Then he outlined his plan.

As I waited for a hearing date before the Appellate Court, Feld would have me officially "committed" to Bridgewater for a period of six to ten months. When I went before the Appellate Court, he would to testify for me once again—but from a new perspective. Committed to the institution, by a board of state certified doctors, there could be no doubt in anyone's mind that I suffered from severe mental health issues.

According to Feld, if I went along with the commitment, he could almost guarantee a substantial reduction in sentence. But aside from the money factor, it was obvious that something else was bothering Feld. His ego had taken a whack, and he planned to make a fool of the Springfield judge.

3.

Growing Up/The Irish Riviera

I have a clear image of a little pink house set back off of Aberdeen Road in Squantum. Squantum, where I grew up, is a peninsular contained within the borders of the city of Quincy. It was part of what was called then the "Irish Riviera," that section of the South Shore where Boston Irish relocated when they'd had enough of the city.

In the 1950s Squantum had an elementary school, library, firehouse, and both a Catholic and Protestant church, where every Sunday, it was standing room only. There was also, on an eastern spit of land jabbing into the harbor, a Nike Missile Range to defend against Communists and an aerial attack, which everyone swore was coming.

Born on February 28th, 1951, the second of four brothers, I am two years younger than Bob, four years older than Ron, and six years older than Scot, the youngest.

My Brookline-born mother, Patricia, kept a tidy house, washed our clothes, and cooked supper every night, which we had to finish because she'd always remind us that, "People in China are starving."

My father, Bob, owned a lucrative auto body repair shop and appraisal business, which he had inherited from an aunt. Auntie Rose had doted on my father, an only child, and the old man hit the lottery when the business became his.

My father, the son of a Boston policeman and his South Boston born and raised wife, Mary, known as May, grew up in North Cambridge in a two family home on Harrington Road. At the start of World War II, at the age of sixteen, he had enlisted in the Navy and spent the following twenty-seven months in the Pacific theatre.

My mother was the only daughter of Georgina MacVarish and, allegedly, never knew who her biological father was. Her stepfather, allegedly a bookmaker, Mum was raised in a succession of Catholic boarding schools. Maybe it was hard for her being away all the time because Mum always seemed angry. And her anger was taken out on her kids.

For the smallest childhood infractions, my brother Bob and I were beaten with belts, electric frying pan cords, wooden coat hangers, or rubber spatulas. I was fed soap and Tabasco Sauce, and burnt with matches for lying or using the wrong "tone." In the end though was her anger that seared me the most. I never understood where it came from. Maybe because her childhood was brutal as were her relationships with men, she became lost in herself and then eventually in the bottle.

When sober, my mother had admirable qualities. She was strict about manners and kept our clothes always washed and pressed. On summer days, she would take us to either Wollaston beach or Nantasket where my brothers and I would ride the amusements in Paragon Park. I can still see Mum standing below us, looking up smiling, as her boys rode the Wild Mouse, Crazy Teacups, or the Congo Cruise.

Although my mother was unable to tell us who she was, she insisted that we knew our own roots. Early on, I was taught that I was of Irish, Austrian, and Scottish descent, which Mum said was, "strong, blood." The only one of us to be born in a Boston hospital, St. Margaret's, it made me feel special.

My father was a good provider, but he was rarely around. It seemed that most nights after work he had other business to attend to, and that was fine with me. In those days I'd catch a beating once a week from my mother, and then another one from the old man when he arrived home.

The next day I'd show up at school or at a friend's house with welts across my face, back and legs. I thought it was normal and was shocked when playmates questioned the damage. I'd become angry and explode, "You're saying your parents don't beat you? Fucking liars."

As result of the beatings, I was scared most of the time. It got to the point where all my father had to do was raise his voice, and I'd shake and cry. I hated myself for reacting that way, but I couldn't control the fear. Anger and fear became the engines that drove me and helped shape the way the way I viewed life—stand up for yourself, take shit from no one, and when threatened in any way, attack.

I learned my first lesson in street justice early. I was playing in the yard one day when Bob approached, his face cover with blood. When I asked him what happened he showed me the wound, a huge knot and gash on top of his head.

He told me that he was playing on Johnny Ward's, our neighbor's, back steps matches and had found a pack of matches. Bob said, "We argued over who was going to show his Mum, and he whacked me."

"With what?"

"A hammer," Bob said.

I was stunned, and then I was angry. Bobby was Superman to me, and Johnny Ward had spit on his cape.

Mum took the news surprisingly well and accepted Bobby's story about building something in Johnny's yard and getting hit, accidentally, with a hammer. He got a few stitches and things quieted down.

A few weeks later, I was in the side yard weeding our garden when Johnny finally showed his guilty face. Bobby was near the wire-fence turning over soil with a pitchfork. Johnny gave Bobby the neighborhood greeting, "Hi-ho, Bob-by," but my brother ignored him.

Undeterred, Johnny approached and leaned on the fence. Out of the corner of my eye, I watched my brother. If he meant to keep working, I would do the same.

Johnny said, "Hey Bob, I was thinking maybe . . ."

Bobby gave the soil one last jab then lunged with the pitchfork, stabbing Johnny in the face. When Johnny lowered his hands, they were bloody. He ran from the yard moaning.

Bobby looked at me. "Don't tell Ma," he said, and went back to work.

Johnny never ratted out my brother because he knew he'd had it coming. It was street justice, pure and simple. If that happened today, police would be involved, and there'd be lawsuits up the ass, but not then. A few weeks later Johnny Ward and the Marinicks were best friends again, and we remained that way until the day Johnny died, at the age of twenty-two, from Colitis.

Small for my age, I was restless, hyperactive, and fell easily into fights. I didn't care if I won or lost; it just felt good to hit someone back. Academically just average but I happened to excel in spelling and reading. I was also good at setting fires. I loved fire and loved watching it spread. I found something comforting in the destruction.

I attended the Squantum Elementary School, and sometimes, before class, I'd set the woods behind it on fire. On weekends I found bigger venues to burn, one of them Squaw Rock, a park about a mile from our home. My friends and I would torch the huge fields of tinder dry grass, burning them to the doorstep of the bluffs that bled down into Boston Harbor.

The Nike missile range also occupied a portion of the park, which always meant lots of security, and nothing beat a chase by the military police. When they'd come for us, we would squirrel up into trees or duck into the eel grass to elude them. I always managed to get away. By the time I was nine I was an adrenalin junkie, and remained one for decades.

Giro's Café

My grandfather, John Marinick, had retired from the Boston Police Department's elite Flying Squad, which was based in Charlestown, in the late thirties and forties. The squad battled street gangs and a host of Irish hoodlums, like the Loopers, who drove stolen cars at high speeds down Bunker Hill Avenue. On the other side of the Charlestown Bridge, the North End, Grandpa also personally locked horns with members of the Italian Mafia. From the nineteen-thirties through the mid- nineteen-nineties, the North End was home base for the all-powerful mob.

Grandpa's wife May was a Southie girl, born and raised. She often referred to the town as "God's Country," and when I'd ask her if God really lived there, Grandma would solemnly respond, "He does." And I believed her. Grandma insisted that I had Southie blood in my veins and that when I grew up, belonged there. Dad disagreed. He saw nothing but trouble if I moved to South Boston.

He must've been psychic.

If Mum was a flare, Grandma was a candle, welcoming and warm, who went out of her way to protect me. But as gentle as grandma was, grandpa was tough, and his no-holds-barred police tactics had once made him the target of underworld figures.

On a day off, while riding his big Indian motorcycle down Massachusetts Avenue, a large black "gangster-type" car came up alongside him. The doors opened suddenly and sent him into a telephone pole. After a month at Mass General, he returned home a man on a mission. No one had ever been charged with the crime, and Grandpa blamed the Italians.

According to family lore, at some point, he and another detective approached Joe Lombardo, at the time Consigliore of the New England mob, while he was seated ringside at a Boston Garden boxing match. Certain that he was connected to the attack Grandpa informed Lombardo that if anything else happened to him or his family, he would hunt him down and kill him.

My father, on the other hand, had a very different relationship with the mob. I couldn't have been more than six or seven years old the first time he took me into the North End. From then on, once a month on a Saturday morning, he would take me with him to Giro's Cafe. As we followed the empty Expressway north into town I took advantage of the rare opportunity I had to be alone with him. We would talk about his life growing up in North Cambridge and, occasionally, his combat experiences in World War II, something he rarely discussed.

Following boot camp, Dad had sailed out of San Francisco Bay on a destroyer and didn't return for more than two years. During his tour, his ship was engaged in several major naval battles and invasions, including the Battle of Okinawa, where he was wounded by shrapnel and contracted malaria. He suffered from its symptoms for the next thirty years.

In my father's old WWII photo album, there is a fading yellow photograph taken in the middle of a Nagasaki street a month after the second atomic bomb was dropped. Those trips to the North End gave me pieces of the puzzle that was my old man.

While in the North End, we would inevitably end up in Giro's Cafe. On the corner of Hanover Street and Atlantic Avenue, it had been an area fixture for decades. From the time I was a kid, Giro's maintained the same facade, waiters, menu, and valet, a wiry, little guy still employed there when I could legally drink.

When you entered Giro's the noise from the streets seemed to melt away, as if it were afraid to interrupt what went on there. On the right was a small dining room and a little further down was the bar. Opposite the bar, a ramp led to a private dining area. At the rear of the building was another large room, where, on Sundays, we ate as a family once a month for years.

Right after I celebrated my First Holy Communion, I went into Giro's for the first time. We got there before the place opened, and Dad had to knock to get in. In front of the tiny bar he introduced me to a huge guy named Joey who was dressed a black tuxedo, the standard uniform of Giro's waiters. Above Joey's eyes was a herd of scars, and his nose was as flat as a snowball on impact. I had never seen cauliflower ears before. I wasn't afraid, but I couldn't take my eyes off him.

"Nice to meet you, Ricky" he said, shaking my hand, and I was even more amazed. The guy had a voice like Yogi Bear.

Dad asked Joey to watch me for a minute and walked up the ramp to the dining area. Joey put his hands on his hips, studying me for a moment, before he said, tilting his head toward the bar, "Maybe you want somethin' to drink?"

A few minutes later my father returned and, taking me by the hand, led me up the ramp into the nearly empty room. Near the back, a balding man in a suit sat at a table, a newspaper spread out before him. A younger guy, dressed the same way, stood a few feet away from him smoking a cigarette. It wasn't until I got closer that the guy reading the paper finally looked up

"JL," my father said, "This is my son, Ricky."

Like I wasn't even, there, JL said over the top of my head, "Who's he look like?"

He tugged his wire-rim glasses down to the edge of his nose, and examined me over the thin ribbons of gold. I examined him back. Around his neck a thin, silk tie, and the collar of his white shirt looked starched to the point that if he turned his head quickly, he might lose it.

"People say he looks like me," Dad said.

JL nodded. "That's good, Bobby, a boy should look like his father."

With his hand, he jerked air toward his chest. "Come over here, kid. How old are you?" he said.

I told him, then shook JL's hand. It was smaller than Joey's, but the grip was the same. JL said, "You can call me Poppa Joe."

"How old are you?"

The guy next to him snorted smoke and chuckled.

I looked at the guy with the cigarette. He winked at my father.

Poppa Joe said, "Ricky, you eaten at Giro's before?"

I shook my head.

"You're gonna. You thirsty? How 'bout somethin' to drink?"

Since everyone was offering, I figured I was. "Okay," I said.

"What do you want, a Coke?"

"Shirley Temple."

Poppa Joe frowned. He wagged a finger at me, said sternly, "Guys don't drink Shirley Temples." He looked at the other guy. "Frankie, get my man here a Special."

When Frankie came back, he handed me a glass filled with ice, ginger ale, grenadine syrup, and a cherry. It looked and tasted like a Shirley Temple.

"How's that?" JL said.

I nodded.

"That's a Special. Whenever you come to Giro's, that's what you order from now on, okay?" His hand shot out and we shook again. "Nice to meet you, Ricky."

"Nice to meet you, Poppa Joe."

I only saw Joe Lombardo a few times after that. Half a decade passed, and on a Sunday afternoon in Giro's, Lombardo was there with the same guy who smoked. When he came to the table to acknowledge my parents, he ordered a round of Specials for my brothers and me. I think my father was more thrilled than we were.

When I was seventeen, I took my first real date, a beautiful sixteen-year-old blonde, to dinner at Giro's. Dad must have called before because the waiters fussed all over us. I ordered my usual, spaghetti and meat sauce, and my girlfriend ordered steak *a la pizzaiola*. When the meal was served, the maître came over and offered to cut her steak into little pieces and, impressed by my friends, she let him.

It wasn't until I was in my late teens that I learned the truth about Joe Lombardo. According to the US Treasury Department Bureau of Narcotics, Lombardo was a member of the top hierarchy of the Mafia in the Massachusetts area, and number two man to the boss of the New England Mafia, Phil Buccola. Poppa Joe's first arrest had come in 1917 for assault with intent to kill. In the following years there were other arrests for possession of morphine, bribery, murder, lottery, possession of a revolver, and a second arrest for assault with intent to kill.

Other known mobsters who frequented Giro's were Frank 'The Spoon' Cucchiara, who attended the infamous 1957 Apalachin meeting in New York, Rocco Palladino, Anthony Santaniello, Henry Selvitella and Ilario Zannino, all of them ranking members of the New England branch of *La Cosa Nostra*.

I never learned the exact nature of the relationship that my father had with these men. In almost every way he remained an enigma until the day he died. But I do know this; he wasn't a gangster or even a criminal. When I asked how he knew Giro's owner, he said, "JL respected your grandfather."

That was it. Period. My father obviously respected those guys too, and it made a deep impression on me. I started to think that gangsters were cool. I mean how could they be "bad guys" if Dad respected them?

Grandpa thought different. I only asked him about JL once; he told me to change the subject.

Blast from the past

Jump ahead a few months with me. I had been returned to Bridgewater, from Walpole State Prison, and had gotten back into a regular routine of exercise, meditation, and work on the Grounds Crew. Time passed quickly. I was even sleeping better until they moved a jerk-off named Jerry next to me.

At least once a week Jerry, who always wore a hand-made pork-pie hat, started screaming in the middle of the night, and shouting the Hail Mary prayer.

I have always been fan of the Virgin Mother so Jerry's version pissed me off.

"Hail Mary. Haaiilll Mary. Full of ggrrrace. Hail Mary. Hail fucking Maaary."

I'd scream through the wall at him, "Shut the fuck up."

"Haaaaaiiiiiillll Maaaarrrrryyyyy!"

"Shut up, you motherfucker!"

There would be silence, and then the grinding would begin.

I was never able to determine what Jerry used but somehow he carved a huge crucifix into our adjoining wall deep enough that maintenance had to come and refinish it. When I asked Jerry once how he managed to do it, he grinned and gulped like he had swallowed a rat.

While descending the stairs of the block one day, I noticed a new guy coming up them. A fit hundred and ninety pounds, clean-shaven, his hair closely cropped, he looked familiar, but I couldn't recall from where. The look in his eyes, though he tried to conceal it, showed that he had recognized me too.

It didn't take long to remember who he was. He was my old pal from my Club Soda days, John Bianchi (you'll meet him later, promise). I did some investigation and found that Bianchi had been recently shipped to Bridgewater from The Hill, Walpole State Prison, allegedly because someone there he had screwed in the past had recognized and tried to kill him. Put in PC, protective custody, he was next sent to the Ranch in the belief he'd be safe there.

What the DOC didn't realize was Bianchi had enemies everywhere.

I had already told Mark the story how, in the past, Bianchi had put the screws to me by outsmarting me at Club Soda. Now there was the opportunity for payback and I wasn't about to let it slip. Moving quickly, with no time to fashion a weapon, I planned to get him in the chow hall, with Mark volunteering for back up if anyone interfered.

At noon, the huge dining area was packed. Half a dozen screws manned posts along the walls on the lookout for anything suspicious. Already seated when Bianchi came in, I watched him move slowly through the chow line. His head swiveled nervously as he picked up his tray and carried it to a table, four rows up from where I sat.

Mark was a row ahead of me, and when he turned around and looked, I gave him the nod. He had never seen Bianchi before, but with instincts honed by years behind the walls, he had picked him right out. Bianchi had picked me out too and glared at me now. He knows he's getting it good, the prick knows he's getting it.

Tightening my grip on the lousy state fork, I started to rise, trying not to draw the screw's attention. Bianchi, his eyes locked on mine, suddenly shot to his feet and then flung his tray sideways, creating a racket. He calmly waited for the screws to rush in and grab him. It was the action of a coward, a real PC (protective custody) move. He was shipped out the next day, but that wouldn't be the last time I saw him.

4.

Body Shop Blues

My father was big on image. He drove Caddies and Lincolns, had a closet full of suits, two dozen pairs of dress shoes, dozens of ties, and between the three-carat pinky ring and the solid gold Rolex, my old man always looked like a stud.

The family growing larger, with four boys now, my parents decided that they needed a bigger house. They purchased a nice one on Wollaston Hill. The new house, surrounded by a tan, granite wall, had flowerbeds and exotic trees. It was as good a place as any to fake the American middle-class dream and, at least from an exterior perspective, we owned the dream. But life in the new house was no different than in the old and my father was around even less now, and my mother drank more. She was also being treated with drugs, like Nembutal, for a host of disorders. With drugs fueling the fire, she directed even more of her anger at me.

At the beginning of my thirteenth summer my father inquired about my plans. Plans? What did he mean? I ride my bike, shoot hoops down the playground, go to Wollaston Beach with my friends.

"I guess the usual stuff," I said

My father shook his head. "No, you're too old to be hangin' around. You start work at the shop Monday morning."

I was floored. I had to work the whole summer?

With little to say about it, I began to put in forty-hour weeks in the family's auto body repair business learning how to sand putty, and tape, prime, and paper cars in preparation for painting. I learned a few other things too.

I got to watch my father in action and saw that he was a hellava businessman. But when I watched him fawn over insurance appraisers and company adjusters, the people responsible for sending us work, or laugh at their bad jokes, I could tell it was forced. His respect for those men bordered on fear and I didn't like it, and I hated them for it. It was clear to me I could never fit into that mold, and being a businessman wasn't for me.

After work, I'd take the Washington St. trolley into town. As it followed Commonwealth Avenue, just before it entered the Kenmore Square tunnel, I would see Boston University students with their book bags on the sidewalk. They seemed so carefree, talking and laughing, and it got to me sometimes. I was nothing like them and I knew it, I would never be college material.

After I'd disembark at Park Street I would take the Red Line to Ashmont station, then the bus to Wollaston Center, then walk a mile home—for fifty bucks a week, and Mum took eighteen for board. That was the start. It took years to realize that I would always earn a shitty wage working for the Roche Co.

Flying

My first love affair began in the Quincy Quarries and lasted for years. In 1825 the quarries were the source of granite for many monuments, including the obelisk at Bunker Hill, as well as for buildings all over eastern Massachusetts. In 1963 they were shut down, and the great open pits filled with spring water and became the perfect swimming holes.

Encircled by immense cliffs, the emerald green pools drew swimmers like lint to a filter but the danger was real. Every summer someone didn't surface after they jumped or, upon impact with the water, broke their back or leg. From my perspective, though, it was the perfect place to test myself, the most wonderful reason to go there.

Every quarry had a name. In the summer of '65 Green Tank was the first one that I swam in and conquered. There were lots of other kids there that day. Some swam naked, which shocked me, while others swam just in their skivvies. Many jumped off the ledges wearing sneakers to protect their feet when they hit the water.

That first day I jumped from two forty-foot ledges, and dove off a thirty-five footer. It didn't matter whether I was jumping or diving; when I was in the air, it was as if I were flying.

The next day, and for the rest of that summer, I was the talk of the playground. Every chance I had, even at night, I would be up the "Q's" perfecting my skills. And it was a skill. You didn't just jump and hope to hit right.

When an experienced jumper steps off a ledge, the first thing he'll do is pull his knees to his chest. His arms extended parallel to his shoulders, out to the side, the "chair" is ridden all the way down until the last twenty feet or so when he opens—snaps his legs out, toes pointing downward while simultaneously pulling his arms to his chest, fists tucked tightly beneath his chin, and enters the water at speeds exceeding sixty miles per hour. Quarry jumping was about facing fear and maintaining control.

It was easy to get hurt. On the way down if you focused on your shadow on the surface of the water you might not open in time. I had been warned if I hit in the "chair" the water could be actually burst your rectum. Or if you jumped and panicked, lost your balance, the result could be devastating. That first summer I saw a kid get knocked out on impact, and drown.

The Quincy police made fruitless attempts to discourage us from swimming, going so far once to dump barrels of dye in the water which turned it as blue as Paul Newman's eyes. But on a steamy, summer day, it didn't stop anyone. Nobody gave a hoot if they emerged with a tint.

Later that same summer, I dove from a cliff face sixty feet high and jumped off every ledge in the quarries except one, Table Top, a measured one-hundred-five feet, the highest point in the Granite Rail quarry. I had often climbed up there intending to jump but each time had backed down, and I wasn't good at backing down.

The summer ended, and after school one September day, I put a note in my pocket and rode my bike to Granite Rail Quarry. As I climbed to Table Top, there wasn't another soul in sight. The air was a cool that day, but the sun and stone ledge beneath my butt was warm as I dangled my feet over the edge, scrutinizing the water a hundred feet below. It had a markedly different color now, and the surface wasn't as welcoming as it was during summer.

I was also concerned about giant logs in the water. Forty feet long and three times the diameter of a telephone pole, they had been used once to haul huge blocks of cut granite from the quarry. During the hot months, entire neighborhoods of kids would straddle and paddled them around, but some were so waterlogged that they skulked, like trap-door spiders, just below the surface. We called them "submarines".

Usually, before anyone jumped, swimmers were in the water below on the look-out for "submarines." But I was alone now, and I didn't know where they were.

It didn't matter.

I took off my sneakers, got to my feet, took the note from my pocket, with my name address, and telephone number on it. I tucked it into one of my sneakers, and then folded my windbreaker and shirt and left them in a neat pile on top. The note wasn't for my parents. I didn't care about them. It was for my friends, in the event that something happened, so at least they would know that I wasn't afraid, that I was up there doing what I said I would.

As I stood at the edge, the wind suddenly picked up and rippled the water. I knew that it was going to be like ice.

One hundred yards away, on a dirt road that snaked behind a colossus of rock that everyone called "Ship", a man walked his Golden Retriever. He stopped when he spotted me. What I must have looked like, alone, a tiny figure on the brink.

I heard him shout something, then I blessed myself and jumped.

As I rode the chair down I tried to see beneath the surface, then I snapped out of it and hit. Twelve feet under, the water numbing cold, I raced the rising bubbles to the surface and light. When I broke through, I whooped loud enough to make the rock face flinch.

I began to swim toward the outcrop that we used as a landing, but after only three or four strokes, I hit something big—a submarine. Moving parallel along its length, I looked back to where I had just entered the water and realized that death had been no more than ten feet away.

On the landing I stood in the sun shivering, and the guy with the dog, closer now, shouted, "Are you okay?"

I waved and shouted back, "Yes." The dog began barking and continued to bark as I climbed up to my clothes.

At school the next day, I told all my friends what I had done. When some of them doubted me, I said, "Go fuck yourselves, I'll go back today and do it again."

I was relieved when no one took me up on my offer.

Despite my daring at the quarries I still never felt noticed by any of my classmates and certainly no adults—with the exception of the last day of school of my ninth grade year.

Mr. Brooks, my Civics teacher, pulled me aside after class and gave me this big gap-toothed grin, his bushy eyebrows more like caterpillars hovering over his thick, black framed glasses. He shook my hand and said, "Richard, I want you come back to see me when you've done something with your life."

I was shocked because, like I said, I'd never felt noticed and here was someone who believed that I might make something of my life. I thanked Mr. Brooks and told him that I would, and meant it.

Marty's Boys

1968

Like every high school, North Quincy had cliques. In my sophomore year, ever on the look-out for action, I joined a gang that called themselves the HOGAS. The HOGAS drank beer on weekends, drag raced cars, and cruised the streets looking for girls; but it wasn't enough for me, I craved action. A mile from Baker's Drug, where the HOGA'S usually gathered in front of, was another gang that called themselves the Marty's Boys.

The Marty's Boys were wild and loved to brawl. If they couldn't find anyone locally to fight, they would drive south to Nantasket Beach looking for trouble, or over the Neponset Bridge into Boston. I thought they were just what I needed and joined them.

In the fall of my senior year a small group of Marty's Boys burst into Cannata's sub shop, home turf of a Dorchester gang, and with bats and golf clubs, wrecked the place. Cannata's owner came out shooting, and a Marty's Boy caught a ricochet and almost lost his eye. It was the last time the MB's fought as a group but, undeterred, I still craved action.

In 1968 I read Hell's Angels: The Strange and Terrible Saga of the Outlaw Motorcycle Gang by Hunter Thompson, and it had a profound effect on me. Tough? The Hell's Angels feared no one, lived for action, and willingly laid down their lives for each other. I now had direction. After graduation I would head to California and become a Hell's Angel.

Then I got to the part of the book that described what was expected of a Hell's Angel "prospect". Most of the stuff I could handle no problem, but there was one thing I couldn't. According to Thompson, when a prospect was presented with his "cut" or vest, every member in the chapter pissed and shit on it, and the prospect had to wear it. Discouraged, I passed on the Hell's Angels. In 2001 I read another Hell's Angels book, this one written by Ralph "Sonny" Barger, one of the club's founders. I laughed because in it Barger wrote that the dirty vest for prospects was a myth.

In the summer of 1968, I almost had a run-in with another outlaw biker gang, the Devil's Disciples. While driving down Wollaston Beach in their World War II era halftrack, one shouted insults at a group of high school kids sitting on the seawall. The kids refused to take it, and one, Brendan Riley, gave them the finger.

The bikers circled back, and one jumped off and smashed Brendan in the head with his helmet. Immediately jumped by twenty angry high school kids, the Disciples became victims of a savage beat down.

The Disciple's headquarters was only two miles away, just over the bridge in Neponset. Grown men with rap sheets, drug habits, and a penchant for carrying guns, they put out the word they would be back to settle the score the following weekend. We needed an army to challenge them—and got one.

Nowadays if some biker smashed a kid with a helmet, his friends would be too busy recording it on cell phones for Fox News to defend him. I was lucky to live in a better time, when people didn't run to the cops or the courts to defend them. To me you weren't a "real man" unless you stuck up for yourself and refused to be bullied. And the fighting part was fun too.

North Quincy mobilized, and the following Friday night there were two hundred kids armed with ball bats, pipes and golf clubs waiting for the Disciples.

The bikers never showed, but the cops did and everyone scattered. My group was drifting toward the Wollaston Yacht Club when a little kid skidded up on his bike and said, "Hey you guys, Southie's in the yacht club and one 'em slapped my sister's boyfriend."

Southie and Quincy were longtime rivals so a bunch of us quickly funneled into the narrow walkway leading to the entrance to the yacht club's just as the Southie kids were coming out, along with two local girls. It was obvious they were from Southie just by the way they were dressed: Barracuda jackets, pressed jeans, Sperry's, and colorful Izod shirts with the collars turned up. Compared to our tank tops, shorts and sneakers. Okay, we were hillbillies, but dangerous hillbillies.

The leader of the pack I picked up the pace and when someone yelled, "get them," we all started running. Almost all the city kids turned tail and bolted back inside, but one stood his ground.

Tall and lanky, with a muscular build, he reached into his jacket and pulled out a gun. I stopped about fifty feet from him and attempted to back up, but momentum had bunched us together. The kid held the gun like he knew how to use it, and when he squeezed the trigger I dropped to a knee expecting a bang. Instead it sounded like a paper bag when it's popped, but doesn't explode. The noise didn't scare me, but the fist-sized ball of flame racing toward me like a meteorite did.

The flare ricocheted off the chest of the kid next to me and splintered into the air above us, and I was up again and running. I chased the gunman through the length of the Wollaston Yacht Club, and out the rear door onto the landing in time to see him leap into an idling speedboat that was packed with his cronies, and the two turncoat girls.

Out of deck, momentum almost carrying me into the water, I watched as he shouted obscenities and gave me the finger as the boat accelerated into the night leaving behind my frustration and rage, and a rising blue cloud of exhaust smoke.

No One Gives a Shit

1969

"What do you mean the *car's* in the water?" I was eighteen years old, and it was the strangest phone call I'd ever gotten.

The Quincy police dispatcher had just said they had found my mother's car at the high water line at Wollaston Beach, but no one was in it. When he asked if I had the money to have the car towed, I said, "Yeah, we got the dough, just have it towed here." It was four o'clock in the afternoon.

The news wasn't all bad, it was early September and still warm outside. But where would I begin to look for our mother? I called the cops back.

Was it too early to file a missing person report?

Yes, she had a drinking problem.

No, she'd never done this before.

Had she ever considered suicide? I never asked her.

"Yeah," I said to the cop. "I'll call you if I see her, okay?"

At 7:30 p.m., it was just getting dark when a yellow cab spit my other out in front of the house. She didn't look bad, I had expected much worse: ripped clothing, sand in her hair, and seaweed. Her eyes were glazed but that wasn't unusual.

As she approached, I said "Hey, where's your car?" She muttered something and blew past me.

I yelled at her back as she walked upstairs, "The cops called the house, Ma. Your car was in the ocean, you know that?"

She entered her bedroom and slammed the door. She would camp there for days, coming out only to use the bathroom. But at least we knew where she was.

A permanent sense of autumn pervaded that house. Nothing bloomed, everything withered: my parent's marriage, my mother's health, the ambitions of my remaining brothers, Ronnie and Scot. Bob had left for college years before and had never returned. Living in that house was surreal. I was like an actor in a movie following a script I knew would have a terrible ending.

For a brief time I dated a new girl, Arlene, and she had introduced me to a friend of hers, Cara. Blonde and beautiful, Cara had legs like Bette Davis had eyes. Her front tooth was chipped, but when she smiled I was blind to everything else—including any allegiance to the Marty's Boys. After we began dating, I rarely saw them.

With her exclusively throughout my senior year, I soon realized that Cara had wandering eyes—while I only had eyes for her. It was a tough thing to handle, especially for a guy whose confidence level had barely reached the bud stage.

In 1969 I graduated from North Quincy High, and most of my classmates were thrilled it was over because they had definitive plans for their lives. They were heading to college, joining the military, or going into the family business.

Me, I was drifting.

It was tough working for my father that summer. From the time, I was a kid, whenever he had a problem with me, he would simply stop talking, for months at a time. Shortly after graduation, I pissed him off somehow, and all communication between us ceased until the end of August.

It was my fifth summer working at the shop and I had mastered an array of skills. I could compound and polish cars, and expertly sand and prime them, but I wanted to paint them and knew I was ready. Earl, the head painter, agreed with me but the owner of the company didn't. It was as though my father were afraid if I learned too much, he would have to pay me more.

At the end of the summer two Marty's Boys took a beating from a Dorchester gang. Arrangements were made to settle the score the following weekend. It would be an all out gang fight at a predetermined place.

I could hardly wait.

As I had in the past I went up and down the beach attempting to enlist others to help us but found no one willing. It seemed everyone had other things to do: barbecues to attend, plans for the Cape, and some just flat out said no. Out of twenty-five Marty's Boys, only five said they would fight for their friends.

The night before the scheduled brawl, I bumped into a former classmate, John "Mugsy" Murray and, after explaining the situation to him, asked if he would help. I wasn't surprised when Mugsy said no. He wasn't a fighter. But what he said next floored me. "Ricky, you don't get it. High school's over, we've graduated, man. No one cares about that shit anymore."

No one cared? I did, but then I realized that Mugsy was right. After this episode, as far as Quincy and Wollaston Beach were concerned, it was over for me too.

The following night, at the appointed time, five of us walked to the designated spot on the beach known as the Black Lagoon. All of us shared the same attitude: we might end up in the hospital, but we'd go down as a crew. It was one of the best nights of my life.

Especially after we waited for two hours and no one from Dorchester showed up.

Quincy Junior College

In 1969, the Vietnam War raged and so did the anti-war movement. In October a hundred thousand people gathered on the Boston Common to protest a war that they believed was unjust and immoral.

I like to think that I'm patriotic, love my country, and if I had graduated from high school in 1967, when the war was largely viewed in a positive light, would have probably joined the Marine Corps raring to fight. But two years later the mood of the country had changed. People I knew, upper class men initially, and later kids from my own class, were returing from Vietnam addicted to heroin and/or psychologically messed up. I was warned not to go but registered for the draft and if called would have reported.

Instead, I decided that I'd give higher education a shot and enrolled in Quincy Junior College. I only excelled in one class, English Composition. The professor said I had the heart of a writer, and encouraged me to keep at it. I think it was the first time I actually thought that I might become a writer someday.

While attending school, in late October 1970, I got a job as dishwasher in a Howard Johnson's restaurant, and busted my ass nights for two-fifty an hour.

I was clueless as to what I would do with my life, until the first time I saw troopers from the Massachusetts State police. Howard Johnson's was located just off the highway in Quincy and occasionally targeted by robbers, so troopers were always a welcome sight. The waitresses loved them, and it was easy to see why.

In those days, the mandatory retirement age for state troopers was fifty, so almost all of them were young, huge, and in tremendous physical shape. Every chance I got I'd pick their brains about the job. The adrenalin junkie (and maybe the hidden writer in me) imagined myself in high-speed chases, entering prisons to quell riots, and investigating homicides. The thought of being paid for it was almost secondary.

But whenever I would discuss the possibility of a police career with my father, his reaction was always the same. "I think you could do better," he'd say, and when I'd ask, doing what? His response? Stay in school and take business courses.

Undeterred, I did my research on the state police. I learned when the exam would be given, and what the basic height and weight requirements were. At five-nine and a quarter, I would just about squeak by on the height requirement, but making the weight would be tougher. At the time minimum recruit weight for a trooper was one hundred fifty-five pounds. At one forty-seven, I'd have to pack some on.

On a break at Hojo's one night, I revealed my plans to a huge, redheaded trooper. Staties generally work the highway alone, but this guy was a trooper "coach." With him was a probationary trooper fresh out of the academy.

When I related my plans to him he gave me a look, like I was out of my mind. Even the young trooper grinned. My cheeks growing hot my focus shifted from one face to the other.

I said, "What? You think I can't do it?"

The senior cop turned his back on me and waved to a young waitress who had just entered the kitchen.

I squeezed past them. I wanted to be like these sons-of-bitches? I don't think so.

But I guess deep down I still did.

The Combat Zone

1971

Cosmo, the brother of one of the cooks at Hojo's, tended bar in a strip club located in the Combat Zone, Boston's notorious adult entertainment district. The bulk of the district was on Washington Street, between Boylston and Kneeland, extending to Stuart Street and Park Square. It had gotten its name in the early sixties when sailors and Marines poured into the three city blocks heavily patrolled by military police.

Within the confines of the "Zone", as we called it, were porn shops, pool halls, massage parlors, peep shows, pornographic theaters, and most importantly, strip joints. The Zone was Disney Land for adults.

Seventeen the first time I went there, I managed, with the aid of a phony ABC (Alcohol Beverage Commission) card, to make it beyond the doorman of the Intermission Lounge. The Intermission on Washington Street was owned by the allegedly Mafia connected Balliro family. Small, smoke-filled and filthy, it was the only joint in the Zone with a carpeted floor but decade of foot traffic, spilled drinks, and blood gave it the appearance of asphalt in high summer.

But I wasn't there for the rug or the décor. A naked girl danced on the Intermission's main stage while go-go girls in elevated cages, either side of it, writhed to the blaring music just beneath the low ceiling that channeled their vibrations like a punch. As I sat at the bar, punch-drunk, sipping my five-dollar beer and worshipping the women, I thought I had died and gone to heaven.

Cosmo didn't bartend at the Intermission, but at another cavernous club named Jerome's Naked i on Washington Street. Next to the front door a sign advertised a "Totally Nude College Review," and above it a catchy neon sign displayed a winking eye over a supine women's crotch.

Cosmo had begun his career as a "bar-back", (a bar-back insures the bartenders have: cases of cold beer, buckets of ice, bottles of hard liquor, dump the trash, bar towels, whatever) then worked his way to bouncer, and eventually bartender. Bar-backs at the Naked i earned twenty-five bucks a night, plus a tip-out, which was a lot better dough than what I was making at Hojo's. Tired of washing dishes and sick of the state cops, I decided to see Cosmo.

The Naked i wasn't hiring but Cosmo was kind enough to make a suggestion. "Try the Downtown Lounge up the street," he said, "and tell Freddy, the manager, I sent you."

It was a few hours before noon when the Downtown's stoned-looking doorman let me in. The place was almost empty. The main room featured a horseshoe-shaped bar that wrapped around a long stage that resembled a lane in a bowling alley. A naked woman, wearing an obvious wig and a red, feather boa draped over her shoulders, grooved to the recorded music, some kind of jazz with little pauses and starts, her head listing to the side, like she was feeling the vibe.

I stood there amazed and watched her, barely aware of the bartender's approach. Cosmo's friend, Freddy, in a white, ruffled, open-collared shirt, said in a bored voice, "Yeah, what can I do you for?"

I told him why I was there and he gave me the once over. "You got any experience?"

I almost lied and told him I did, but shook my head.

Freddy said, "Just yesterday we fired this little Spic bar-back. Should have shit-canned him six months ago, but the owner liked him. He didn't like to show up for work. You gonna? What's your name?"

I told him my name, quickly adding that I'd show up on time. He gave me a second once over then shook my hand. "A friend of Cosmo's huh?"

Two nights later I began as a bar-back at the Downtown Lounge. Since I'd be working the same hours as Hojo's, I never told my parents I'd quit.

The new job kept me hopping. Like most Combat Zone strip joints, the Downtown's doors popped early, eight in the morning, and didn't close again until two the next morning. I worked the busiest nights—Thursday through Saturday.

The place was huge and usually jammed, and running ice and beer up the narrow stairway from the basement, then through the crowd was a lot tougher than washing dishes.

But Hojo's couldn't hold a candle to the energy of the place.

On weekends the club offered a live band with guys playing saxophones, trumpets, electric guitars, and drums, and an old guy in a tuxedo introducing each act. "Ladies and Gentlemen, for your viewing pleasure, a woman of beauty, mystery and sen-sual delight. A former Rockette and Las Vegas showgirl, please welcome La-dy Mis-ty."

He'd back out of the spotlight and the band would kick in playing a song like, "Big Spender" and Misty would make her entrance in a sequin encrusted robe, and every eye in the joint reflected its sparkles.

Sometimes the headliners used props like a chair or small couch, and the dance would tell a story. Headline acts, like The White Savage and Pink Champagne, followed the stripper circuit across the country and always worked the main floor. The new girls, the up and comers, or the older dancers, would work one of two stages in the back of the club.

The Downtown's clientele was a cross section of society. College kids with phony ID's, white and blue-collar workers, cops, ex-cons, and gangsters.

The Zone might have pushed vice, but it was also in one, the handle wrenched by the local branch of *La Cosa Nostra*, which was always referred to as "In Town". I don't think there was a business down there that didn't make regular payments for protection. It was rumored that the owners of the club paid two grand a month rent, like a tax, a huge sum in those days.

Other people had to be paid off as well. City fire inspectors, cops, inspectional services personnel all had their hands out, but the club owners raked in so much cash, no one seemed to care. Cash, not credit, was king in those days and, at the end of the night, the owners left with shopping bags full of it.

It didn't take me long to realize that there were opportunities to be made with the wiseguys who frequented the place. I saw them as fruit trees waiting to be plucked. It was forbidden fruit sure but, young and hungry, and searching for that adrenalin rush, I didn't care where the produce came from.

Over the next few months, I got cozy with a couple of East Boston wise guys. They were just younger versions of the North End gangsters my father knew, and they didn't attend college or have business degrees. They took shit from no one, were rich, and I thought that could work for me.

When they'd walk into the place I'd flatter them, make a big deal about their suits, the watch on their wrist, or the quality of the lady on their arm. I was a kid, with a good sense of humor, so I got away with a lot. When I'd make a remark like, "What a fucking knock-out, Paulie, but man would she look better with me." Paulie would shake his fist and say, "Know something kid? You got balls for a bar-back."

And that was exactly what I wanted him to think, I had balls.

When I made Paulie and his pals laugh, I saw it as just another way in, and I found it easy to make those guys laugh. When they'd walk through the door I'd be on them like stink. I'd say, "Hey you guys, how're doin'?" Shake their hands and make a big fuss over them. It wasn't all show because I was genuinely happy to see them. Other men kissed their ass because they feared them or owed them money, but to me these men were the real deal, hard guys, and I wanted to be just like them.

One morning after a shift, I was home eating breakfast when my father came into the kitchen and said, "So, how was *work* last night?"

My stomach jumped because I thought that he thought I was still working at Hojo's.

I started to answer but he stopped me.

"You think I don't know what you're doing," he said. "If I believed for a minute you were drinking in that dump, you'd be out of there, understand?"

But my father knew that I didn't drink.

"You making any money?" he said.

"I'm doing alright."

He waved a finger, "Okay, we won't tell your mother, but when you're there, you work, and you don't get caught up in the bullshit, okay?"

"Okay."

And that was that. I was in.

When I had first started work at the club there were night when Paulie would hand me a thick, legal-sized, envelope, with one end folded over and secured by elastic, to give to the doorman. One night after he handed it to me, he grabbed my arm as I turned. "Not the doorman," he said. "You, I want you to do this." He then gave instructions for me to run up to Essex Street, near the Playland. "There'll be a guy in a gray Mercury, Phil, got a moustache. Give it to him. And make sure ain't cops around when you do."

I ran like a gazelle through the weekend crowd, located Phil and returned. When Paulie, standing at the bar, turned around and saw me he was shocked. He said, "Ricky, what the fuck? The guy's waiting."

"He got it," I said and his eyebrows jumped, and he pulled out a roll and peeled off a twenty, but I refused to take it.

"Just glad to help," I said, and went back to work.

From then on it was me running with an envelope, and some nights I'd make multiple trips. I'd run to the Intermission, the Pink Pussycat, Jerome's, The Mousetrap, or some other joint to pick one up. At Paulie's insistence I was taking the twenty dollars for every delivery. Twenty dollars at that time was a good score, worth about one hundred dollars today, so some nights I was making three or four hundred bucks. Not shabby for a kid, but I wanted more.

I tried to impress my father with my new contacts, believing that he would be proud, but when he learned about my friends, it made him uneasy. I was confused. Was this the same guy who always told me stories about his hoodlum associates when I was a kid?

Then one night as Paulie was getting ready to leave, he pulled me aside and made a proposal. "I'm opening a business with some guys from the North Shore. You got a car, I can put you to work. Interested?"

I was and didn't ask what I'd be doing because I didn't care. But I needed a car.

The next day I told my father that I wanted to buy a car, but when he asked me the reason, still trying to impress him, I stupidly told him. He gave me two options: quit the club or get out of the house.

I couldn't buy a car and remain home so I figured I'd ask Paulie, who was great at working angles, what I should do. That night Paulie never showed up, but at one in the morning, my father called looking for me. I figured, okay, he's probably just checking to see if I quit. But when I went to the office to pick up the phone, the look on the manager's face said no, it was something more

Friday nights my father played cards with his friends, at least that's what he told us, and rarely came home before one. When he got home that night he'd found my mother unconscious on the bedroom floor. He was calling from Quincy City Hospital, where she'd been admitted into the ICU for a drug overdose.

My father said, "You better get here."

I had sand in my guts as I sped back to Quincy.

I left my father in the visiting room and entered Mum's cubicle in the ICU. I examined her from the foot of the bed. Beneath the thin sheet was the outline of a body once vibrant but now bird-like and reduced to the sum of wires attached to it and the stainless steel box with blinking lights next to her.

There was a calmness to her face that had been absent for years, but when I reached to touch her, I paused. In the curious ICU half-light, I stood there watching her breath and thought about the good times we had shared, the crazy birthday parties, the trips to Nantasket Beach, the candy-filled baskets on Easter mornings. All the brilliant snapshots strung, like Christmas lights, above the years of brutal beatings.

Behind me a nurse stuck her head through the curtain and said, "Don't worry hon, she'll be okay. She's got a strong heart."

I thanked her and pulled up a chair and, sitting down, placed my hand over my mother's. "It's Ricky, Ma," I said and stayed until the sun rose.

Kenmore Square

1970-71

My mother bounced back from the overdose and after completing a drug and alcohol program was admitted to the psyche ward of a private hospital, the Human Resource Center in Brookline.

My father was busy juggling between his job, visiting our mother, and attempting to maintain a semblance of control over my younger brothers, Ronnie and Scot. In an effort to help out I passed on Paulie's offer and quit my job in the Combat Zone.

After completing my first year of college I decided to drop out. I remember the look on my father's face, the disappointment when I told him in his office at the John Roche Co. He tried to talk me into staying in school, but I'd made up my mind.

He said, "So what do you plan to do with your life?"

"How about I work here for you, and really learn the business," I said.

But that kind of talk made him uneasy. He said I could work at the shop *for* him, but that was it, I'd be performing the same tasks I had been for years. Unable to see any options, I took the job.

For the next two months, twice a week after work, I'd return home and pick up Ronnie and Scot, and we'd drive to the HRC (Human Resource Center) in Brookline to visit our mother. Along with my father, and sometimes our older brother Bob, we would sit through 90 minutes of family counseling. I didn't mind the sessions. It was obvious that our mother, sober and relatively happy now, looked better than she had in years but the crazy thing was she honestly believed, incorrectly, she could still save the marriage.

For my father, it was done. He had a longtime girlfriend whom I would see skulking around the shop when I worked, but girlfriends were nothing new for him. In the past, especially after a night of the two of them drinking, I would hear my mother accuse him of cheating, and they would fight over it, the fights sometimes becoming physical.

Cara returned from school out west. Crazy in love with her before she left, my passion had cooled. I had been dating other women but for reasons totally lost to me now I started to see her again.

At the shop there was a painter named Eddie who liked to party weekends in Kenmore Square. Packed with universities and colleges, the area was white hot with nightclubs that catered to the younger set. Within five city blocks, over a dozen clubs sprouted like sponges eager to soak up their energy, money and, occasionally, blood. Students from all over the country flocked to places like: Oliver's, Kings Row, The Ark, Copperfield's, City Club, The Up and Up, Pooh's Pub, Lucifer, and a place called T.J.'s Lounge. T.J.'s, formerly known as The Rathskellar, was located 528 Commonwealth Ave in the center of the square, and had the reputation of being easy to get into.

On a fall night in 1971 I walked into the upstairs lounge just as a fight broke out. Three red-shirt bouncers and a stocky guy, with a Mediterranean look and eyebrows thick as ferrets, battled a suburban softball team. The T.J.s' crew was tough and as the bouncers dragged the players out by their feet, one of them wrapped his arms around a balcony column. As the bouncers yanked his legs, stretching him out like a clothesline, I stomped the guy's wrists.

I watched them toss him out and a voice behind me said, "Nice move, you react fast." I turned around and saw the guy with the thick eyebrows. He grinned and offered his hand. "Thanks, I'm Tommy Matook. I manage this place."

Right off I asked him for a job, bouncing, but T.J.'s wasn't hiring. Matook said, "Listen kid, I'll keep you mind, but for now why don't you go downstairs and check out the band."

After descending the narrow stairway to the left of the main entrance, I entered a room that pulsed with the sound of heavy metal. Packed with stoners, bikers, college kids in t-shirts, and mini-skirted bleach blonds with too much mascara, the humid air was ripe with the scent of rancid beer, body odor, and Aqua Velva.

I made my way to the bar and ordered a coke, and then searched for and located the band, which played on a tiny stage fifty feet across the room. Above a sea of pumping fists, their heads and vertical guitars were changing colors under the lights.

I looked back at the door and saw Matook come in with a bar-back behind him lugging a bucket of ice. Bobbing like an icebreaker on a frozen sea, he worked his way through the crowd. Tommy approached, placed a hand and on my shoulder, and signaled someone over. It was a tall kid whom I had spotted earlier standing at the drink rail. He had been eyeing me since I came in. Tommy shouted into my ear, "Rick, meet Rich Torsney, everyone calls him T. T's from Southie and one of our bouncers."

I looked into T's eyes. "Southie?" I said, my hackles rising. "I've had problems with guys from Southie."

T's eyebrows went up but he still stuck his hand out. "Well, any friend of Tommy's won't have one with me," he said.

There were no openings for bouncers but T still showed me the ropes of the place, the hot spots, and tough to get out of areas when fights broke out, and Torsney knew about fighting. He was the current New England Middleweight Golden Gloves Champion.

At the end of the night, just as I was leaving, T let me in on a secret. He had had problem at a Quincy yacht club the summer before. "On a lark," he said, "I took the flare gun from the boat with me, and it ended up saving my life."

What?

I sat down and motioned for T to take the seat across the table. "You and me got something to discuss," I said.

Bank Robbery and Other Job Opportunities

1972

T.J.'s Lounge in the early 1970's was what was called "unaffiliated," which made it unique. It meant that no one controlled the place, not the Mafia or the Irish Mob, but the average T.J.'s customer ran the gamut of underworld types who were used to working more angles than a kaleidoscope. There were dealers pushing just about every drug: meth, weed, coke and whatever hallucinogens happened to be around. Whether you wanted an eight ball or a kilo, an ounce of weed or a bale, someone in T.J.s would take your order.

A skinny, black kid named Ace passed counterfeit bills, Hank the bartender/resident bookie, as well as a crew of bank robbers who used the lounge as a private clubhouse.

Frank Rossi was a regular customer and a favorite of mine. Seven years older than me, Rossi was the undisputed leader of the bank robbing crew. He was funny, articulate, drank but wasn't a drunk, and tough but rarely fought. Frank had money but never flashed it, except for his penchant for new Cadillac Eldorados.

Frank and his crew would disappear on "road trips" and whack a string of out-of-state banks. When they showed up again, the celebration lasted for days. To me they were like rock stars. Now I felt the hell with the stuck-up state police, I wanted to be just like them.

At the end of the summer of '71 I took my first pinch. The bar fight wasn't a big deal, both sides had landed punches, but a half an hour later one of the "victims" returned with police and two of us were charged with assault and battery. I got lucky later in court when the case was dismissed.

Less than a year after her hospitalization, my mother relapsed and overdosed again. By this time my father was long gone, so it was one of my brothers who found her. It was more of the same thing; she went to Quincy Hospital ICU, a detox, and then a long stay at the Human Resource Center.

Eight months later things got worse. My mother went on a bender for days; the only reports that she was alive came from my brothers who would see her, like a character out of a John Carpenter flick, creeping from the bedroom into the john.

One morning after work at the club the previous night, I slept in until eleven then got up and was rinsing my face in the bathroom when I heard the gunshot, followed by the sound of falling, broken glass. I burst into my mother's bedroom. The air was filled with the stench of body odor, burnt hair, and cordite and my mother was in a corner sobbing uncontrollably, arms hanging loose by her side, one hand gripping a revolver. She had put the gun to her head and pulled the trigger but, at the last second, had turned away. The bullet had passed through her hair, the large mirror on the bureau, and ended up in the wall.

I screamed at her, "What the fuck are you doing?" and lunging around the bed ripped the gun from her hand. My mother crumpled on the edge of the mattress, sobbing and rambling, but some of what she said made sense.

"I can't take this. I can't take this anymore, any-mooore. I can't I--"

I grabbed her arm and yanked her to her feet.

"You can't take it?" I said. "You? What about us? I've fucking had it. We've all fucking had it. Next time do it right and kill yourself, get it over with."

It was a terrible thing to say, but I meant every word. All she had put me through as a kid, everything that I had tried to move on from was bubbling up now like pus from a wound. I was tired of the trips to the hospital and the bughouse, tired of the nightmare of her pacing around drunk. I snapped the shade up and called for an ambulance.

I walked my mother to the flowered chair by the window and sat her down, and as sunlight washed over her. "Last stop, Ma," I said. "This is it, no one's helping you anymore. You have to do it yourself or you're done. Understand?"

She gave me the same look she always did just before she entered a detox. I searched for and failed to find something different in those eyes. The ambulance came and took her away.

It was the first day of my mother's recovery.

Flix

Days were spent working at my father's shop, and I bounced in the club nights. In early spring, my father stopped talking to me again for some bullshit reason. This time it dragged on for months. Finally, I quit the Roche Co. and within a week landed a new job as head painter at Concord Auto Body, a large facility in Concord, MA.

I had also quit TJ's Lounge then wrangled a doorman's job at a new club down the street called, Flix. Flix occupied the first floor of the old Hotel Somerset on Commonwealth Ave. and catered to an upscale crowd.

From the start, the place was a smash. Part of the attraction had to do with its indoor swimming pool, four fully stocked bars, regulation as well as bumper pool tables, and the images of famous movie stars that covered the walls of its Hollywood themed interior.

Along with regular customers, underworld players frequented Flix. People like George Pappas, a reputed killer and drug trafficker, whom I met for the first time while I was working the door.

I had been having a problem with a group of young, North End hoodlums who were all juiced up on steroids and coke. I viewed them as trouble waiting to happen but needed an excuse to bar them.

I said to them, "I'm sorry guys but house policy says no sneakers."

All of them looked at their feet, even the ones that had shoes on. "Fuck you," one of them said, "we're from the North End and connected, you motherfucker."

"Connected" meant they had ties to the mob, but usually it was bullshit. My usual response would be, "Yeah, connected to my dick." But this time I kept my mouth shut. There were five of them sweating, and with their eyes bugging out. If something kicked off, I'd be dog meat in seconds.

They began moving up the steps and then stopped, their leader focused on something behind me.

George Pappas stood there, grinning like a nasty genie. Pappas threw out energy like a Tesla coil, and he must have fired a couple of bolts because collectively the North Enders took a step back. The leader, the crazy in his eyes replaced now by fear, said, "Hey, George, what's up?"

Pappas came up next to me, shoulder to shoulder. He said, "Why you guys givin' the kid a hard time?"

One of the punks shouted, "Hey, who the fuck are--?" but a glare from the leader shut him up quick.

The leader sheepishly said, "George, we weren't bustin' the guy's balls, we just--"

"It's the sneakers," I said. "We got house rules against them."

Pappas shrugged his thick shoulders and shook his head. "Sorry guys, it's their policy, and their house, and everyone knows you can't beat the house."

The pack sullenly moved down the street, and as Pappas returned inside I shouted thanks at his back. Without turning he said in his gravelly voice, "You're welcome. I'll get us a drink, you deserve one."

When he returned, he handed me a glass filled with an amber liquid and ice cubes. I asked him what it was.

"Dubonnet on the rocks, a gentlemen's drink."

I drank it but didn't like it, but I liked this new guy Pappas.

Quincy District Court

I had just arrived home from work when my mother informed me that George Burke had called. "He wants you to go over and see him," she said. Burke was a neighbor on Wollaston Hill. He was also the District Attorney of Norfolk County. As a kid, I had worked on his early campaigns passing flyers out door-to-door and I guess, in a small way, helped him move up the political ladder. Little did I know then about the depth of his memory, or how generous he could be when it came to rewarding his friends.

Burke's wife, Sandy, let me in their house and directed me to the living room. I stopped at the entrance to the room. On the tube the Celtics were playing the '76'ers, and Burke, a former Celtic, was glued to the screen. I stood there a moment watching him watching them before I said, "Mr. Burke?"

He snapped out of his trance, grinned, and motioned me over with one of his big hands.

Burke had good news. There was an opening in his office for an administrative assistant, was I interested in the job?

He said, "Listen Rick, I think you'd be great. You can trade in that painter's uniform for a shirt and tie, work in a nice clean environment, earn a bigger paycheck, and learn about the criminal justice system. I'd say it's a slam dunk."

I was almost leaping out of my skin as I returned to my house that night. Imagine me a professional in the DA's office? I couldn't believe my luck.

Two weeks later I started work for the DA's office in the Dedham Superior courthouse, the same building where Sacco and Vanzetti had been convicted fifty years earlier. Within weeks I was transferred to busy Quincy District Court that had one of the heaviest, criminal caseloads in the Commonwealth.

In Quincy I was lucky to have a great boss, Peter McGonnigal. I was assigned to the courtroom, where my job was to monitor the proceedings, and keep track of the findings for our office. I got a close look at the vaunted American judicial system. As I performed my duties, I also heard police officers from various departments testify in criminal cases. I got to see who was prepared and who wasn't. State troopers appeared to have the most on the ball, which renewed my interest in joining the force.

In 1972 I took the tough written exam, survived the background investigation, and passed the state police physical test, which included, running a sub six-thirty mile. Put on the waiting list, I waited four years.

The comedian Lenny Bruce once said, "In the halls of justice the only justice is in the halls." Four years in a courtroom convinced me, he was right.

I had grown up believing TV courtroom dramas like *Perry Mason*, *The Defenders*, and *Ironside* depicted the way that the system actually worked, but the reality was vastly different. Wealthy defendants rarely saw the inside of a jail, not even rich *sex offenders*. Case overload was another reason the system was broke, and for the sake of expediency, many deals *were* hammered out in the halls.

At the time, much like today, most judges were just highly connected political hacks. Some may have been qualified, but many weren't. I saw judges that rushed through their daily caseload so they could leave and play golf. One went so far as to announce in open court that he had a three o'clock tee-time, and the ADA had better not make him late.

The courtroom could also be funny. There was a case involving an eighty-year-old black man named Morris in court for assaulting his wife. With Morris on the stand, the ADA put it to him directly. "Mr. Morris," he said. "Did you, or did you not, strike your wife in the face?" Morris gave the crowd a big shit-eating grin and said, "Hit her, counselor? Man, I nailed her with a shot that would have knocked out Mo-hammed Ali." The courtroom went wild.

And other things happened that weren't so funny.

One morning I was surprised to see my Flix friend, George Pappas, in the courthouse crowd. The look on his face said he was in trouble. I asked him what was going on, and Pappas replied he had been written up for motor vehicle violations, what would be called "road rage" today. It would not have been a big deal—if Pappas weren't already on probation for something more serious. I said to him, "Why didn't you mention this at the club?"

Brushing it off, he said, "I handle my own shit, and don't like to bother people with the small stuff."

But the small stuff wasn't small. The previous year he had been convicted of assault and battery and given a suspended sentence of one year in jail, with probation for another two years. Pappas was no stranger to jail, and a year wasn't a big deal, but he had a wife and kids to support. If convicted on the motor vehicle charge, Pappas was gone.

I had a friend in Probation pull Pappas's record and was surprised to learn, considering the terrible things I'd heard about the guy, that his criminal record was far from extensive. It consisted mostly of minor stuff, with a couple of short stints in the county lock-up. In those days criminal records were typed onto index cards, and Pappas's only filled two, mostly motor vehicle infractions, with a third card almost empty, except for the assault and battery conviction.

When I began work with the District Attorney's Office, I was schooled that in our world there were only two sides, and we were the good guys. But after working in the courthouse, as well as in nightclubs for years, I realized that things weren't that simple. Pappas was a friend. On more than one occasion, he had stood shoulder to shoulder with me at the club facing down trouble and had never once asked for anything in return. Even at this juncture, resigned to the fact he was going to jail, he did not ask for help.

He didn't have to.

I took the third probation card, with the assault conviction on it, and stuck it inside my suit coat pocket. Pappas pleaded guilty to the motor vehicle charges later that morning and when the judge looked at his record, with no assault conviction on it, all he received was a fine and short loss of license

Later, outside the courthouse, I watched his jaw drop when I told him what I'd done. He said, "Man, I thought I was going to jail; I knew you were up to something. Thanks kid, you got balls, I owe ya." But Pappas owed me nothing. In the past he had my back, now I had his. That was my only misstep in the four years I worked for the Norfolk DA because I did not believe in playing both sides.

When I returned inside, Braintree police Sergeant John Graziano approached me. John and I were friends and Pappas happened to live in his town. "Rick," he said, looking concerned. "I saw you talking to Pappas, how do you know him? Do you know he's bad news?"

I explained how I had met Pappas at Flix. I admitted that I had heard about his reputation but had never fed into the gossip. John said. "He's not someone you should be associating with." I assured John that I didn't plan to and, at the time, meant it. Little did I know then how my life and Pappas's would eventually cross, and run parallel, just a few years down the road.

The Rat

In 1975 I left Flix and began working in a new rock and roll joint called The Rat. My pal, Jim Harold, a bruiser who loved to brawl and former top UMass football player, had leased the downstairs of the former TJ's Lounge and had been booking bands playing a new kind of music. They called it punk rock.

In the early days crowds at The Rat were sparse and consisted mostly of scruffy camp followers of the bands that played there. Money was tight. Most weeks Harold barely made enough to pay the staff wages.

Less than a year later things were quite different.

Like a top Las Vegas odds maker, Harold developed a knack for picking the right bands to showcase in the club. Whatever hot group was playing CBGB'S, the New York City punk rock mecca and the Rat's alter ego, Harold conned into playing the Rat. On weekends, and sometimes during the week, the line in front of the place stretched down the block.

I ran the door and the floor security. There was a cover charge at the door, and when name bands like: The Ramones, The Talking Heads, or The Police played, bribes to get in were common. They came in various forms: money (my preference), sex (for some bouncers blow-jobs in the balcony were part of doing business), and drugs.

I had managed to avoid LSD, Quaaludes, Black Beauties, and every other drug of the era. I only recently begun to drink again, just beer, and that's all I did, until I tried coke.

A friend from Dorchester, Bobby, was a frequent Rat customer. He was a hustler and thief who specialized in stealing high-end cars: Porsches, Mercedes, Lincolns, and Caddies, which he shipped out of state to waiting customers. Bobby made a ton of dough, lived the fast life, and loved cocaine. He always had it on him, offered it to me, and I always refused.

Then one night I didn't.

I left the door and followed Bobby upstairs to the Rat's balcony, where we sat at a table and each snorted a long line of something that tasted like bubble gum. The Peruvian flake hit me like an uppercut to the chin.

Back on the door when I laughingly asked Bobby about the danger of addiction, he responded, "Hell, everyone does it man. It's a party drug. You think everyone's a fucking addict?"

It made sense. No one that I knew was addicted to cocaine. At least not until later that night when, after I pissed, I gazed into men's room mirror.

6.

Okinawa

September 1977

When I was fourteen I began to study karate. I got hooked after watching Frank Sinatra, in the 1962 movie *The Manchurian Candidate,* chopping tables in half with his bare hands. I had suffered abuse as a kid so I thought that if I could master karate, no one could ever mess with me again.

My first school was The Mattson Academy in Braintree and in 1975, after ten years of on and off study; I earned my black belt in Okinawan Uechi-Ryu karate. Then, searching for new challenges, I decided I'd travel to Okinawa, Japan, to study under the Grand Master of our system, Kanei Uechi. I was twenty-five and he was the closest thing I had to a hero at the time.

Within a few months of my marriage to Cara (we were married in September 1976), although she was opposed to the trip and we had fought over it often, I left for Okinawa. To a certain degree though Cara was right. It was selfish to leave her and to spend all that money but the trip, in the planning for years, was something I thought I had to do. It had taken a decade to earn that black belt, and I wanted to test myself against the best in the world.

As the plane circled the island preparing to land I looked out the window and watched the white ring of the East China Sea pounding Okinawa's coral shores, and thought of my father the Navy man. Only thirty-three years earlier, as part of the largest amphibious assault of World War II, his ship and hundreds like it were in those same waters and under attack by swarms of Japanese kamikaze pilots. The bloodiest naval battle of the war included five thousand naval personnel among the fourteen thousand allied dead.

After a twenty-six hour flight I got off the plane in Naha and it felt like I stepped into an oven. I hailed a cab and told the driver to take me to Futenma, where the master's dojo was located.

After a few days to recover from jet lag, I showed up at the dojo and found it very similar to the ones back home. There was a heavy bag, some free weights, iron sandals to strengthen your legs, but in one corner something I had never seen before, a small Shinto shrine.

Monday through Friday I attended a four hour class, and sometimes another in the evening. Despite Okinawa's daily average temperature of a humid ninety degrees I trained my heart out.

Whenever I performed a series of kicks, punches and blocks correctly, the old man, Master Uechi, then in his late sixties, would smile and nod. But when I screwed up a strike, block, or God forbid, one of the katas (formal exercises), he'd wince and shake his head, and it would cut me to the core.

It wasn't all hard work, a guy had to relax, so on weekends I partied hard. I had been there for a month when I met Arbie Kenefick. Arbie, an American, had been on the island four years studying under the master.

Weekends would find us in local bars and sometimes bars not so local. A few miles north of Futenma was Koza. When the Vietnam war raged, Koza, with it massage parlors, strip clubs, and brothels, was a favorite R&R destination for thousands of American servicemen.

One night, following a visit to a Koza strip club, we found Arbie's '73 Honda blocked in by two cabs. Earlier I had warned him not to park in an "Oky" cabstand because the drivers had a ferocious reputation. A short distance away a large group of them huddled and squinted at us through cigarette smoke.

Arbie ordered me into the car. I figured okay he'll start the car, then we'll sit and wait. The cabbies, after making their point don't park here again, eventually will saunter down and move their vehicles. But Arbie had this crazy glint in his eyes as he turned the engine over. He said, "Put the seatbelt on, Rick," and revved up the engine, and I knew we were in for a hellava ride.

Shifting into reverse, he popped the clutch and blasted into the Toyota behind us, knocked it back three feet. Then he shifted back into first and rammed the car ahead crushing the taillights. A plastic, ruby shower, rained down on the hood.

I howled with laughter and had just managed a, "One-more-time," when the first punch, through the open window, flattened my ear.

"Fucking GI son a bitch." My assailant's fingers were wrapped around my throat now, and he was trying to pull me out. Grabbing his shirt, and a clump of hair, I savagely yanked him into the car until our faces were inches apart.

I gagged on his fish breath as Arbie rammed the car behind us again.

"Fucking Jap fuck,"

"Fucking GI."

"Aaahhhhhh!"

"Aaahhhhhh!"

I was busy breaking knobs off the radio with his head when Arbie was yanked out by the mob of enraged cabbies. Then I was next. It turned into a bad night.

The next morning I woke up just after seven, body aching and head pounding, to the sound of sirens. I walked out onto the second floor balcony in my underwear and gazed down the street. Less than a block away I saw the flashing lights of emergency vehicles.

I slipped on a pair of shorts and flip-flops and headed toward the action. Okinawan cops and Marine MP's from Camp Butler, the base across the street, had blocked the road off with bright orange cones. They ordered the gathering crowd to stay back as they redirected traffic up a side street.

The road had been under construction for the past month, part of an island-wide multi-million dollar sewerage project to accommodate the region's growing population. Huge lengths of concrete pipe were being installed and a deep trench hugged the road for miles.

During my stay I had made friends with quite a few Marines, mostly karate students from Camp Butler, and as I circumvented the ring of police and MP's, I spotted one of them, a Gunny sergeant named Norm holding with a camera to his face.

I shouted, "Hey Norman, what's up?"

He lowered it and ordered the cops to let me to pass. When I came up beside him he said, "Ordinance, Rick, got a thousand pounder in that trench."

Then I saw it too, less than fifty feet from where we stood. The huge bomb looked more like a fat torpedo and may as well been made out of sugar the way a Marine bomb disposal team, and others, scrambled over it like ants.

Norm jumped into the trench and tossed the camera to me. He said, "When I heard this baby was out here had to get me a shot." And scrambled toward it, yelling over his shoulder, "Take a few of me, Rick, and I'll get you."

It seemed like everyone had cameras. A Marine posed with his foot on what was left of the bomb's tail-fin, then he switched up with the picture taker who scurried to the front, squatted, and kissed the bomb's head while giving the thumb's up.

Hell, this was exciting. I jumped into the trench and caught up with Norm. When I commented on how fired up everyone was, Norm gave me this look like what, don't you get it?

He said, "God-damn, Rick, we're Marines. You know how many of us were lost on this pissant island?"

He gazed at the bomb like it was an Angora kitten. "Look at her sleeping there, a thing of real beauty, but hell, she wakes up the whole fucking block goes. Weapons like this saved Marine lives, probably your Dad's too."

The bomb disposal guys were really getting pissed now. They were screaming and yelling at people, especially at a young Marine who had cut the line and was down on all fours licking the bomb like a cherry Popsicle.

I snapped a photo of Norm straddling the bomb grasping invisible reins. Then someone else got the two of us squatting near the tail. A half hour later the bomb guys defused it and carted it away. I heard it ended up as a coffee table in some colonel's office.

A week later at the same time sirens woke me again. In the process of fire hydrant installation, on the opposite side of the street, workers had dug up another huge bomb, this one even closer to my building. From the balcony I scanned the crowd to see if Norm and his camera were there. They weren't. I went back to bed and slept until ten.

I had been studying hard for three months when Master Uechi, who had taken a liking to me, recommended I be tested for Nidan, second-degree black belt, at the end of another six weeks of training. I wanted that belt, but I also missed my wife. I had written her weekly and we talked on the phone often, but it wasn't enough. I said good-bye to my training partners at the dojo, Gunny Sergeant Norm, my drinking partner Arbie, and Master Uechi and boarded a plane back to Boston.

Cara had no idea I was coming. When I walked through the door of our M Street apartment. I put my bags in the bedroom and, exhausted, fell asleep on the living room couch.

A few hours later, I heard a key in the lock, the door open, and Cara gasp when she noticed me on the couch.

Within days I received information that would have made Cara gasp again.

While I was in Okinawa, Cara had started a new job in a bar, Ames Plow, in Boston's hot Quincy Market District. A friend knew an a guy employed in a pizza joint inside the same complex. The guy, a regular at Ames Plow, had told my pal that Cara had been plowing one of the bartenders there.

I was angry and hurt. I had been faithful to her. Sure, I had been lonely too, and there were beautiful women in Okinawa, but I had taken my marriage vows seriously. My friend had no reason to lie but I still lacked proof, solid proof, my wife had been unfaithful. It was years before I realized that real evidence existed.

My father had never trusted my wife. Maybe because over the course of his own life he had dated a string of Cara's, and could tell one a mile away. While I was gone he had hired a friend, a private detective, to follow her but wisely kept his findings to himself, at least until after Cara and I were divorced. When I was a kid he was a lousy father, but making up for it now.

In hindsight it was a good thing that I was such a trusting idiot. Had I known about Cara's cheating, it might have distracted me from the toughest test of my life that hovered just around the corner.

MSP

Cara was in the shower just off the kitchen when the yellow telephone on the kitchen wall rang. She shouted through the cascading water.

"Richard if that's work, tell them I can."

I was hardly working so she had been volunteering for extra shifts at the bar.

When I picked up the phone, in no mood to talk with anyone from Ames Plow, the voice on the other end surprised me. "This is Trooper Davidson from the State Police Academy in Framingham. Could I please speak to Richard?"

"Speaking," I said, realizing quickly what the call was about.

"Richard, you've been on the list for over four years. We're planning another class, the 60th Recruit Training Troop, beginning in February. Are you still interested in joining the Massachusetts State Police?"

I was dumbstruck. Home less than two weeks, I had returned to work at the Rat. Beyond that, I had no plans for my life. At the nightclub I made decent money but the job had no future.

Now a future had been dropped in my lap. Aware that state police earned peanuts, I asked the trooper, "How long is the training, and will I get paid while I'm there?"

"The academy runs for twenty-two weeks and, yes, you'll get a stipend."

Maybe it was an omen, but on the day that I was supposed to report to the academy, eastern Massachusetts was hit with the Blizzard of '78, and the starting date pushed ahead.

When I reported the following week, it wasn't long before I learned that the drill instructors, many of them former Marines, believed that none of us would ever qualify to wear the boots and breeches of the Massachusetts State Police, the oldest organization of its kind in the nation. The first day I did over seven hundred push-ups and damaged a triceps muscle so badly I was unable to bend the arm for days.

And the torture didn't let up for twenty-two weeks.

A month into the training, Cara told me she was pregnant. It was unplanned and I was shocked. All I could think of was how could we afford a child with her tending bar and me barely working, and soon we would be reduced to one income.

Three months later, while at the academy, I was called downstairs one night and informed that Cara had suffered a miscarriage. A weakness in her cervix allowed it to open prematurely and the baby had dropped.

The only comforting news was that Cara was at my mother's house at the time, and my mother had been sober for years. When I got the house, I did my best to console Cara.

Physically she seemed to be okay but she resented the fact that I wasn't distraught. She was right, I wasn't, but there were reasons.

It's painful to admit now, but I knew that I wasn't mature enough to accept the responsibility of a child. And there were selfish sentiments; I wanted more time to be alone with my wife to see if I could really love her again.

The next day as I sat on the wall in front of my mother's house, a car pulled up with my brother and some of his friends. Possibly in an attempt to lift my spirits someone tossed a lit pack of firecrackers out. When I went back inside Cara called me a heartless monster, implying that I was celebrating the death of our child.

I couldn't return to the academy fast enough.

East Bum Fuck

In mid-July 1978, I graduated along with the other members of the 60th Recruit Training Troop from the Massachusetts State Police Academy. Three elements determined class rank: physical training, academics, and perhaps the most coveted, the instructor's rating. The top rating meant the instructors had come to a consensus that a particular recruit had all the qualities that might someday make him/her the best cop in the class. When I was chosen for that honor, it was one of the proudest moments of my life.

The process which began twenty-two weeks earlier with a hundred and twenty-four women and men, ended with eighty-four graduates. Out of the thirteen original female candidates, only one had made it all the way through.

Forged in the fire of the state police academy, each graduate had a sense of *esprit de corps* and a fierce pride in what they'd accomplished. But pride wouldn't pay the bill at the supermarket checkout counter. We'd be among the lowest paid state troopers in the nation. At the time there were troopers with children collecting food stamps to get by on.

The starting pay for my classmates and me, at least those with only a high school diploma, was $10,700 (in today's dollars an annual gross of thirty-nine thousand). Twice a month I'd get a "draw check" for one hundred and forty dollars then, at the end, receive the balance owed with interest. Within a year a proposal in the state house, allegedly, would increase the starting salary to fifteen thousand dollars, still lousy but better than nothing.

Aside from the obvious problem with wages, the MSP was plagued by other problems due to budgetary constraints and a governor, Michael Dukakis, who hated his troopers. There was a shortage of almost everything: cruisers, gas, tires, uniforms, and even ammunition. Most of the cruisers—none at the time had air conditioning or even a security cage—were falling apart. In the hot summer months engines had to be left constantly running, shift after shift, because if turned off would never start again.

There was something else too. I hadn't joined the force with the same starry-eyed view of the equity of the criminal justice system that most of my classmates had. Nor did automatically view those of us on "the job" as the "good guys." That perspective was too simplistic because over the years I had met some good bad guys, and some really bad cops. As a police officer, I planned to take everything on a case-by-case basis, testify honestly in court, and let the chips fall where they may.

Regardless of my point of view, I was pumped up knowing I was now part of an elite force, ready to hit the streets, and excel in a road troopers job: multi-car accident reconstruction, apprehension of drunk drivers, speed traps, and drug running interdiction. I wanted to tear into the heart of it, get into the action, and make a difference in somebody's life.

But my superiors had other ideas.

Due to my class rank, I assumed, incorrectly, that I would be assigned to a really busy barracks. Just before graduation we stood in formation, and Sgt. John DiFava went down the list of individual barrack assignments ". . . Long, Norwell Barracks; Glasheen, Andover Barracks; Lilly, Bourne Barracks; Marinick, Topsfield Barracks." My heart skipped a beat, and then bounced off the asphalt.

Topsfield? I'd been assigned to East Bum Fuck.

Topsfield, a small rural town off Route 95 close to the New Hampshire border, had about the same crime rate as an Amish barn, and was a far cry from the action outpost that I had envisioned. With little choice, I reported for work and was assigned to a "trooper coach," the veteran cop I would ride with, and who would train me during the three-month probationary period.

I found that most of the cops I worked with were great. Staff Sergeant McAuliffe ran a tight but fair ship. If you did your job, which included writing a strict minimum of eight citations per shift or "eight for eight" as they called it, McAuliffe wouldn't bust your balls. But there were other, less desirable men, like Corporal Arnold "Arnie" Ellis.

For some reason right from the start Corporal Ellis was on me. My accident reports weren't comprehensive enough, my hair was too long, I didn't log the correct mileage of my cruiser, etc. And I didn't like Ellis with his greasy, slicked back hair and the way he talked out the side of his mouth like a gangster.

Ellis led an extravagant lifestyle for a trooper at the time. New Lincoln Continental, nice house, and I heard that he liked to bet on the ponies, a lot. He allegedly also owned a racehorse somewhere. I was a street guy, and every instinct told me that this little toad was rotten. I tried to avoid him as much as I could.

There were other shady things about Topsfield. A year or so earlier, before I was assigned there, the barracks itself had been the scene of a crime. Hundreds of pounds of confiscated marijuana had disappeared from a locked storage bin in the basement. What amazed me more was no one had ever been prosecuted for the theft. Hundreds of pounds stolen from a police station and no one was arrested and charged?

I was learning a lot more about the good guys and the bad.

When I first heard about the pot heist, I jokingly mentioned to my trooper coach that maybe Arnie Ellis was involved. He didn't appreciate my comment one bit.

"You shouldn't talk about another trooper like that," he said. "Arnie's a character but a damn fine cop."

I didn't take his word for it, and time would prove me right. In February of 1982, Ellis was arrested after reporting to work as shift commander at the Topsfield barracks and charged with conspiracy to smuggle 33,000 pounds of marijuana, as well as supplying guns to the rest of a gang. Arnie Ellis got a pony ride to a federal penitentiary.

October 1979

I pulled the cruiser up to the curb in front of Quincy's Central Junior High School. I got out and, after climbing the familiar steps to the first floor, for an instant was thirteen again. I thought about Mr. Brooks who had told me to come back when I'd done something with my life. Would this fit the bill, me in a statie's uniform?

I pushed through the swinging doors, turned right, and entered the principal's office. The lady behind the desk smiled. "My, my, a state trooper," she said. "What can I do for you, sir?" I explained why I was there, and she tilted her head to the side then said, "No, there's no Mr. Brooks here now, and I've been at Central eight years."

I heard footsteps behind me and turned to see my old gym coach Mario Casali standing there, smiling. I remembered Casali as someone who was very well liked and who commanded respect from his classes. I greeted him and was amazed when he immediately placed me.

He said, "You were in Larry Bray's and Bobby Sleeth's class, correct?"

I answered affirmatively and his smile grew even wider. He said, "It's looks like you're doing pretty good for yourself."

I asked Casali about my former Civics teacher, and he told me that Brooks had retired over a decade before. Then he added, "Richard, you were one of those quiet, shy kids, with great athletic ability, but I don't think you realized it."

He was right, I hadn't. But here was someone else that had seen my potential. I wondered if I would ever live up to it.

The first three months solo, assigned to the day shift, I averaged over two hundred miles a shift on my cruiser, and rarely, with the exception of the occasional serious accident, did anything of substance happen. It didn't matter that criminal activity in the Topsfield area was almost non-existent, I was still was required to make the eight for eight quota and aggressively searched for something, anything, that would allow me to meet it.

Then one day I found it.

On a Sunday afternoon while traveling west on Rt. 495 in Haverhill, I noticed a guy hitchhiking on the East bound side. On the asphalt next to him was a leather valise. There was something about the guy, the way he looked at me when I passed, that made me suspicious. I accelerated to the next exit, a quarter of a mile away, then swung back onto 495 east.

I had gone about a half-mile without seeing him and assumed either he had been picked up or he was hiding. I pulled into the breakdown lane and backed up, keeping an eye on the woods, then spotted him in the tree line about fifty yards away. He bolted as soon as I got out of the cruiser.

Among the three fastest milers in the academy, I ran him down quickly, a kid about twenty in jeans, a dark t-shirt, and sneakers. I patted him down and asked him where the bag was.

He gave me a look. "Bag? What bag?" he said.

I said, "The one you ditched before you took off running."

We were almost to the cruiser when I spotted the bag, caught up in some thick brush fifty feet away. I cuffed him and sat him in front of the license plate.

I said, "I'm getting the bag, don't fucking rabbit," pointed at busy Rt. 495. "Run that way you're road kill," I aimed a finger at the woods. "That way you catch a beating. Don't move."

When I got returned with the zipped, leather valise, I noticed the kid had shifted position and was underneath a headlamp now. He was distancing himself from something so I looked under the car, and spotted a wallet, that I probably would have missed if he hadn't moved.

I went through its contents and found three driver's licenses from three separate states: Florida, North Carolina, and New York, each with his photograph but a different name. The kid had been busy.

I said, "Like to comment on which one is real?"

He pouted and looked down between his knees, but when I picked up the bag and dropped it on the hood, it got his attention.

I unzipped the bag and it was instantly Christmas.

On top was a knot of dirty tee shirts and socks and beneath them a bundle tightly wrapped in plastic. Slicing it open, I found four pounds of high quality, super-compressed weed, and under it wads of banded money, over twenty-five hundred dollars in small bills. At the bottom of the bag, there was a four-inch, nickel-plated .38 Smith& Wesson revolver, fully loaded. The gun had obviously been fired, a lot, because the cylinder, trigger guard, and barrel interior were black with burnt cordite and badly needed cleaning.

On the return trip to the barracks, the kid started talking and admitted that the name on the Florida license, Andrew Daly, was his. Daly said as we entered the barracks, "If I have an outstanding warrant on me from another state, will I be sent there?" I told him that it depended on the nature of the crime.

There were no computers in those days, so a Teletype machine was used to trace the driver's license information and, almost immediately, there was a hit from Florida. At least as far his name went the kid was telling the truth. Now with his real name and social security number, we put a bulletin out on the NCIC, the National Crime Information Center, to see if Daly was known anywhere else.

NCIC, launched in 1967, has been called the "lifeline of law enforcement". According to its website, it is "an electronic clearinghouse of crime data that can be tapped into by every criminal justice agency nationwide 24/7". Three hours passed and we got another hit.

We learned our guy, originally from Virginia, had hitchhiked across country and ended up in Colorado where he somehow had gotten a job at the Air Force Academy. He worked in the kitchen a few months then was transferred to the officer's club where he waited on tables, performed general clean up, and developed a reputation as a reliable worker.

It wasn't long before his superiors trusted him enough to take the weekend deposits to the bank Monday mornings. Since everything then was paid for in cash, the deposits, at times, were substantial.

Whether it was Daly's intention all along will never be known, but following a long holiday weekend instead of taking fifteen grand in receipts to the bank, he continued to the airport where he boarded a flight to Miami. That was where his trail went cold until his arrest on Rt. 495.

Once Daly started talking he was difficult to stop. He told us that he bought a car in Miami then followed the coast line north, stopping in New York City, then later in Buffalo where he bought the gun and pot, before continuing to Providence, Rhode Island. After totaling the car outside Providence, he abandoned it then hitchhiked into Massachusetts, where our paths crossed.

The day after the arrest, on the ride to the courthouse, the kid opened up even more. Relaxed and seemingly optimistic now, Daly seemed more like an average kid who just happened to screw up. After he was arraigned on drug distribution and weapons charges, a hearing date was set for bail.

With outstanding warrants in Colorado, I never believed that Daly would be allowed bail. I was amazed when bail was set at twenty thousand dollars, and even more so when relatives from Virginia came up to post it. Daly jumped bail and was never seen in Massachusetts again.

A month later we received a ballistics report on Daly's weapon from authorities in Buffalo. It seemed that the gun had been used there in a double homicide, but due to a time-line differentiation, Daly was not considered a suspect.

The months passed quickly. The pay raise came through, but the promised fifteen thousand dollar starting wage had been whittled down to just under twelve. Now instead of a hundred and forty bucks a week, I was getting a check for a hundred and sixty-five and change. Disgusted and furious, I wanted to quit.

Assigned now to the eleven to seven graveyard shift, I found it tougher than ever to make the eight for eight moving violation requirement, and even harder to make arrests. No arrests meant no court-time, and no extra money coming in. Overtime, snapped up mostly by senior troopers, was almost non-existent.

My head was filled with other thoughts too.

Cara had left Ames Plow and worked now at a new nightclub, The Flying Machine, in the Holiday Inn not far from Boston's North End district. The Flying Machine was a flashy meeting place for gangsters, gamblers, and drug dealers, and the Las Vegas nights run by Jason Angiulo, son of Boston Mafia chieftain, Gennaro Angiulo, always drew huge crowds. Among the underworld types who frequented the place was my pal, George Pappas, and his henchman, a known killer and Winter Hill enforcer named Brian Halloran.

When she was home, Cara liked to talk about work, how the previous night some gangster had told her how beautiful she was, and how he wanted to take her to Las Vegas or London to show her the lights. Cara seemed focused on the money they flashed, these cool friends of hers who had never worked an honest day in their lives.

Cara wasn't rubbing it in, she was just relating facts, and it was a fact that she was beautiful and that these gangsters had everything, and her husband had nothing. What bothered me more was I knew I could do anything they could, and probably better.

I began to question what I was doing driving the highways alone at night searching for broken tail lamps, and expired inspection stickers. I also wondered, as my cruiser sliced through darkness at three in the morning, what Cara was up to.

One night I had just reported for work and the desk officer called me over. Shaking his head he said, "Rick, you're not going to believe the report I just got. Remember the kid you pinched that ripped off the Air Force Academy?"

"What about him?" I said, right away feeling uneasy. My first thought, they had tied Daly to the double homicide in Buffalo. The look on my face must have given me away.

"No, not the homicides," the trooper said. "It's worse than that."

When he related the story, aside from the actual horror of the tale, my mind returned to the time when I had chased Daly through the woods. Out of wind he had finally stopped running, then turned around and faced me. I remember his eyes, the emptiness in them that seemed to mock me. At the time I had chocked it up to exhaustion.

After making bail Daly went on the run, and then on a crime spree. In a small southern town he had pulled a string of B&E's and when that wasn't enough, had broken into a home and savagely beat and raped the female occupant. Luckily her son was able to escape through a window and call 911 from a neighbor's house.

After holding the woman hostage for hours and threatening to kill her, with a SWAT team poised to make their assault, Daly had put the gun to his head and, at the age of twenty-two, took his own life.

When I had chased him that day, it was just an adventure. I'd never considered the danger or felt the need to draw my weapon. No one wore Kevlar vests back then. What if Daly had turned around with the .38 in his hand? It was sad to think that he had wasted his life and hurt so many in the process. I was also troubled that I had lowered my guard. It could have cost me my life.

Reckoning

The middle of December and I was parked in front of a shuttered diner facing Rt.1 northbound. I checked my watch; it was 3:00 a.m. The blower on high in my idling cruiser, the hot air blasting, my soggy wool overcoat was beginning to dry out along with my wet leather boots. The snow, falling for hours, had turned from wet flakes into icy birdshot whipped by an increasingly violent wind. With another four hours to go in the shift, I knew that the highways would soon be sheets of glass.

Two hours earlier I had responded to a five-car pile-up on I-95 north in Topsfield. Luckily, no one was hurt, just twisted hunks of steel to be towed away. Now, half asleep behind the wheel, I was settling into what was usually the calmest time of the night, the predawn hours between three and five. Just before four I received the first call.

The desk officer told me that a civilian had called in on her CB to report a collision between a tractor-trailer and a private vehicle on Route 495 west in Amesbury. The woman insisted that the accident had involved serious personal injury.

It was important to get the scene as quickly as possible, a few minutes could mean someone's life, but the driving conditions were a lot worse than I had imagined. Doing about fifty, with both front tires nearly bald, I struggled to keep the car on the road. As the minutes passed, the desk officer fed me more detailed information. A large, tractor-trailer rig had jack-knifed across the three-lane highway and a vehicle was lodged beneath it.

On 495 west, at the bottom of a long hill, I could barely make out the outline of the truck through the falling snow. The entire rig painted white, it was in an L-shaped position across three lanes. I skidded diagonally to a stop across two lanes and prayed that I wouldn't get pancaked from behind.

Barely out of the cruiser the truck driver approached. "Trooper," he said, turning and pointing behind him. "The guy over there's dying, or maybe he's dead." Through the heavy snow I could see he was crying. "It wasn't my fault," the driver said, "the fucking snow, it wasn't my fault."

I said, "Listen, I need your help, you have to calm down, okay? How many in the car?"

"Just one."

I called for an ambulance and two tow trucks, then went around and popped the cruiser's trunk, grabbed an armful of highway flares and passed them to the driver.

"Light 'em and spread 'em out in a line across the road," I said. "When you're done, I want you to stand over there in the breakdown lane and wave one high if you see a car coming, but stay off the road." I didn't need a *double* fatality that night.

A quick examination of the crash site revealed the Ford Torino was stuck dead center beneath the trailer with its windshield sheared off and the roof crushed back like an accordion.

The driver was slumped over the console and missing most of the top of his head. Amazingly, he still was breathing but gurgling loudly. Unable to open the driver's side door, I leaned over and pulled him upright then, covered in his blood, skidded back to the cruiser and grabbed an old blanket from the trunk.

When I got back to the victim, I noticed that the snow had collected in the cup of his open skull. I prayed the cold might somehow help him. Medically there was nothing I could do for him so, after dabbing the snow from his face and chest, I wrapped the blanket around him. I was so focused on doing my job the way I had been trained, at no point did I panic or even become nervous.

By the time the ambulance and tow trucks arrived. I had drawn up a diagram of the crash scene, and interviewed the truck driver. I had also located the witness, the CB lady who had called the accident in, and interviewed her as well.

The EMT's arrived and attempted to stabilize the victim, but I knew that there wasn't much hope. It wasn't until they removed him from the car that I noticed something on the rear seat, a brown, paper bag lunch. The man had been on his way to work.

I should have been accustomed to the carnage, my third highway fatality since I started the job, but I was numb that night on the way back to the barracks. It wasn't the guy dying that haunted me as much as the lunch on the rear seat.

I thought about the woman, most likely his wife, who had made it for him earlier that night. Somewhere she was sleeping comfortably, oblivious to the fact that her husband was dead. I wondered who would give her the news.

Back at the barracks, an hour into the previous night's paper work, I received a call from another trooper. His uncle was the crash victim, the driver of the Torino. The only thing he wanted to know was did his relative suffer?

I told him that as far as I could tell his uncle probably never knew what hit him, and he never regained consciousness. I think that it gave my brother trooper some peace.

The paperwork completed, I grabbed my orange raincoat off the back of the chair when a veteran trooper said, "Rick, you might want to wash that thing before you wear it again."

In the basement of the barracks, the orange raincoat draped over an old trash barrel, I hosed off blood and bits of brain. I watched the stream snake its way into the sewer and thought I had to be crazy a hundred and sixty bucks a week, for this?

On my way back to South Boston, as the windshield wipers muscled slush from the glass, my thoughts were focused on leaving the job. Not long after I made the second biggest mistake of my life, quitting the state police. It would take years to learn the value of perseverance and patience.

7.

Cool Cash

1980

I hadn't seen George Pappas for over a year when he walked into the Rat one night with two other men. One he introduced as Mike. About my age, Mike wore a nice pair of slacks, stylish shirt, and sport coat. He was definitely overdressed for the place.

The other guy, introduced as Brian Halloran, had thinning, brown hair that hung like creeping vines over the width of his huge forehead. He was tall, two hundred plus pounds and mean looking, and sweating like he had just run a mile. Casually dressed in sneakers and velvet Nike workout gear, he kept using the same finger to wipe his brow.

I got Pappas to the side and asked about them.

When he said, "They both work for me." I drew my own conclusions.

Pappas inquired about the state police, what happened with them, and I told him about the crazy hours, lousy equipment, lack of money, and then added that I was broke. He grinned and gave this deep belly laugh and wrapped an arm around my shoulder. "Don't worry about money kid, we can fix that," he said. Then he leaned in closer. "You still got a gun permit, right?"

As he got ready to leave a few hours later Pappas pulled me aside. He said, "I got a security detail the middle of next week that could use a guy with a gun, a legit gun. You interested?" Adding quickly "Ain't like I don't got my own, but the heat's on, brother, and I'd hate to take a pinch packin'." He explained then how a few weeks earlier he had almost been busted in a drug sting.

Pappas said, "I'd bring the goon," tilting his head toward Halloran, who was at the end of the bar talking with Mike and a couple of young girls. "He got no problem with this." He put a fist next to my head and curled the index finger like he was pulling a trigger. "But he got three strikes against him already: he's Winter Hill, not too bright, and got no gun permit."

"What am I going to be doing?" I asked.

"You'll be watching something for somebody else."

"Are we watching or taking it?" I said.

"Watching, just watching," Pappas said. He buttoned up his jacket. "The guy's a good connection, trusts me."

The following Wednesday night, Pappas picked me up early, around six o'clock, at the South End condo that Cara and I—we were married in 1976—had bought the year before. As we drove through the city toward Brookline, he talked about the ways he could put me to work: cocaine distribution, weapons sales, loan sharking, whatever interested me.

Pappas made the bulk of his money peddling coke, but with my own habit surging I knew that I couldn't be around it. Pappas was a friend, but a dangerous friend and I didn't want to end up on his bad side.

That night we agreed that I would pick up work from him as it came along: delivering product for him one day, transporting weapons occasionally, mostly to Chinatown, or helping him to collect on his shylock debts. He told me that he could pay me in either cash or cocaine.

In Kenmore Square, as we went by the Rat, I saw the bouncer known as Andre the Giant manning the front door. I wondered if I'd see him again because, more than likely, I was heading into a situation where somebody, me maybe, could get shot.

Outside of Kenmore, as we followed Beacon Street toward Brookline, I thought about what we would be guarding, a roomful of coke--and maybe someone got word that they might be ripped off? Suddenly the .380 in my pocket, and two extra clips, didn't seem like much back up. I wanted to bring my shotgun, but Pappas had nixed it.

"Unless it fits under your coat, leave it," he said.

After passing a block of stores, we turned right off Beacon Street and entered an enclave filled with huge homes. I said to Pappas, "Police keep an eye on neighborhoods like this, maybe your guy won't need us tonight."

Pappas smirked, "My guy's pals with the mayor too, but it don't mean shit. Believe me he needs us."

He continued to drive, seemingly in circles, for another ten minutes, and I was convinced he was trying to confuse me because he didn't want me finding my way back.

Eventually, we pulled over front of a big house set back about a hundred feet from the road. Pappas was pissed the gate to the driveway closed. He said, "He was supposed to leave the fucking thing open. See," he said, jabbing a finger at me "you took that shotgun and got out with it, a nosey neighbor looking out the window might spot it and call the cops."

He glanced at his watch, popped the door. "We're here until six tomorrow morning. We mind the house, watch TV, he's got food and soda, we stay awake all night and you get twelve hundred bucks." He winked. "And if you keep *me* awake maybe a bonus."

I asked, "You think the pistol's enough?"

"He got more in the house," Pappas said.

"What are we guarding, can you tell me now?"

George looked at the house. A light had just blinked on over the front door. "He's waiting, let's go. Cash," he said.

I said to him over the roof, "Is your pal expecting trouble tonight?"

"Far as I know, no, we're just insurance. He don't have what it takes to hold what he's got and needs people like us to help him."

The guy who greeted us at the door looked like Danny DeVito, but with less hair. He also had a huge gravy stain on the front of his sweatshirt. He seemed more like the help than the owner.

Pappas introduced him as Carl. Carl said, "Georgie," with obvious relief then gave him a hug and eyeballed me. "You guys are right on time," he said. "The others just left."

The foyer to Carl's home was huge like a Las Vegas mansion with a black marble floor that glistened. Tall blue vases with flowers bursting from them like fireworks stood on either side of a stairway that rose in a wide curve toward the second floor. At the top, on a landing, was a life-sized bronze statue of a naked girl and a swan.

Pappas introduced me. The guy checked me out like I was a tree on a Christmas lot. "He'll do," he said finally. "As long as you trust him."

Pappas said, "Remember the guy I told you about in the courthouse who saved my ass?"

Carl's eyebrows went up. "Him?"

"Him."

Carl chuckled. "Hope he ain't working for the DA," he said and pointed toward a room at the end of a long hallway, "It's in the closet down there," he said, motioning for us to follow.

He said over his shoulder, "You guys hungry? I got a cold-cut platter from Mike's Deli and there's milk, Dr. Pepper, and ice coffee in the fridge. Eat it all up. I'll be gone for four days."

Pappas said, "You're leaving what time?"

"Probably earlier, but by six the latest, I want to beat the traffic on the Pike."

We entered a room that looked like a library, with lots of shelves with books. There was a huge projector TV in one corner and a black leather couch tucked against a wall beneath a long, narrow, glass-block window. As Carl moved toward what appeared to be a closet, he pointed at a cabinet next to the TV. "There's a VCR inside with a bunch of movie tapes, including *The Godfather*. I've seen it ten times," he said.

Pappas chuckled and said to me out the side-of-his-mouth, "Wise-guys watch it to learn how to be wise-guys."

Carl tugged the closet pocket door aside, revealing an interior filled to bursting with heavy leather and fur coats. On the floor below them was a large Carrier air conditioner box. He sunk down and tugged the obviously heavy box out, then looked back over his shoulder at Pappas. "You tell him?" he said as he opened the top.

Pappas squatted beside him. From where I stood I could see that whatever was inside was wrapped in heavy, clear plastic with lengths of red tape forming a cross on top. Dropping down, I saw through the plastic banded packets of hundred dollar bills.

"All hundreds?" George said.

Carl shrugged. "Hundreds and fifties," he said. "Thing's heavy, weighs about forty pounds." Without looking back at me he said, "Ever seen a million dollars, Rick?"

After making a hundred and fifty bucks a week with the state police, the sight of all that cash made me dizzy. If you applied the currency inflation rate to it today the box would contain almost three million dollars.

"Whatsamatter?" Pappas said. "You okay?"

Carl said, "The kid's not used to money, George? Maybe we can change that."

Pappas said, "That's what I said on the way over."

A major cocaine dealer, and one of Pappas's main suppliers, Carl Bernstein, left for New York City the following morning with a million in cash behind the driver's seat of his new Porsche. Less than a week later, thirty-five kilos were delivered to a restaurant parking lot off Rt. 95 outside of Providence, Rhode Island. Pappas and Bernstein transported it back to Boston in a borrowed Ford parts van.

The following morning we drove back into Boston. We were on Mass Ave in the South End when I casually mentioned how in the future, if we got the same chance, we should hog-tie Bernstein and take the money.

Pappas screwed up his face like he smelled something foul. "You know," he said, "I'm gonna pretend I didn't hear that because you just made me nervous. Are you the same guy that told me before he would never betray his friends?"

He had a point. While I was still in the state police academy, Pappas had stopped by the Rat on a Saturday night with Brian Halloran. He said he was checking in to see how I was holding up, and he was curious about something else.

He pulled me into the coat checkroom and closed the door. His voice low, he said, "Something to think about, Rick. Once you're settled in as a cop, ya know, information, the kind you'll have access to eventually, will be worth a ton of money."

It was obvious what he was getting at. Bu it wasn't for me and I told him, "Not who I am, George. I would no more betray the guys I work with than I would you. For me it's one side or the other, I can't work both."

Pappas seemed to understand and I understood that he had to ask. He was a hardcore criminal who saw an opportunity.

Still, regarding Bernstein I said, "Hey, George, we're talking a million fucking—"

He slammed his fist on top of the wheel. "Shut up! Shut the fuck up. I'll tell you this once. You give your word to someone, that's it. I'd no more take money from Carl than you. You hear what I'm sayin'?" He turned sharply onto Tremont Street and neither spoke again until he pulled to the curb in front of my house.

"See ya later," I said. I opened the door and started to get out, but Pappas grabbed my arm.

"Since we're working together, I'm gonna school you. Two things in this world you never do, fuck your friends or ask me about murder. Any questions?"

I had none, got out and closed the door. As I turned from the car, the passenger window went down. "Hey, Rick, re-lax," Pappas said.

When I turned, he was grinning. "I'll be back around four. Be here, you're gonna love it."

He had changed just like that; one minute wanting to punch me out and now he hinted at some kind of gift. I was learning the code of the street and realizing there actually was one. Nowadays when some criminal justice "expert" mentions that honor among thieves is a myth, I laugh because I personally experienced it for years.

When Pappas showed up again at my door, I was shocked by his appearance. He stood grinning in this all white tennis outfit that looked straight out of GQ magazine. He hoisted the expensive, leather gym bag in his hand. "You letting me in or what?" he said.

To my knowledge Pappas never worked out. "What's with the outfit?" I asked as we entered. "I had no idea you played."

"I don't," Pappas said. "I met a broad at the Kenmore Club a few nights ago. Fucking knock-out, told me she plays racquetball. I told her I'd meet her at the club today."

"Then what?"

Pappas shrugged. "I dunno, I'm thinking maybe I'll tell her I twisted my knee, offer to buy her a drink?"

We both laughed. Pappas was a character, a real funny bastard most of the time, but then, like a switch was thrown, he could become serious as cancer.

In the kitchen downstairs he dropped the bag and said slyly, "Don't play what she does, but I can tell you about racquets." He unzipped the bag and yanked out a small, black machine gun with a thin metal folding stock. The barrel was filled with holes.

"It's a Smith and Wesson model 76," George said. "The clip holds thirty rounds."

He tossed it to me. The gun was light, maybe six or seven pounds. I handed it back and asked why he had it.

He mentioned something about trouble with some North End guineas, then laughed and yanked the receiver back. He said, "Fuck with me, I'll drive down Hanover Street with machine guns chatterin'."

The scene was surreal. Six months earlier I was a trooper assigned to Mayberry. Now I had a guy in my house with a machine gun, seriously talking about killing people.

The weird thing was I was comfortable with it.

He put the gun back in the bag and fished around like some kind of devilish Santa Claus before he tugged out a huge, black revolver, a Smith and Wesson .45 ACP with a six inch barrel; it looked just like Dirty Harry's. He handed it to me and its weight surprised me. It was hefty enough to slug down an elephant.

"Like it?" he said.

I nodded and gripped the gun with both hands, lined up the sights.

George beamed. "Brand new and it's yours, pal, got one for the goon too."

I took it that he meant Brian Halloran, the Winter Hill enforcer that I'd met at The Rat.

A trained shooter, I practiced regularly with the pistol and carried it everywhere until I lost it one night to the Boston police, but that's a story for later.

Pain Spotting

My cocaine use escalating, to keep the high going I was now stealing hundreds of dollars a week from the door of The Rat. I had no illusions about what I'd become. It was cocaine as soon as I reported to work and cocaine into the late morning hours. The months passed quickly like one long night.

It took a long time for Rat owner, Jim Harold, fighting his own demons, to finally realize that he was losing his shirt. Actually he had lost it and was down to his wife beater because everyone was stealing: bartenders, waitresses, bouncers, and managerial staff. Even customers were walking out with cases of beer.

Any semblance of control I had once held over the Rat's ferocious staff was gone. Now guys I had personally hired were mangling customers for the smallest infractions. Yanked off the front door for fighting, I was exiled to work as a bartender downstairs, where I continued to steal and grow progressively more paranoid.

In an effort to stem the hemorrhage of cash, Harold hired professional "spotters" to keep tabs on the bartenders and feed him reports. This was bad news for the customers because everyone looked like a spotter to me.

The Nervous Eaters were playing that night. Steve Cataldo was blasting, *Talk to Loretta* to a house packed tighter than a fresh pack of Marlboros when I first noticed the little prick that looked like a spotter.

Three of us worked the bar, me on the last station across from the rear door. I eyeballed the spotter on a stool in front of the draft taps. He was nursing a Miller Lite and tapping his butt on the edge of an ashtray. Yeah, he watched me too, but tried not to be obvious.

I grabbed one of the bouncers, Feenzo, off the floor and ordered him to take over the bar. I needed a good blast of Columbian so I could handle the situation in a responsible manner. On the second- floor landing I snorted a rail long enough to choke an ostrich then, as I descended the steps and the lightning kicked in, all I thought about was the rent-a-cop spotter.

Behind the bar again, unable to feel my fingers, I fumbled my way through a batch of mixed drinks, and cursed out any customer with the balls to complain. Fuck with me you son-of-a-bitch, don't like your fucking Cape Cod-DER? I'll Visine your drink and give you the shits.

Then, in walked in a solution in the form of two Southie boyos. "Tornado" Joe Earner and Kevin "Mini-Mac" MacDonald were, as usual, chomping at the bit looking for trouble. I mentioned the spotter and promised free drinks for the night if they took him outside and tore him a new asshole, tossed him into the "Blue Motel"—what we called the dumpster out back.

They were nineteen and thirsty so, within seconds, they grabbed the guy, who left fifty bucks on the bar, and dragged him up the back steps. A few minutes later Tornado returned, blood splattered across his cheek and forehead, with Mini right behind him almost pissing himself laughing.

Tornado said, "Rick, he's in the motel but who knows for how long. One of them chinks, from the restaurant next door, came out and dumped garbage on him."

Fast-forward a week. I'm on the bar when the same guy comes in and plunks himself down in front of me. Above one eye was a shiny, pink line, the width of a shoelace, where stitches had been. His nose, a brand new curve to it, still swollen.

"Remember me?" he said hopefully

"Nope."

"Ah, you worked here that night."

"What night?"

"Oh, come on man, last week. You were right there when two guys dragged me up the back steps, called me a cop, and kicked the living shit outta me. I woke up in the dumpster a rat on my chest."

"You know how many guys get tossed from this place?"

"I also left fifty bucks on the bar."

Hey, that was work related. I had split it three ways; I was supposed to pay for the beating myself?

"Never saw it," I said and pulled him a draft beer. "Here, have a beer and relax. I'll have the bouncer keep an eye on you."

The guy shook his head. "I'm a bus driver for chrissakes, work for the T."

"Like a *shot* with that beer?"

****

In 1980 my drug habit finally got me canned from the Rat. But I was an addict, and a good addict never blames himself. It's always someone else's fault. Me? I blamed the Rat's owner, my former friend, Jim Harold, for singling me out. Sure, I was stealing and getting into fights, but no more than everyone else, right? I asked Pappas to straighten it out.

I met him the next day in a coffee shop outside Kenmore Square, and he told me to relax, he would get me my job back and, by the way, did I want to become manager? I was in no shape to manage anything, and when I pondered the reasons I wanted the job back couldn't come up with a single one. Every dime I made went up my nose and the bar had become too violent, even for me.

Punk rockers were a constant source of trouble, and more and more Southie gangsters frequented the place now. One night two associates of Jim Bulger's tried to shake down the owner, Jim Harold, for monthly protection payments. To his credit, Harold refused the gangster's advance, but the move created tension between us.

And on the home front things weren't much better. Cara had been cheating on me with a married North End bartender. After he dumped her, she wanted me back. The Miller Lites and piles of coke must have deep-fried my brain, because when I should have passed went along with the idea.

In the end I wouldn't put down my drugs or crazy friends, and Cara wouldn't put down her lovers, so our attempt to make the marriage work failed, again.

8.

Bump and Run

Summer 1981

When not working with Pappas, I ran with a crew of thieves based out of the Old Colony Projects in Southie. Every day I learned new ways to feed my addiction to action; but the small wins, and there were many, set me up for dangerous falls like when I was a kid up the quarries. I'd make a dangerous jump and be immediately challenged to make the next even more deadly one. The problem was I never backed down. I was surfing the crest of a tsunami even then.

The boyos from the OCP dipped their mitts into everything hot: computers, Gillette razors, sneakers, clothing, gold jewelry, diamonds, booze, and even cases of frozen lobster and expensive beef—anything that could be turned quickly into cash. A good way to get the swag was by something called the "bump and run".

As the sun came up Frank "The Tank" MacDonald and I would leave the projects in a hot box and drive into the Financial District looking for targets. At that time of day small delivery trucks, usually box trucks, were out making deliveries to the huge downtown office towers. We would single one out and follow it until it stopped.

Parked at the curb a half block behind it, Tank and I would wait until the driver got out. When he threw up the rear door we'd approach and check out the contents. We looked for specialty items with labels like: IBM, Xerox, RCA, Radio Shack etc., and if there was nothing, we recognized we'd pass on the truck. If we saw something we liked, we moved to the next phase.

Traffic moved slowly through the maze of the Financial District's narrow streets, so it was easy to keep up with our prey. We would wait until the truck was stopped the first in line at a traffic light, and then smash into it. We didn't nail it hard enough to cause damage, or draw civilian attention, just enough to make the driver get out, usually leaving the engine running, and rush to the rear to examine the damage. As the driver of the car, I'd be out too, and as we screamed accusations at each other Tank would jump into his truck and drive off. The guy would chase after him and I'd jump in and drive away.

Safely back in Southie it was Christmas all the time as we unloaded dozens of computers, photocopiers, ink cartridges, and TV's into other vehicles. We'd bring them to a warehouse in Chelsea owned by a fence who took everything we stole. Life was good, and getting better all the time.

Cold Feet

By 1980 I was a full-blown cocaine addict while my mother, the alcoholic, had been sober for years. An active member of AA now she had completely turned her life around and was even active now in "commitments" at jails and state prisons, including maximum security MCI Walpole, where she helped bring AA's message of hope and sobriety to the men. I saw her rarely then, usually only after I had been on a bender a few days. My mother desperately tried to help me, but I had become her and rebuffed her advances.

My marriage on its last legs, one afternoon Cara returned to our South End condo to find me in a rage. Earlier, I had found a greeting card, from one of her boyfriends, on a closet shelf. Written inside: "Had a great time in room 307, let's do it again soon." I went ballistic.

When she walked in I confronted her, and the argument raged back and forth until I stuck a gun in her face, threatened to kill her. I wasn't stupid enough to shoot her, but planned to kill her boyfriend when I found out who he was.

A month later, on New Year's Eve, I returned home at three in the morning, high as a lab rat. Cara was supposed to have met me at a party earlier, but never showed up. When she waltzed through the door, just before four, we went at it again.

Cara's girlfriend, Nancy, a Pennsylvanian transplant and the mistress of a wealthy, married Ford dealership owner, was staying at our home for the weekend. Cara was also high, so she didn't display her normal reserve when confronted her with her cheating.

When she laid back into me, I gave her a slap, the first time I ever laid my hands on her, and she screamed and Nancy called the cops. When they showed up, I was mad enough to kill someone, and didn't care if I died. I grabbed the pistol and was almost to the front door of the building when a cop, peeking through a side window, spotted me and screamed to his partner, "He's got a gun!"

It was too late.

I opened the door and pointed the gun at his head. I was screaming, I don't remember what, and his partner was behind me with his gun to my head. He was yelling at me to drop it, then another cruiser pulled up and those cops jumped out.

My cop was dead, I was dead, everyone was dead.

It was freezing outside, and I was out there in my socks and my feet were cold, so, after a minute, I let the cop go and lowered the gun, but didn't want to drop it—it would ruin the bluing—but finally I did and was tackled.

Handcuffed in the back of the cruiser, I looked out the window to see Cara in the small crowd gathered. "Be careful of him, he's dangerous," she shouted. "He's a boxer and has a black belt in karate."

A court date was set and my father stepped up to the plate and hired a good attorney, who hired a psychiatrist to evaluate me for my defense, temporary insanity. I was insane that night, but it was due to an eight-ball, and a case of Bud Light. The psychiatrist thought different. After two weeks in a private institution in Brighton, I was diagnosed as suffering from a bi-polar disorder.

In the end Cara stood up. She only wanted to move on with her life and refused to testify against me. And what about the Boston cop? I got lucky with him too. When he learned that I was an ex-cop, he didn't push the charges. I was grateful and sincerely apologized to the guy for my behavior.

For that, I received a sentence of a year in jail, suspended, with two years' probation. The judge, thinking I was really crazy, ordered me to see a shrink for a year.

That should have slowed me down, but it didn't. Not even a little. The more I reflected on what I had lost, the angrier and more frustrated I became. And I didn't have to search for targets to blame: a screwed up childhood, lack of education, lousy marriage, my scuttled my job with the MSP, and the fact I was now a full-blown addict.

I was a funnel cloud looking for a place to touch down.

One night my love affair with coke almost turned deadly. Whacked out when I came home, I ate a mixture of Elavil and Valium to come down, and the unexpected happened. As if I were looking into a narrow pipe, my world began to shrink, then my legs went numb and I couldn't stand up. I hadn't spoken to Cara in weeks, but I called her and told her I needed her help. She arrived and took me to the hospital where my stomach was pumped.

Afterwards, a doctor came into the room and interviewed me, asked if I was suicidal; I laughed it off. But later, all alone in the room, I wondered if the doctor was right.

Chinatown

The Four Seas Restaurant on Beech Street, owned by Chinatown's top mobster, Harry Mook, was a late night watering-hole for all types of skids: cokeheads, gangsters, band members, nightclub bouncers, and people who'd been drinking and drugging in Boston's club scene all night. George Pappas and I met there Saturday nights, between two-thirty and three in the morning, to discuss our plans for the upcoming week.

In 1981 Pappas's federal drug case was finally adjudicated with Pappas pleading guilty to all charges. The charges he faced stemmed from the night that his apartment was raided by the feds, and I was supposed to have been there too. A DEA agent named Stutman, the lead agent on the case and such a hard charger he was later appointed special agent-in-charge of New York City, had been after Pappas for years. That night I was supposed to have picked up a load of coke for delivery to Pappas's North Shore customers. I also moved his coke to former Rat bouncer, and Southie drug dealer, Jack "Polecat" Ferris, for distribution on the streets in that part of town.

At the time, as far as I knew, Jim Bulger had nothing to do with dealing cocaine. Apparently, he made enough from his own lucrative rackets: sports betting, extortion, loan sharking, race fixing, and hijacking, while also shaking down major marijuana smugglers for tens of thousands of dollars a month.

Ferris and I had come up with a plan. In Southie there had to be thirty independent coke dealers. We agreed they should come under one umbrella, and that we'd be the ones holding the handle. If everyone bought their product from Ferris he'd go, in a matter of weeks, from moving ounces to kilos. The sound in the distance was a cash register ringing. All we had to do was get Jim Bulger on board.

In the late nineteen-sixties a criminal empire arose in the town, and James "Whitey" Bulger, who was never called Whitey except by the press, was its undisputed chieftain. Bulger, a survivor of a savage war between the Killeen and Mullen's gangs, ran the town with an iron fist. Step a little out of line you'd catch a beating, step out a lot you were dead.

Southie was Bulger's town, and unless he had a healthy respect for you, as he did for fellow mobsters like Pat Nee and George Hogan, no one made a serious move without an okay from him. Ferris said that he could clear our proposed move with Bulger by offering him a cut, twenty per cent of the gross.

A few days later I was shocked when Ferris told me that Jim had nixed our plans. Bulger was concerned that a few dealers might not fall in line easily and would have to be *persuaded*, which could get messy and "messy" brought heat, and Bulger didn't like heat. He told Ferris to give me a message: "Don't think about doing it behind my back."

The next day Tank and I were stretched out in the sun on a bench at the edge of Fifth Street Park when Bulger, in a tight-fitting V-neck t-shirt and jeans, pulled to the curb in his dark, blue Malibu.

The passenger window went down and he barked at me to get into the car. Maybe because I was an ex-cop, I rarely had any direct contact with Bulger. It was usually someone else in the crew, Jack Ferris or Mini-Mac, who dealt with him.

One hand gripped the wheel as he leaned across the seat until his face almost jutted outside. Sunlight reflected off the large, gold Jesus head that dangled from the heavy chain around his neck. "Get in the car," he growled. "Getinthecar."

I got in and stared straight ahead as the window went up and Bulger put the car into gear. The tension thick enough to chew, he glanced at me as we turned onto D Street. At the light at West Broadway we stopped and an old man, on the opposite corner, recognized Bulger and waved. Bulger responded by lifting just his fingers off the wheel and it wasn't until after we turned and passed the Pen Tavern that he looked at me again.

"I like to eat healthy," he said, "You?"

"I, uh—"

"No," waved a finger at me "don't answer," he said.

He stabbed his chest with his thumb. "Me? I eat lean meats, organic, a little dairy, no junk food, and I-don't-drink." Seemed to catch himself as we went by the Lithuanian Club, and gave this weird little grin. "Okay, maybe a glass of wine now and then."

I might have glanced at him once as we drove up Big Broadway, Bulger going on about the importance of avoiding guys who could land you in jail, and the benefits of staying in shape. He was lean and fit with a kind of energy that pulsed from him and made me uneasy, like when your ears are about to pop. I wanted to get out of that car or at least to lower the window, Bulger's breath reeked of onions and sardines.

We turned onto Dorchester Street, then right onto West Fifth making a circle toward the park where Tank was waiting.

"Rick, you were in shape once, healthy," Bulger said, looking at me more than the road. "You should get off that shit you're snortin', put down the beer." His face grew crimson, and the veins in his neck bulged.

"Hey, Jim, listen, I—."

"Shut-up!"

Further down I could see Tank getting up from the bench and walking toward us. Bulger sneered, "That thing with Ferris? Your fucking *plans*?"

He savagely cut the wheel to the curb and stomped the brake, almost launching me into the dash, as he screamed into the side of my face, "They're over, understand? You fucking understand?"

Tank was almost to the car when I said, "Yeah, I understand."

"Good, do it next time you ride in the trunk, get out. Get the fuck out."

I got out and we watched him roar off. Tank chuckled. "Probably means you ain't pals anymore?"

The next day the crew was gathered at the same spot when Bulger approached again in the Malibu. This time Kevin Weeks, his chief lieutenant, rode shotgun. We gave him a wave; Bulger liked to be recognized, and down went the window and he slowed, but didn't stop.

"Got a nice day, gentlemen, enjoy it," he said. And the funny thing was, Bulger meant it.

A week before the DEA raid on Pappas's apartment the Tank and Mini-Mac had done a "bolt-job" (grabbed merchandise and ran out the door) in a Newbury Street jewelry store, and got away with a huge diamond ring. It had retailed for eighty grand and they ended up splitting about seventeen thousand. We'd been partying a few days when I remembered that I was supposed to call Pappas. He had asked if I could make some deliveries over the weekend.

I left Tank's apartment and called from a pay phone outside Dirty John's Sub Shop on Old Colony Boulevard. When Tricia, Pappas's wife, picked up I asked her in code if the stuff was in, and, like Bob Barker on the old *The Price is Right* show, she said, "Come on down."

I told her I'd be there soon, but out-of-my-mind high, never made it.

Late the next morning, feeling guilty as hell, I dragged myself out of bed and used the pay phone across the street to call the apartment again. Screwing work up wasn't my style, but as months passed coke had sunk its talons deeper into me. I couldn't even recognize when I was fucking up.

Tricia answered on the first ring, but as soon as she began talking, I knew something was up. I said, "Hi, Trish, sorry about—"

"Oh, *hi*," she said.

"Ah, yeah, about last night I—

"Yes, yes, I know," she said, and that's when I got it.

I asked, "Is someone there?"

"Yes, and she told me that you said the same thing about her."

My first thought cops were in the house. The woman had antifreeze in her blood.

"See ya later," I said and hung up.

Later I learned that less than an hour after I called the previous night, a team of DEA agents led by Stutman had raided the apartment. But Pappas was no dummy. He had previously installed a special steel front door and frame in the apartment that was almost impossible to knock down. He had also switched out the bathroom toilet and replaced it with a high-pressure unit. One flush would suck down a cat.

While Stutman and his frustrated cronies sledge hammered the door, it held up long enough for Pappas to flush three kilos of coke down the john. The agents found nothing.

The next morning, as Trish and I spoke, the cops were still in the house drilling holes in walls and floors. Pappas was arrested on conspiracy charges, but less than a week later released on bail. During the raid Stutman couldn't find any product, or Pappas's machine gun, hidden inside a secret compartment beneath the refrigerator.

Pappas eventually plead guilty to distribution charges and was sentenced to five years in federal prison, the judge suspending execution of the sentence, a practice not uncommon at the time, and giving him three weeks to get his affairs in order before he had to surrender himself.

The next time we met at the Four Seas restaurant, Pappas, out on the town earlier that night, was in a good mood. He seemed to study me as we talked and asked how I was doing with the coke. We had never discussed that before, and he had never seemed concerned. The night ended with Pappas telling me where to meet him the next day.

The following day we met in a Chinatown parking lot off Beach Street. Pappas was outside his car and wearing the same clothes as the night before. After we laughed about him not making it home, he quickly turned serious and seemed to study me again, as if he was checking for cracks.

In his gruff voice he said, "So, how're we doin' my friend?"

I said, "I'm alright, George, what's up?"

He leaned against the front of the car and talked about things that I already knew: he was going away but figured he'd be out in just over three years. It wasn't good news, but at least he was getting out. If Stutman had found the machine gun, and coke, Pappas could have been a lifer.

Then he told me something that surprised me; he was the biggest coke dealer in Chinatown. I was shocked even more when he asked me take over the business and keep it running until he got out.

Making deliveries for a few bucks and enough coke for my own head was fine, but become a full time dealer? I reminded him that I was bad around the stuff, but he said it didn't matter, because I always got the job done. There was no one else he could trust he said.

It was nice being asked, but it wasn't for me. I was a coke fiend, and good decisions and drug abuse don't ride the same bus. Besides, I only knew a few guys in Chinatown, and Pappas's connections were his. He couldn't expect me to trust the same men.

Then a car pulled up beside us. The door opened and a uniformed Boston cop got out, a Chinese cop. Pappas's eyes lit up when he saw him. The guy, in his mid-thirties and in decent shape, put me in an eye-lock as he shook Pappas's hand. Pappas said to him, "This is the guy I told you about."

It was surreal. Pappas said, "Rick, this is Felix."

Felix? I'm thinking a Chinese named Felix didn't ring true, it wasn't his real name. Felix measured me up and nodded.

George put his hand my shoulder. "You do this, Rick, Felix's my guy, you'll work everything through him."

Felix looked at me and nodded. He shook Pappas's hand again and said, "We'll talk, soon." Then he left.

I had no intention to take Pappas up on his offer but decided to pretend I was thinking about it, tell him when we met at the Four Seas later that night. Pappas said to be there at ten and I could give him my answer. I was also curious but not alarmed when he said I should, "Bring a friend." Which meant a gun.

That night I had brought along a chrome plated, .32 five shot revolver and as Pappas and I talked and ate, his former associate, Brian Halloran, walked in. I was caught a little off guard, but Pappas seemed cool, even though I knew the two of them had a falling out, months before, and gone their separate ways.

Pappas switched to my side of the table to give Halloran, a big guy, the chair. Halloran settled in and glared across the table at me. Lifting his chin he said, "What's he doin' here?" Pappas calmly explained that I was in there ordering take-out and he had invited me over.

Halloran was his usual whacked out self. His pupils big as plates, he chewed gum like he was keeping time to a song in his head. There were no amenities, nothing, they just got into it.

From what I determined, Halloran owed Pappas money for coke. Five thousand was the figure with Halloran insisting that he had already knocked it down to twenty-five hundred. But Pappas said five thousand, and since he was going to prison in less than three weeks, he wanted his money, now.

While I picked at a plate of rice, voices rose on both sides of the table. I was careful not to stare at Halloran because I didn't want to set him off. The guy had a vicious temper and was a known killer, but I was comforted by the pressure of the gun in my belt.

Halloran worked himself up to the point where he was teetering, on the verge of losing control. With a thick finger, he stabbed air over the table. "Fuck you, five grand," he said, "I gave you an envelope outside of King's Row."

As Pappas denied it, I ran the napkin across my lips, flattened it out on my lap before sliding out the pistol, and aiming it under the table at Halloran's belly. If he jumped up or went into his coat, he was getting it.

Dealing with Halloran's emotions was like riding the Giant Coaster at Nantasket Beach. Whip cracking furious one-second he could be calm as the Mona Lisa the next. Halloran backed off for a moment. Pappas took a sip of tea and glanced at me, then down, and his eyes caught the glint of the chrome-plated .32, and went "Pfffft," spraying tea, then chuckled.

Halloran's shifted his glare between us. "What's so fucking funny?" he said.

I slipped the gun between my thighs and pressed them together, holding it.

The tension broken, Pappas bumped me with his shoulder and said, "Nothing, the kid's got a good sense of humor is all. Brian have a beer for Chrissakes. Relax, we'll straighten this out."

I looked at Pappas, shrugged at Halloran.

But it still wasn't over. The Iver Johnson five shot had a tiny, black, plastic grip, and when Pappas bumped into me the weapon had dropped a few inches. Now it dangled, like a stalactite, a foot above the floor. If it fell there'd be a shit storm.

Luckily a waiter came in that recognized Halloran. "Ah, Mr. Brian," he said, approaching the table. When Halloran turned to acknowledge him, I stuffed the pistol under my crotch.

That night Halloran left the Four Seas with a promise to give Pappas two grand within a few days. Not long after Pappas told me over the phone Halloran had given him fifteen hundred dollars, and he was optimistic that he'd get the rest before he had to surrender himself.

Six nights later, at three in the morning, Pappas met with Halloran again, and also another man, alleged Mafioso Jackie Salemme, at the Four Seas. At five a.m. the Boston police found Pappas in a pool of blood face down on the table. According to the coroner's report, he'd been shot once through the eye from a distance of somewhere between three and nine feet.

The first thing I thought was the murder was the result of Halloran's temper, problems with coke, and the money owed Pappas. But then I thought about it more and it wasn't that simple.

Back in April Pappas and I had planned take a business trip to New York City, but the trip was put on hold. Pappas had told me that he and the "other guy", who I assumed was Halloran, had been hired to do an "out of state contract." Certain that Pappas was talking about murder, I asked him nothing more about it.

A week later Pappas told me that the trip to New York was back on because he and "the other guy" were no longer involved in the "out of state business." He said someone else would handle it.

In May of 1981, Roger Wheeler, an Oklahoma businessman, and owner of the World Jai Alai Association, was murdered for allegedly uncovering an embezzlement scheme. Apparently, members of Boston's Winter Hill Gang had skimmed thousands of dollars a week from his parking lots. Wheeler had to be stopped before he went to the feds, and following a game of golf, as he returned to his car in a country club parking lot, he was, shot twice in the head.

The Boston Kraken's tentacles were long.

When I read about the murder, my first thought was that this probably was the out of state contract Pappas that referred to. The way I saw it, Pappas knew too much and was viewed by some as a potential threat, which had to be eliminated.

Within days of Pappas's murder, Halloran, along with alleged South Boston Top Echelon Informant, James Bulger, put word out on the streets that Pappas was killed because he was a rat.

I knew that it wasn't true and it made me furious because Pappas had always stressed the importance of not snitching.

In the end, it turned out Halloran was the rat. Following the Wheeler hit and the murder of Pappas, he was concerned about his personal safety as the single weak link that could connect Jim Bulger to the Oklahoma killing. He cut a deal with the feds, then doubled his error by talking to corrupt FBI agent, John Connelly. Unbeknownst to Halloran, Connelly was Bulger's buddy, and after Halloran filled Connelly's ear, Connelly filled Bulger's and the hunt for Halloran was on.

On May 11, 1982 Halloran, along with his friend Michael Donahue who had innocently offered to give him a ride, were machine gunned while sitting in Donahue's car outside the Pier Restaurant on Northern Avenue. Donahue, part of his head blown off, died instantly, but Halloran, although mangled by bullets, still managed to stagger from the vehicle before collapsing in the street. The hit car backed up, and a gunman stepped out and finished the job.

It has been alleged that at the time of the murder, a block away on Northern Ave, Connelly sat in an unmarked police car watching the show.

It was the way of that world. Good guys got labeled while the real rats ran free. Not much has changed.

Nuts and Bolts

With Pappas dead, I had to find new ways to support myself, and my drug habit. Everything that I needed I found in the OC, the Old Colony Housing Project, among the most physically distressed sites in the Boston Housing Authority's federal portfolio. Covering more than sixteen acres, its eight hundred and seventy-three apartments were housed in twenty-two brick, three story walk-ups.

Within the OC's borders was a collection of characters more bent and twisted than the ancient elms that lined Patterson Way. Along with average working stiffs that lived there too was a collection of: stick-up men, hijackers, tailgaters, drug dealers, strong arm enforcers, and top lieutenants for the Southie's Irish mob.

There was almost a carnival atmosphere about the place, a feeling that anything could happen. Need a hot box? A C-note would buy any make you wanted. Hot goods? Tailgaters along the Old Colony's northwestern border on Dorchester Street used dummy cars to slow trailers trucks down enough so their locks could be cut off and the rear doors sprung open. As it moved through traffic tailgaters would jump inside, tossing the cargo into the street to be scooped up by the occupants of the chase car that followed.

Almost anything could be had: leather jackets, sneakers, guns, cigarettes by the case, fresh meat and fish, hard booze and beer, TVs, razor blades, vitamins, toys, and cosmetics for a dime on the dollar.

But that was just the tip of the underworld iceberg.

It was the era of the Boston Irish mob, indisputably the most powerful organization of its kind in the nation. Even the local arm of the Mafia, immensely powerful in its own right, avoided conflict with them. Instead they sought an alliance. It was a decision they would come to regret.

If Southie was a sea we, the "working men," were the undercurrent with Bulger and his boyos the waves breaking in your face. A constant fixture around the town in his blue Chevy Malibu, rumored to be armored plated and equipped with James Bond-like equipment, Bulger was the envy of everyone I knew.

Everything that I'd been taught about the value of hard work, getting a good job and paying my bills, flew in my face as I watched Tank and Mini in action. I began doing "bolt jobs" with them all over eastern Massachusetts, Rhode Island and New Hampshire. A "bolt" involved a targeted store usually located on the first floor of a strip mall or shopping complex because you had to be able to run, literally *bolt* out of there quickly.

Posing as customers, the Tank, Mini-Mac or myself, would take turns entering a shop and, depending on what it specialized in, ask for either gold chains or diamonds. If expensive gold chains, I'd tell the clerk I was interested in looking at two, as a wedding gift for an older brother and his fiancée.

First, I would ask the clerk to show me the women's eighteen-inch collection. Then I would request the twenty-inch chains, so I could "comparison shop" for my brother. Usually the jeweler, sensing a fat sale, would eagerly unfold two, long velvet bags containing up to forty gold chains each: serpentine, rainbow, flat gold, link etc. and lay them, side by side, in front of me on the counter.

It was important to keep the jeweler relaxed, the conversation flowing. "Oh, they're having their reception at the Parker House in Boston, honeymooning in Tahiti."

This reinforced the notion that I came from money, and of course, I always looked the part, wearing, nice slacks, a Polo Shirt, and either a knock-off Piaget or Rolex Presidential on my wrist. Jewelers fell for it, but maybe wouldn't have had they noticed my track shoes.

Once it was laid out: a tray of diamond rings, bags of gold chains, envelopes stuffed with loose diamonds, I'd make my move. I'd look the sales person dead in the eye and very sincerely say, "Thank you very much." This confused them long enough for me to grab the booty and *bolt*.

Lightning quick on my feet I'd run out the door, often with the jeweler in hot pursuit, accelerate down the sidewalk, and dive through the open rear door of the getaway car as it pulled away.

That spring and summer we did at least twenty bolts with the retail value of the booty north of a million dollars. Never once did we come close to getting caught, which reinforced the notion that crime *did* pay. But no matter how quickly the money was made, it always spent faster.

The downside to jewelry heists was the return. A "fence," an individual that trafficked in stolen goods, would only pay us a fifth of the retail value on diamonds, a seventh on watches, and for gold, unless it was sold privately, all we'd get was *penny weight*, the weight of real gold in an object. The fences made fortunes off us, for basically doing nothing. Years later, while I was in Norfolk Prison, a fence we had used told me that we had made him a rich man. It wasn't something I wanted to hear.

Mini-Mac's girlfriend, Andrea, was from Newton, an affluent community west of the city. Andrea was wealthy and wild and the summer before she and her girlfriends, attracted to bad boys, began slumming with Southie project rats. The bad boy aura quickly eroded when the Southie boys began showing up at their house parties, beating up their boyfriends, and ripping the safes out of their parent's walls. Everyone of them beat feet for the hills, except Andrea.

Andrea was a coke-head and, like me, an adrenalin junkie. She loved to ride along with us on scores just to sit in the car and watch. She and Mini-Mac eventually married, and Andrea remained a fixture until the bitter end. In 1984 Kevin 'Mini-Mac' MacDonald, along with two other men, robbed a Framingham jewelry store at gunpoint and later, indirectly, it cost him his life.

We stopped doing "bolts" after an insurance industry flyer, circulated to jewelers all over New England, described our appearance and the way that they worked. When a five thousand dollar reward was offered for information leading to our arrest, it was as good a time as any to quit.

On the drive back to Boston after a final diamond heist in Gloucester, we passed a construction site where a trooper worked a detail. Recognizing him as one of my classmates I sunk into the seat, and my heart sunk too. The thrill of the robbery fading, I said nothing to the others, but still had enough humanity left to feel a sense of shame.

Off "the job" for two years, in a free-falling coke high, I'd been reduced to the level of a common thief and under no illusion I wouldn't sink lower.

Billy the Greek

The Greek lived in the same building, 7 Patterson Way, as Tank, but two floors below him. Tank said the Greek was a stick-up guy and that he was stand-up as a wall. Built like one, heavy set and solid, with the temperament and swagger of a badger, the Greek had dark, deep-set, twinkling eyes, but when the twinkle went missing, watch out, the werewolf came out and only a blanket over the moon could stop him.

My new tutor was an old school criminal with a natural aversion to cops. When I told him that I had been one he gave me this look, then relaxed and said, "Okay, we'll try to work with that."

The Greek said what he would teach me would get me into trouble, then asked if I could handle big trouble. When I told him I could, he gave me the same look that George Pappas had once. "Alright," he said, "I'll give you a shot. How're you at stealing cars?"

And that's how it started.

We began small, the stick-ups mostly in barrooms and restaurants, because cash registers in those places were usually up front. I was the driver. I'd sit outside the place and wait with the engine running, listening to music. When the Greek came out with the cash, he would have this calmness about him, like he was leaving the men's room after combing his hair.

I learned that this new game had definite rules. An important one, no dawdling, you go in and get out as quickly as possible and, above all, remain calm. The worst thing you could do was panic people because frightened people are tough to control. And that's what robbery's about, control, lose it you're in trouble. The Hollywood version, where a robber enters a bank, shouts and shoots into the ceiling is bullshit. Whether it's a supermarket or armored car it's all about getting the money.

Usually around dusk I would pick up the Greek in a burner (stolen car) and we'd drive around take a tour of the city. If we found nothing promising we'd head over the Mystic Bridge and explore the North Shore, or follow the interstate to Malden, Everett, or some other town in search of targets. I'm talking about little scores here: mini-marts, package stores, barrooms, and chain restaurants.

The Greek was a smooth talker. He'd enter a place with the register right there and sit close with his eye on the cash draw. He'd order a drink and chat with the bartender. He had a snake charmer style that got them to relax and at that time of night, early evening, the place wouldn't be crowded.

At some point he'd ask the bartender for change for a twenty. Then he'd slide off the stool and pull out the pistol, lean over the bar and say, "And give me all the rest of it too, including the "day bank." See, oftentimes, the day's receipts were kept under the bar. We'd be a block away before the first head poked outside the door.

Then one night the Greek said that it was time to break my cherry. He would do the driving while I went in with the gun. The target was a Store 24 that had just opened on Commonwealth Ave. near the junction of Brighton Ave in Boston. It had never been hit. In those days when receipts reached a certain amount they were placed in a "drop" safe set into the floor. That way if the store got hit it wouldn't be for more than a few hundred dollars.

The Greek wasn't concerned about money that night; he was schooling me. This was an evaluation, to see how I moved and handled stress.

When I entered, the only customer in there was on his way out. I made a quick visual sweep then headed for the counter. Disappointed, I had hoped for a guy but standing in front of me was a girl, about twenty. I didn't want to point the weapon at her.

I wasn't concerned about overhead cameras because, wearing a stocking cap, jacket, and sporting a two-week beard, I almost looked Latino. I pulled a paper bag out, snapped it open, and put it on the counter. But when I took out the pistol, displaying it in my palm just to show I was serious, she started to freak.

"It's all right," I said and stuck it back my pocket. "I'm not going to hurt you, just put the money in the bag."

I think she wanted to move, but couldn't. She stammered, "I . . . can't."

Jesus.

"Why? C'mon, just gimme the money."

"But I can't open the register, unless I first make a sale."

I had picked a lunatic.

Then a customer walked in and came up to the counter. I stayed right where I was, just a friend of the girl stopping by for a visit. The guy was in his early thirties. He had a street look about him. He turned his head and looked at me, his eyes lingered a few seconds, before he turned back to the girl and said, "Pack of Marlboros" and set a five dollar bill on the counter.

When he checked me out again, I tightened the grip on the gun in my jacket pocket. Pivot my hips and I'd be aiming right at him.

The girl's eyes were popping out now and glued to *me* as she handed him the Marlboros, rang up the sale. I said, "Give him a pack of matches," and she did and he nodded at me, thanks. I am certain he knew something was up, but he took his butts and left.

Okay, one more time.

I said, "The money, empty the draw into the bag, now."

The girl was actually vibrating, her eyes on the brink of bubbling over.

"Please, I can't," she whined. "Unless I make a sale the register won't open."

Frustrated, I raised my voice. "Then pretend I'm buying a pack Marlboros." Relief flushed her face like the Ex-Lax had kicked in, and her mouth formed an O as she punched in the sale, scooped the money, and dumped it into the bag.

"Now, go to the back room and stay there," I said. "And don't come out 'til I'm gone."

I grabbed the bag and watched her disappear through a curtain in the wall. I threw Yodels and Slim Jims into the bag on my way out the door.

When I got in the car, the Greek said, "What the fuck, what was up with that guy? Man, you were cool." Then suddenly he pointed across my chest. "Jesus Christ, look."

Turning my head I saw the girl at the door, palms against the glass, mouth open wide enough to inhale a Big Mac. We roared off heading west up Brighton Ave.

In the first of a long string of hold-ups, I had demonstrated control, calmness, and the ability to think fast on my feet. It was easy and exciting and although the take, three hundred dollars and a box of Slim Jims, wasn't great I realized, with a gun, there was no limit to what I could earn.

The small scores were a training ground, and they didn't cut it for long. People who sold drugs, especially cocaine, were everywhere and making big money, and the Greek and I thought they should share it.

For a portion of the take, usually a fifteen per cent cut, tipsters would give us addresses of mid-sized cocaine dealers. I also had my own sources, Pappas's old customers. We'd come knocking, hitting the lock squarely with a short-handled sledgehammer, and the doorframe exploded.

The problem with those scores was the take was generally lousy. Some coke fiend or a dealer, up to his eyebrows in debt, would guarantee a pound or two was in an apartment, and we'd bust in and end up with two or three ounces, or worse Inositol, what dealers cut the product with.

For a long stretch we got nothing but bad information but whether good *or* bad, drug rip-offs were dangerous. We could get shot coming in or busted going out, so at any time our walking days could be over. And it wasn't just drug scores. We got lousy intelligence on other scores too: supermarkets, meat and fish wholesalers, the occasional nightclub "drop". It was obvious that this would end badly. Uncomfortable with the odds and lousy pay-offs, I was ready to shift gears.

Club Soda

I decided I'd try the nightclub business one last time. In 1983 Club Soda was a cool little disco-themed bar owned by a thirty-five year old "dig me" from Rhode Island named Steve DiSarro. A successful Boston condominium developer, DiSarro had, allegedly, also made millions selling cocaine. And there was one other thing, supposedly he was a godson of Raymond L.S. Patriarca, the boss of the New England Mafia.

"The Man", as Patriarca was known, had run the New England branch of La Cosa Nostra with an iron-fisted grip since 1952 when power had shifted from Boston to Providence, Rhode Island. He wasn't a guy to mess with, and DiSarro, a Mafia wannabe, had no problem flaunting his connection.

Club Soda catered to an upscale crowd. This wasn't the Rat where the doormen wore tank tops, suspenders and steel-toed shoes; the door of Club Soda was guarded by suits. On the first night, I worked with a big, redheaded, former boxer from Revere named Joe Lake. Joe was edgy like me, in good shape, and took lip from no one. They had partnered me up with the perfect guy.

A doorman screens out riff-raff and keeps the place safe from potential problems. Club Soda hired a lot of flunkies, friends or cousins of the owners, so Joe and I kept a close eye on each other's back.

Along with its regular customers, Soda was loaded with half-assed gangsters, coke dealers, and women who liked to associate with half-assed gangsters and coke dealers. One of them, a coke dealer named "Joel," had an apartment down the street on Commonwealth Ave.

Joel wasn't just a dealer; he also sold jewelry, guns and a lot of other weird stuff that people gave him in exchange for his product.

One night after work, a bunch of us went to Joel's apartment. Everyone was whacked out on coke and watching MTV when Joel jumped up from the couch suddenly and ran into the kitchen. He came back out juggling a pair of live hand grenades and everyone was like *whoa*.

The grenades were smooth, not the Sgt. Fury pineapple type, but Joel said they would cut you in half, so I gave him a hundred bucks for one.

Club Soda was more than just crazies. With one of the best sound and lighting systems in the city, and a great DJ, Joey Carvello, Soda was packed from the moment it opened. There were beautiful women, successful businessmen, fashion mavens and, on weekends, a line of limos delivered Columbian coke dealers. Working the door, I felt like a kid peeking in through a candy store window.

While allegedly large cocaine deals took place in the basement office, Joe and I shook down smaller dealers at the door, charging them a "users fee" that allowed them to push their product and keep their teeth. But it was chump change compared to what the owner was making.

Most nights when DiSarro strutted in, he would barely acknowledge us. I was envious of this little grease-ball, who I thought had the world by the balls. Good looking, dapper, acting like a movie star gangster, he sold drugs but wasn't an addict like me. I resented him, hell in those days I resented almost everyone, including myself. I had brains but felt like a loser, *was* a loser, and my response to this knowledge? I hit the coke harder.

I'd work four nights at the club, get a paycheck, and then spend every dime the same night on coke, maybe DiSarro's coke. When I got up the next morning, the flush I heard was my life going down the toilet. It couldn't get worse.

Then it did.

It was a Friday night before a busy holiday weekend when John Bianchi pulled in front of the club in a new Porsche 944. From the cut of his clothes he looked like another Mafia wannabe, which wasn't unusual. Just about everyone who worked there, or came into the place acted as though they were "connected".

At six feet and a solid two twenty, Bianchi looked about thirty years old, and right off was way too chatty and friendly. My Spidey senses should have tingled more, but I was too distracted by what he had on.

Covering a thick, hairy wrist was a gold Rolex Presidential, while the opposite one was strangled by a chunky, gold and diamond bracelet. Huge diamond pinky rings adorned both hands, and around his neck was gold chain as thick as a bicycle tire. Immediately, I made plans for this big, grinning *target*—wearing at least fifty grand worth of bling. If I found out where he lived, he would pay for my next Florida vacation.

We played cat and mouse. He told me his name, and I, thinking there was nothing to fear, gave him my real one. The guy's real cute and I'm pumping him for information, but at the same time he's pumping me back. When we got to the what do you do for a living part, he whispers to me that he's an undercover state cop. I knew the prick was lying so I said to him, "If you're state police, what's your RTT?"

Now that's a question only a real trooper can answer. RTT= Recruit Training Troop.

Mine was the 60th. If you don't know your training troop, you're not a trooper. Bianchi was baffled.

When I told him that I was a professional doorman, who had bounced in a lot of clubs, it really perked up his interest.

"Like where?" he says, offering me gum.

I take it and, chewing, go down the list, but when I got to the Kenmore Club, the huge entertainment facility across the street from the Rat, he stopped me. "Yeah, yeah, I like Narcissus," he says. "Go in there a lot, the manager's—what's his name—a really nice guy."

I jumped right in. "Jimmy Olsen," I said, "Ya, Jimmy's cool."

Bianchi then tells me that he's originally from Cambridge, but that now he lived in the North End, the home base of Boston's mob. He raised his eyebrows when he said the North End. Oh, I get it, you're a *gangster* is what you want me to think. I played along and continue to blow smoke up his ass.

I say, "Oh, you kind of look like someone—now *my* eyebrows go up—who *lives* in the North End." He likes that and pats my shoulder and pulls out a wad, peels off a twenty. He slips it into my hand and says, "I'm gettin' a drink, how about watchin' my car."

When he leaves an hour or so later he said nothing. I watched him drive off, and it was like watching a fat goose slide under a fence. Okay, I'll get him the next time I thought; when he comes in, Joe will ID him and get his address that way.

The following Tuesday I report to work, but the minute I walked in, Tom, the manager, grabbed me. Tom's got this cat-ate-the-canary look on his face. He had always resented Joe and me because he couldn't control us, but his eyes aren't showing resentment now, something inside them is saying *I got ya*. "Steve wants to see you downstairs," he said.

Steve didn't know I existed. "Yeah, what about?" I said, standing there swinging my tie in my hand.

"He wants to *talk*."

"After I put on my tie."

"The hell with the tie he wants to talk, *now*."

Fuck it, I had done nothing wrong, so I went downstairs to the office, knocked, and went in. Right off I spot DiSarro behind his fancy desk talking up to a guy standing next to him. He's middle-aged and wearing a suit, and looked like he *lived* in the North End for real. The conversation stopped, and DiSarro's glaring at me.

Behind me the door closed, and I looked back, and there's a creature about six-eight in a black suit and white open-collared shirt standing there. Built like a Transformer, he's blocking the door and his nostrils are flaring like a cartoon bulls.

DeSarro says, "You motherfucker, you thought you could get away with this?"

The giant makes a move to grab me, but I circle block his hands away and savagely shove him into a filing cabinet, barking, "Keep your fucking hands off, me," then turned back to DeSarro. Now I'm angry. "What the *fuck* is going on?"

The giant moved in again, but the other guy put up a hand and stopped him. DeSarro's was on his feet and waving a sheet of paper, one of those composite sketches police make of suspects. "Know this fucking guy? You know him?" DiSarro said, trying to act tough.

I looked at the drawing and my stomach jumped; it was the guy with the Porsche, Bianchi. DiSarro's screaming now but the words aren't making sense, I'm feeling dizzy, sick. I've been had, but how?

"... anchi, the name's John Bianchi. How'd you know this piece of shit?" DiSarro says.

I told him the story of how he had come to the club, and we had talked for an hour, about his jewelry, and the plans to rob him.

The guy in the suit, his eyes have this twinkle now, he's getting a kick out of the way I was thinking. Then he speaks for the first time and his words are s-l-o-w and deliberate, like it's important that I understood every word.

This is what he told me.

Around five the previous evening, Bianchi went to the Kenmore Club. Two bartenders were inside cleaning, setting up for the evening shift when Bianchi rapped on the front door and used my name to get in. He said Rick Marinick, from Club Soda, had sent him down to meet with the manager, Jim Olsen, about a job. Olsen had been already contacted and expected him to be there.

Once inside he pulled a gun and tied up the bartenders. Then he sat at the bar and calmly sipped a coke as he waited for Olsen to arrive. When he did, around six, Bianchi got the drop on him too. He escorted him to the upstairs office and forced him at gunpoint to open the safe.

In those days cash was king, so the weekend take was substantial. Bianchi left the Kenmore Club with eighty-five thousand in a bag. Jesus, I'd been had. Here I thought I was setting him up and he was setting me up better—and making huge score.

The word was that the Kenmore Club owner, Henry Vara, paid a lot of money "in town" so things like this didn't happen. Wise guys, like Mafia hit man Joe Russo and capo regime Ilario Zannino, came into the place, and brought their friends, so this was considered personal—and I was in the middle. There was a chance I wouldn't leave the office alive.

I had nothing to hide so I did what I always did, went on the offensive. I said, "You think I'm dumb enough to get involved in this shit?" The funny thing was the previous year I had thought about robbing the Kenmore Club, but considered it too risky in the end.

Fearing possible retribution you would think I would have quit Club Soda right there. Friends had told me to but I disagreed. If I did I'd look guilty or, worse, afraid, and since neither one worked I stuck to my guns, literally, and began carrying a piece everywhere.

I took other precautions. My O Street apartment shared a common basement with the three-family next door so, securing it against a possible attack, I duct-taped the hand grenade I had bought to the door knob, straightened the pin, looped the wire through the ring and nailed both ends to the door frame. If someone forced the lock and came through, boom.

The first time that Tank saw it, on his way to the kitchen, he said, "Fucking grenade, why Rick? You got nothing to steal, everything goes up your nose." We laughed about it but Tank was right and he said this concerning any problem I might have over the Club Soda fiasco, wiseguys, and Bulger's connection to them, "Bulger kills for those guys, you had a problem it would be over by now." He was right.

The following weekend the crew: Pole Cat Ferris, Andre the Giant, Ozzie Ort, Mike

Blythe, the Greek, Red Shea, Tank, and I were enjoying a night out at Street Lights on Big Broadway, our unofficial headquarters. The house was jammed and everyone was on the dance floor boogying to the jungle beat with crazy Southie women. Tank was moving with a little blond a few feet away when he yelled over, "Rick the bomb gotta go."

"What?"

"That thing on your door," he burst out laughing. "You're too fucking paranoid."

Back at the table he said to me, "Been thinking about it. Your bed is what, eight feet from the cellar door?"

"Yeah, with a wall in between."

"Fucking sheet-rock. Someone breaks in you're as dead as the mook coming through, just a thought."

The grenade was a defense against someone entering, and laying for me while I was *out*. It never crossed my mind they might try while I was there. Later that night, Tank and I drove to Kelly's Landing, in his big Lincoln Town car, and tossed the thing into the harbor. Even submerged it was loud.

10.

Tale of Two Banks

The Greek had a friend who worked for Brink's Armored Security. The guy, a gambling degenerate, was up to his eyes in debt to shylocks—and looking for a way out. He gave the

Greek the address of a bank in Malden where an armored truck made a drop-off off of a hundred and twenty-five thousand. We went and watched the play.

Medford's Wellington Circle Plaza is a medium-sized mall located on the corner of Route 16 east and 28 South. Fifty yards from our bank was another, the fort-like Guaranteed Trust. Behind the banks, at the rear of the large parking lot, ran a row of retail shops like the crest of a wave.

At nine am the Greek and I sat in an Audi sipping coffee half way between the shops and banks. Removing his sunglasses the Greek scrubbed the lens with a cheap paper napkin. "According to my man," he said, "delivery's at ten but occasionally, to fool guys like us, they mess with the schedule but I'm counting on ten."

"Don't like sitting here," I said.

The Greek slid the glasses back on, and looked into the review, adjusting them.

"Relax, cops come you know what to say."

When "clocking", doing surveillance work, it was important to have a cover story down pat, in case police came around snooping. The story had to be simple so, if separated, we both could repeat it. If cops asked we'd tell them that we had met some girls, locals, the night before at—insert the name of a local nightclub here—and they had agreed to meet us in the parking lot for coffee. There was a coffee shop in the mall and also a Dunkin Donuts down the street. Most cops, being men, would understand this no problem.

As we waited we discussed the two ways to take out the guard—outside in the parking lot or inside the bank. Both had pros and cons.

Outside there was a good chance, with people around, there'd be witnesses but the main threat was the driver who could blast away through the gun ports. To avoid getting shot our timing had to be perfect, ambush the outside guard at just the right angle to the rear of the truck so the driver would be unable to get off a clean shot.

If we hit him inside there was a good chance there'd be no shooting but bank employees were guaranteed to hit the alarm, and a police station was less than a quarter mile away.

The good news? We only planned to grab one bag. It was a 'get well' score to get us back on our feet, fatter ones would come later. But on that overcast morning, as we waited for the truck, I had no idea how quickly *later* would come.

Or what it would cost.

A half-hour before 'our' truck was due another truck, a red and white Wells Fargo, swung into the mall and stopped in back of the Guaranteed Trust. Strangely, after positioning itself directly behind the rear door it sat idling for five minutes before a guard finally got and entered the bank. A minute or so later the rear door opened and the guard, along with a guy in a suit, came out.

After taking a good look around the parking lot he rapped on the rear door and it opened and another guard jumped out. That was three, including the driver, when armored bank transports usually only have two. It wasn't long before we saw why the extra was needed.

While the guy we assumed was the manager made notations on a clipboard, for the next fifteen minutes moneybags in a steady stream, some of them huge, were passed hand-to-hand from the bank to the truck. I had never seen so much money.

I looked at the Greek. "This is the one," I said. "There's three million there maybe more." The loading completed the truck was on the move again rolling toward Rt. 28. I put the Audi into gear and said, "Let's see where they're going," then eased out behind it.

The next stop was right over the town line in Medford. If you turned left on Mystic Ave the Baybank Trust was a short distance down on the left. We turned into the parking lot and drove past the truck that was stopped and sat idling next to the bank.

I parked the Audi then got out and went around the opposite side of the building, entering the tan brick, two-story structure through a side door. After climbing a flight of steps I looked out the window. The truck was fifteen feet below me.

The guard was just getting out and when he opened the side door I could not believe my eyes. Covering most of its floor were bags stuffed with cash, in a layer three deep. I was looking at millions.

I can say from experience that some armored car guards are alert, cautious, and ready to react quickly but most are stuck in the rut of routine—like the guy below that wasn't looking anywhere but inside the truck. He took a dolly out and wheeled it into the bank.

Back at the car I told the Greek that we just had the score of the century dropped in our laps. I said, "The guard came back outside with three bags. I say we hit him when he's loading them in."

The Greek started the car and sat there and stared through the windshield a moment before he said, "I don't know" twice before he put it in gear.

As we pulled out of the parking lot onto Mystic Ave and headed back the way we had come I said angrily, "Don't know *what*? What the hell are you talking about?" We had been scrambling for nickels and dimes for *months* and now we've got a crack at millions, and he's *scared*?

He said kind of whiny, "I dunno, ya know? I got kids, a new baby."

I felt sick and started to say something but stopped. We'd been through some hard times, made a lot of money together, partied hard, the guy was my friend—but it just wasn't in him to do this. Knocking off a lone guard was one thing but taking an entire truck, another.

For a while neither one of us spoke. Certainly the potential was enormous, but so was the risk. We'd be hitting an armored car within fifty feet of a heavily traveled road—a road that could bring police in an instant.

We couldn't, like we had in the past, just grab the money and run. For this we'd have to take control of the driver, guard, or guards, before we began to empty the truck. There was no room for error. Everything had to be perfect.

The traffic on Rt. 93 South was light on the way home. As we passed the Boston Garden on the right the Greek said, "Yeah know, you do this you'll need at least three of ya's."

We entered the South Station tunnel and, like a switch was thrown, the sunlight blinked off and my eyes adjusted to the artificial light. The Greek was right. I would need a team to pull this off and knew just where to find them.

Badger and Flashlight

I was looking at a huge score where the take could set me up for years, but I needed a crew. Putting together a solid crew's never easy. You can't take out a want ad in the newspaper, or even talk much about what you're planning to do. Tell the wrong guy and police will know as much as you do. When you do find the right individual it's all about approach, and you have to feel him out carefully. You start off low key with something like, "We might have something in the works, any interest?"

Inevitably, if they do, they'll ask what their end of the take will be. Throw out a quarter million dollars and it piques their interest pronto, or scares the shit out of them.

Frank the Tank was the first person to learn about the proposed armored car heist, and as usual, he was in. I expected no less. In fact, the Tank would have been pissed if he hadn't been asked first.

Next we needed a driver so we both decided to ask in his brother, Mini-Mac, which turned out to be a huge mistake. The kid had balls, sure, but he was a petty thief who had never moved up. My biggest mistake, I thought I could trust him.

The three of us drove to Medford to watch the play, observing the action from the same second floor from where I had a week earlier. Again I was amazed by how lackadaisical the guard was, totally unaware that fifteen feet above him three faces watched his every move.

When The Tank saw all that money he almost leaped through the glass, but Mini's reaction was very different, and right off he started complaining. "Geez, there'll be hundreds of pounds of cake," he said. "How're going to move it?" Then he said, "I dunno," twice as in I don't know if I can do this.

Here we go again I thought.

On the return trip to Boston Mini passed on the score and I was pissed at myself for inviting him in because Mini had a big mouth—add a little coke and it got bigger than Mick Jagger's. Soon everyone in Southie would know about our plans.

Next guy I asked to drive was a stick-up kid named Flabo. Flabo did the right thing though because, aware of his limitations, he turned us down flat.

Becoming desperate, a bad thing when you're planning bad things, I reached out to an old friend from the Rat days. When it came to a street fight, Spider Guy was as tough as they came but my mistake was equating a willingness to fight anyone with the fearlessness it took to overpower armed men in broad daylight. The two things as different as a badger and flashlight.

If we could find a driver, the Tank and I would handle the heavy stuff; me taking the heaviest load as point man, the first one out to get the drop on the guard. Frank wasn't a killer and neither was I, but I had firearms training and would know when to shoot, and wouldn't miss.

If everything went smoothly we would hit the truck and be gone in less than three minutes, with at least twenty bags, and Mini was right about one thing, money was heavy.

Today when I watch a crime movie and see a character easily carrying a suitcase that allegedly contains two or three million dollars, I laugh because I read somewhere once that a million dollars in brand new hundred dollar bills weighs about twenty-five pounds. Circulated hundreds? Add another five pounds. Brand new fifties? You do the math, money's heavy. If we grabbed one-and-a-half to two million dollars, even with large bills like twenties, fifties and hundreds, the load would weigh over two hundred pounds.

Be Prepared

Once a week, for the next month and a half, Tank and I watched the play at the Medford bank. In an effort to help us, the Greek suggested we bring along his old bank robber buddy, turned major cocaine trafficker, Hobart T. Willis, to watch the play and then pick his brains after, but Tank and I nixed the idea. Willis was too close to mob boss Jim Bulger. The Tank and I feared that if Bulger learned about the heist he might demand a piece of the action, which we had no intention of giving.

Besides, too many people in Southie already knew that something big was up. It got to the point where I would be approached, in a barroom, by a drunk talking out the side of his mouth asking if the "big one" was still on. It freaked me out, and if I had a thimble full of wits about me then would have passed on the score. Tank was having second thoughts too.

In Street Lights one night he pulled me aside and suggested we pass. What he had said made sense, but Tank had money. For me this was it. Consumed by the prospect of making one of the largest hits in New England crime history, I was deaf to his advice, and we argued over it. I told him that he had lost his balls and suggested he stick with moving drugs. We went our separate ways and didn't speak again for almost two months.

The next time we did it, after I banged into him in a Southie after hours joint, we discussed the heist once more and agreed to put our differences aside. To do it right though, we would need real firepower.

Mini-Mac was tight with Jim Bulger, enough so that when Mini got married Bulger was his best man. We got Mini to ask Bulger if he would "rent" us, for ten thousand dollars, two machine guns with extra clips and three Kevlar vests for one day. If the guns were used,axax and had to be disposed of later, we would give Bulger twenty-five grand.

It took a week for him to get back to us through his top lieutenant, Kevin Weeks. Weeks said that Jim, as Bulger was known, never Whitey, had thought it over but decided to pass. The guns were in "a hide" he said and difficult to access. In retrospect, I can't blame Bulger for being hesitant to put weapons like that into the hands of what he must have viewed as a gang of maniacs.

Now Bulger knew that something big was going down, but I wasn't concerned. At the time he was like a god to street hoods like us. Hell, we trusted him enough to ask for *machine guns*. I suggested that after the score, to avoid repercussions, we toss Bulger twenty-five grand.

Tank said, "What are you fucking crazy? We take something at gunpoint then hand it to him? We give him twenty-five he'll ask for a hundred, then what?" Tank was right, and we decided that Bulger would never get a dime from us, and he never did.

We found a driver, a tough kid from the projects with a hell of a reputation named Sean, and the three of us began "clocking" the score weekly to insure the truck followed the same routine every time.

To determine the best plan of attack, we had to be certain that the truck parked in the same position each time because the slightest difference could throw everything off. When it pulled into the lot and backed up to the bank, did it park angle or parallel? Were the guards the same every week and were they alert? We had to learn their habits. Different men? We had to learn theirs.

At the risk of exposing ourselves, we followed the armored truck four stops past the Baybank Trust to see if the routine changed at all and, after watching for weeks, found that it didn't. We understood our quarry completely, but civilians were another matter.

The Baybank Trust was located inside a commercial building that contained other businesses, so we monitored foot traffic and traffic flow through the parking lot and at the bank's drive-thru window.

A score needs stolen cars called "burners", or "hotboxes." For me, out all the criminal activities that I was engaged in, stealing cars by far was the most stressful. In the past I had always relied on local car thieves; a couple hundred bucks got any make I wanted. But for bank heists, and now an armored car, the vehicles had to be stolen by the gang, which meant me, because if the heist turned ugly and heat from law enforcement became intense later, the guy who stole the cars might flip if arrested.

We had to travel to places like: Marshfield, Revere, and as far away as Cape Cod to steal what we needed then drive the cars back to Southie and scatter them throughout the neighborhoods. We would move them around every couple of days so that citizens wouldn't get suspicious.

For the Medford score we would need three cars: the hit car, switch, and the second switch car, but by the time the actual robbery occurred, due to set of peculiar circumstances in which car after car disappeared, I had already stolen twelve. Always a believer in omens and signs there were lots of things about this score that were really starting to spook me.

For example, I would boost a car and find it missing the next day. I'd steal another and that would vanish too. We factored in that we would lose some to police, or to other car thieves, but the rate at which they were going missing was blowing my mind.

On a single June night in 1984 we lost two of the three cars we had stashed for the robbery. With no other option I went out and stole more. Talk about stressful.

The most important part of any score is the getaway and after days of pouring over local maps, studying terrain and checking out every alley and side street in the area around the bank, we believed we'd come up with the perfect escape.

Following the heist, we would exit the parking lot onto Mystic Ave, heading south. Two-tenths of a mile down the road we would turn left into a driveway that took us behind an industrial building where we would pull into a chain-link enclosure, the rear of which formed a portion of the perimeter fence of Rt. 93 south.

The money and guns, already packed into large plastic trash bags, would be taken from the car and through a hole in the fence cut the previous night. An ascent up a small incline took us to the breakdown lane where the switch car waited with the hood up, appearing to be disabled.

The switch complete, we would take the highway south a few miles then the Storrow Drive exit, then the first exit off it and pull into a public parking garage where the third car, a station wagon, waited. A quick transfer of the loot into that vehicle, and in another ten minutes, we'd be back in South Boston with close to two million dollars.

No one doubted that it was a beautiful score.

Killing Field

Game day came on a Tuesday the last week in June 1984. We left the Tank's apartment early, around seven, exiting through the back of #7 Patterson Way into the courtyard with its busted asphalt and clotheslines drooping from rusted poles. With the temps in the high seventies and humid, I still wore a tan, nylon windbreaker to cover the .357 in the holster on my belt. Underneath one arm was a chopped, pump shotgun covered by a twist of beach towel.

Behind me the Tank and the driver, Sean, both packed handguns beneath their windbreakers. The third switch had been put in the parking garage the night before so we were set and ready to fly.

It was nerve wracking driving two stolen cars, loaded with weapons and violent intent, in the heart of the morning commute. People all around us were heading to work and sipping coffee, as they listened to mindless talk radio and weather reports. I didn't hate them the way I usually did. They had made conscious decisions to lead dull, boring lives while, within a few hours; I would be rich, in a jail cell, or dead.

The switch car positioned in the breakdown lane, I opened the hood and poured anti-freeze under the bumper, it was for the police in case they stopped to investigate. Under a windshield wiper was left a small sign that read in black marker, '*Please don't tow—overheated—gone to get help*'.

The three of us were in a four-door Torino tucked into our spot next to the bank when the truck arrived, exactly on time. But this time it stopped where it never had before. Tank and I were seated in back while Sean watched the action in the rear view mirror.

He said, "Whoa, why they stopping there? He's backing up now."

I said to Sean, "When it stops how far away is it?"

He said, "Okay, he's stopped. It's about sixty feet, Rick."

Sixty feet. Was it too far to travel?

We're in a stolen car, armed to the teeth, and adrenalin was pumping like 100 percent octane. Should we hit it? The original plan called for forty feet. Could I cover the extra twenty and still get the drop on the guard.

Then Sean said, "Guard's getting out."

I yanked off my mask. "Fuck it, we pass," I said. "We'll do it next week."

Which was easier said than done.

It meant that we had to grab switch car out of the breakdown land and drive it back to Boston, then retrieve the other in the parking garage. Then both cars had to be put in brand new locations for one simple reason. An old lady sipping tea in her living room might have already noticed the strange car parked across the street from her house, and then if she sees it again the following week on the afternoon news, and it's tied to an armored car robbery?

"Hello officer? I have something to report that may interest you . . ." and an army of cops swarms into South Boston.

In 1984 armored car heists in the Boston area—the armored car heist capital of the country—were mostly pulled off by "Townies" Charlestown hoods. Nothing against Charlestown but we preferred that Charlestown and not Southie would be the first, and hopefully last, place the cops would look for suspects.

The following week came and when another one of our cars went missing—something like the tenth at that point—that was the final straw for me. The Tank had backed out once, now it was my turn.

When I told him I was done, he tried to talk me out of it, but I was adamant and spooked, mostly spooked, and it wasn't drugs. I had been completely clean for over three weeks, my regular routine before any big score. No, I couldn't avoid the feeling, which clung like blistered skin, telling me if I did this I wouldn't come back.

Dead End

The weight of the Baybank heist off my shoulders, I began to feel optimistic again, especially after the Greek and I mushed a coke dealer from Somerville for over four grand. Less than two weeks later though I was right back at zero.

Things weren't rosy for Tank either. Problems caused by Mini-Mac had so infuriated him that he savagely beat him up in the street outside of Southie's Bayside Club. If Jim Bulger hadn't intervened Mini, more than likely, would have been killed. Tank's sterling reputation as a stand-up guy, who took care of business, remained intact because most people that knew Mini thought he had it coming. . But there was one business Tank refused to let go of.

On an early July Sunday morning, less than a month after I'd pulled out of the Medford heist, I woke up to someone banging on my door. Then I heard, "Rick, wake the fuck up."

I sat up, who the hell? The mail slot creaked open and Tank's laughter filled the hallway outside my bedroom. "Rick, it's me, get the fuck up you lazy bastard."

I opened the door and shuffled back to the bedroom. "What do you want," I said, collapsing back onto the mattress. "It's ten o'clock."

"So what," Tank said. "I've already done three hundred sit-ups, two hundred push-ups and ran the fucking island, twice."

I covered my eyes as Tank plunked his ass down on the clothes hamper in the corner. "So what's so fucking important?" I said.

"I'm thinking the score, Rick, we *gotta* do it," he said, slapping the side.

"What?"

"Yeah, I've been thinking it over, a lot. We can't give up. *You* can't give up."

I sat up and swung my feet to the floor. The Tank was up now too, pacing in the narrow space and giving me, point by point, the reasons why we had to do Medford.

The biggest one? Money. There was well over a million dollars at stake and, according to Tank, I was the only one who could take out the guard. "Come on, Rick," he pleaded. "Come on, man, we can do this. Damn getaway's foolproof."

I ran my eyes around the dump I called home. Every dime I made went up my nose, and I was three months behind in the rent. I was a grown man and made my own decisions, but what he said made sense, except for one thing.

"We're fucking car-less," I said, "We can't do it without cars."

Tank threw his hands up like he was tossing confetti. "Car-less, who cares? We go out and steal more." He burst out laughing and pointed at me. "Come on man, you're the fucking car thief. We can do this. You're with me, right?"

I looked at my feet and nodded, the score was back on. I was with him, right to the end.

Later the same day I drove out to Weymouth to visit my mother. I rarely saw her much in those days usually only getting in touch by payphone just before a big score, in case something happened. I figured this time I'm going to be killed.

I arrived at her home around two and she fried up some baloney and made us sandwiches. When she voiced concern over my weight, I told her that I had only lost muscle because I wasn't hitting the gym anymore. She gave me a look, you're lying.

In contrast my mother had been sober for years and looked wonderful. Everything about her shined while her son was a black hole sucking everything in, without a hint of light escaping. I would make money, a ton of it at times, and wouldn't even take my mother to lunch. The only time I visited? Right before I thought I might die. I look back and that was about me too, the visits softening the guilt of a selfish addict for being such a lousy son.

The next day, within the space of four hours, the Tank and I stole three cars in three different towns and drove them back to Southie. In those days all you needed was coat hanger, bent just the right way, to get past the door lock. Then a "DP" (auto body shot dent puller) was screwed into the ignition and the lock ripped out. A screwdriver, used as a key, started the engine and off I'd drive.

Back in Southie we'd wipe the entire car clean of fingerprints. Using solvent soaked rags, we hit places the average person might not consider: gas cap, radio knobs, behind the rear view mirror, under the edge of the hood, the seat adjustments. Then we'd run it through a car wash and vacuum it after.

Months before, as a defense against police pursuit, we had stolen two dry, chemical fire extinguishers from a hotel. If pursued the plan was to blast them out the rear windows leaving a thick, white trail behind like a crop duster.

Late that afternoon I contacted Sean, our driver, and told him that the score was back on. The only thing the kid wanted to know was the time we were picking him up.

At six the next morning, I felt strangely calm as I sat in the Tank's apartment emptying tubes of Crazy Glue onto a plate. Using a watercolor brush each man applied the clear liquid to their fingertips and palms, the dried glue making it impossible to leave fingerprints behind.

Next we sat around a table wiping down the guns and bullets and going over the responsibilities of each man. Before the truck's arrival the Torino would be parked beside the bank, facing the street. The Tank and I seated in back, with me behind the driver.

After the truck passed it would pause approximately twenty-five feet away, back-up then stop at an angle to the bank. The Tank and I would continue to stare straight ahead while Dennis watched the target in the rearview mirror, giving a blow by blow. After months of observation we knew our man well.

Some guards performed surveillance before making their move. Others don't, because they're stuck in a routine, but it's a routine that could get them killed.

We had watched the guard closely to see if he acted nonchalantly, kept his head down like he hoped to see no evil? There was no indication that our guard was a hero. He appeared to be a guy who just wanted to go home to the wife and kids, booze, pot, card game, whatever—it was the driver that troubled me. Unable to observe him closely, there was no way to know what he was thinking.

On game day we'd wait for the guard to exit the bank with the dolly and when he opened the side door and put the dolly in, then start to climb in after it, that's when it started. My job as lead man was to catch him at just the right moment, while he was pulling himself up.

The guard under control, Dennis would back the Torino up as close as he could, and Tank would jump out and climb into the truck and begin tossing bags to Dennis, who'd load them. The planned take was fifteen bags in less than two minutes. Twenty or more if everything went smoothly. On that hot July morning we would leave the parking lot with a minimum of one million five hundred thousand dollars, over three million in today's money.

At 9:30, after we positioned the switch car in the breakdown lane, the others drove off, and I hopped over the guardrail, dropped into a crouch halfway down the embankment. Using a small pair of binoculars, I scanned the roof of the bank building as well as surrounding buildings. Wary of a police ambush, I looked for workmen, people who looked like they didn't belong, but nothing stood out.

After I reunited with Tank and Sean in the Torino on the short drive to the bank, Sean turned the radio on, the disc jockey going on about a new song he was about to play on Boston radio for the first time.

We were parked next to the bank, when the song came on, and my ears perked up when I heard, for the first time, the chorus of Ann Wilson and Mike Reno's ballad *Almost Paradise*— which removed any doubt I was a dead man that day.

"Whoa-oa … ALMOST PARADISE. We're knocking on heaven's door."

Sean snapped off the radio as the truck rumbled past, his eyes were glued to the rear view mirror. "It's stopping," he said, "this time where it's supposed to. Whoa, the door's about to pop and the guard's getting out, opening the side door, here comes the dolly. Loading one bag, two bags, three … Jesus, another one, he's lugging four in today, not a bad hit either. Wheeling it into the bank."

The Tank and I put plastic masks on and tugged stocking caps down over our ears. From a short distance away, the masks almost looked human. Sean pulled a ski mask over his head.

Hard Ball

  I looked at Tank and nodded. "Ready?" He nodded back. Since the first time I saw that mountain of cash, I knew it was mine. Now only two men were keeping me from it, and a hatred boiled up for the Wells Fargo guards.

  Sean whispered, "He's coming out of the bank . . . he' back at the truck."

  I lifted the door latch and shouldered it open, swung out my legs.

  "Side door's open, dolly's going in, hit him, Rick, hit him."

  I said what I always did when leaving the car, "Let's get these motherfuckers."

  What happened next took less than forty-seconds.

  I was out and running, on Indian feet, toward the truck. I covered the short distance in seconds. The guard never heard me coming. He was almost inside when I reached up, grabbed his shoulder, and savagely yanked him backwards.

  He yelped and then grunted as I rammed the shotgun into his neck, pinned him to the side. "Move and you're dead motherfucker. Move and you're dead."

  He whimpered, "Please, please," as I dragged him along the side to the passenger door, and pinned his head against the window. I shouted at the driver, "Put your hands up you fuck or he's dead, put 'em up." He glared at me then reluctantly raised them.

  The Torino braked to a stop behind me and I snatched the guard's gun from the holster, and tossed it over the hood. The Torino's door opened and I thought we got this as I threw the guard down and pinned him with the shotgun. I had my eyes off the driver only for a second when I heard it. A sound like toy caps, the kind we used to play with as kids, exploding.

But these weren't caps. They were highly muffled gunshots; someone was shooting at us from inside the truck. My first thought was somehow I had screwed up; there were three guards today.

I turned to see Tank leap from the truck and I fired into it through the side door toward the rear. Buckshot, like killer bees, ricocheted around the interior and created a spray of shredded paper and canvas. I stepped to the side and fired again, toward the driver's compartment this time.

As I backed up toward the Torino, everything seemed to move in slow motion, and I saw things with a clarity like under microscope: every bolt on the truck, the vividness of its colors, and the sideburns of the driver through the bullet proof door glass as he fired through the gun port, attempting to kill me.

I fired back and heard the snap of his bullets passing my head, and re-pumped and pulled the trigger but nothing happened. Somehow my hand had shifted and hit the safety button behind the receiver. I was unable to fire the weapon.

I tried to back in through the rear door but was shocked to find Tank right behind me, when he should have been all the way inside. The guard fired again and I whacked him in the shoulder and yelled to get in. He did and I slid in beside him and Sean hit the gas and we fish-tailed, the door slamming shut, toward the street.

Ripping mad and trying to comprehend how it all unraveled, I looked at Tank. "What the fuck happened?"

With effort he turned his head and looked at me and I noticed a thin veil of crimson spread across his cheek and neck. "Rick, I'm hit," he said, then vomited a column of blood so dense it looked like Jell-O.

Over the roar of the accelerating engine, I shouted to Sean "Frankie's been shot." We turned off of Mystic Ave. and raced behind the industrial building. "We gotta get him to a hospital," I said as we skidded to a stop inside the chain-link enclosure. I heard sirens in the distance.

The Tank's head rested against the door glass now, his eyes were closed, his chin on his bloody chest. Dennis was already outside the car. He opened the rear door and said, "C'mon man, he's dead, look at him. Get the money, let's go." There was a moneybag on the floor. Tank had tossed out three, but Dennis had only managed to load one before the shooting erupted.

I grabbed Tank's jacket, his body limp and heavy now, and pulled him into an upright position. His head remained down but at least he wasn't vomiting blood anymore. I passed the shotgun to Dennis and, as he disappeared through the hole in the fence, grabbed the moneybag and followed him.

All the months of meticulous planning concerning our actions after the score, the best way to approach the breakdown lane, our hats low eyes on the ground, went out the window because nothing mattered now. I didn't care about cops or who saw my face.

Dennis was already inside behind the wheel when I tossed the bag in back, then turned and ran down the hill, through the trees and tall grass as he shouted behind me, "What you doin'? He's dead, man, he's dead."

I thought the hell with the third switch we'll take Tank to Mass General Hospital, right off Storrow Drive, and drop him in front of the emergency room entrance. But when I got into the car and started to drag him out he felt like an anchor, like he weighed a thousand pounds. I had been right all along; death was in the air on that hot July morning.

When we left Tank's apartment he had carried two guns. I scooped the automatic off the seat, but his back-up piece, a five shot .38 Smith Wesson, its former owner a diamond importer robbed months before, was missing.

The plan had called for the money to be bagged up before we transferred it to the car so a dozen Hefty Steel Ply trash bags were strewn about the rear floor. I searched the seat for the gun then the floor, tossing the bags, but never found it.

A half hour later police found the car.

Shit Storm

We never went to the parking garage, opting instead to drive directly to Southie. Both of us were still in shock, but certain things we knew for sure. Prior to the shooting, I had total control over the outside guard and, realizing this, the driver had put up his hands and surrendered. There was no way for us to know that the driver, safe behind bullet-proof glass and armor plate, would willingly jeopardize his partner's life to protect his payload. Someone told me later, although this was never verified, Wells Fargo offered a ten thousand dollar reward to guards that stopped a robbery in progress. If this was true, then everything made sense.

Back in the "counting room" of my O Street apartment, Dennis and I divided the ninety-two thousand dollar take and agreed not to see each other for two months. He left, and I stashed my end in a bag then hid it in the basement under some trash. I still had to get rid of the shotgun and car.

On the drive to the Mass Avenue Bridge I struggled to wrap my mind around what just happened. A close friend was dead and it was only due to shit luck, and a shotgun, that I wasn't dead along with him.

When we had raced from the scene, I didn't care about cops or being arrested, but one-hour later things had changed. Facing a shit storm from both sides of the law, my survival instincts had kicked into high gear.

I stopped the car in the center of the Mass Avenue Bridge and, at the first opportunity, took the shotgun from the trunk and tossed it over the railing into the Charles River. I drove back into town and ditched the car behind a South End building, then walked back to Southie.

I crossed the Broadway Bridge and took the loneliest walk of my life up West Broadway attempting to feel something, anything, but thoughts of my friend on a slab in a city morgue had turned what remained of any emotions to wood.

Other than Sean, I was the only person in the world who knew that Frank "the Tank" MacDonald, a well-liked local celebrity, was dead. At the time Southie was a proud, close-knit community, a place that you didn't go into unless you were from there. It had taken me years to prove to locals that I had what it took to be accepted, and I had been, but there wasn't a soul I could talk to now.

Then I remembered the one friend I had left.

Red Head Ginger Bread

Elaine Cunniff was a friend of my former wife, Cara, and we met for the first time in 1977, right after my return from Okinawa. I was kicked back on the living room couch reading a copy of *Ring Magazine,* when I heard Cara call me from the sidewalk outside.

From the doorway of our tiny M Street apartment, I looked down the brick steps at Cara's new friend, Elaine, standing there on the sidewalk gazing up at me. She was a skinny little twist of redheaded fluff in a black beret, jeans, and dungaree jacket. Cara introduced her and Elaine gave me this cute little grin. She said, "Hi, Richard."

"Yeah, how ya doin'," I said and went back to the couch.

For me, that was it, there was nothing else to talk about. Certainly, there wasn't any physical attraction. Sure, she was beautiful, thin and long-legged, but Elaine was a redhead and redheads, at the time, did nothing for me. I had this thing if I kissed one, she'd probably taste like rust.

Rust aside, Elaine and I went on to become good friends, and, now and again, she would stop by the nightclubs where I worked, places like the Rat, and then later Club Soda to visit. She rarely drank and didn't do drugs. She would come in with a girlfriend just to see me and *dance*; a little strawberry-blond whirlwind on the dance floor for hours.

Most of the time Elaine was away from the city traveling on business, but when she returned to visit her parents, if I heard she was around, I'd give her a call.

"Hey Elaine, how ya doin'? Want to grab a cuppa tea ?"

When I was broke, which due to the coke habit was fairly often, she would take *me* out to lunch. One night, in 1983, she took me to see my first real play, *Shear Madness*, at a small Boston theatre. I remember walking out with the crowd afterwards blown away that people actually lived like this. They went out to eat around other civilized people, watched plays and movies together unconcerned about where the next high would come from, or who might be trying to kill them.

Elaine was different from any girl I had ever met. Always encouraging, she often told me that from that from the first time we met, she saw promise in me, and a goodness I was unable to see in myself. The most important thing when I needed her, Elaine was always there.

In 1982, whacked out on drugs one night, in Chinatown restaurant, I was stabbed through the hand during a fight, and later arrested. Following the operation on the damaged tendons at Mass General Hospital, and after the arraignment the following day, I hit the streets, unable to even afford the antibiotics I needed.

I reached out to the only person I could and Elaine rushed over, picked me up in the South End, took me to a pharmacy, and paid for the drugs. No questions or lectures, just love.

Southie born and raised, she was aware I was involved in criminal activities but had little idea of their depth. She never judged or condemned me, but would often say in a confused way,

"Richard, what's wrong with you? Can't you see that you're better than this?" And I'd look at her like she was crazy.

I'd say "Better than what? I'm doing just fine," thinking she was just a hippy chick who didn't get the streets, or what it took to survive them.

I had left West Broadway and was cutting through back streets on the way to my O Street apartment when I made the decision. It was a long shot, but I would swing by Elaine's parent's house to see if I could catch her in.

After climbing the huge granite steps of 760 East Fourth Street, I rang the bell and was shocked when Elaine opened the door. I looked past her down the long, dark corridor leading to the kitchen, where her mother, Ursula, was mopping the floor. I guess by my look Elaine knew something was wrong. "Richard?" she said, staring into my eyes.

"Hey, Elaine."

Her eyes continued searching. "You okay?"

"Can we talk a minute?"

I descended the steps and Elaine called back to her mother that she was going outside. I was sitting at the bottom when Elaine settled beside me and waited.

It was a hot summer day, and as I gazed toward L Street, less than a block away, waves of heat shimmered over the roofs of parked cars. With no easy way to say it I just did, "Frank MacDonald's dead."

Elaine exhaled sharply. "What do you mean? I just—

I hadn't looked at her, but then I did and explained what had just happened.

Long before I finished, her eyes had filled with tears. "What are you going to do now?" she said, staring straight ahead, arms around her knees, squeezing.

"Got no idea," I said, standing up. "Right now, I'm grabbing the dough and going someplace, I don't know where. Just wanted you to know that I'm okay, and what happened."

Elaine stood up and hugged me. "Richard, if there's anything I—"

"No, forget it. You see me, keep away, Elaine. Far away, I can take care of myself."

"Richard."

"I'll see you again, don't worry," I said, and then started off toward M Street. Near the corner I turned around and looked back. Elaine stared at me from the top of the steps. Neither of us waved.

11.

Mind Field

When the news concerning Tank's death finally got out, South Boston, the neighborhood where I had always felt safe, yanked the welcome mat out from under me. My apartment no longer secure, I grabbed the money, a handgun, and walked out the door. But you can't walk around with fifty grand in a bag; I needed to find someplace to stash it.

Alby Santos (not his real last name) lived in the Villa Victoria apartments in the South End. Santos, of Puerto Rican and Italian descent, was a fitness freak and originally from the

Bronx in New York. The apartment, where he lived with his wife and son, was only a block from my former Tremont Street condo.

I had first met Santos at Club Soda, where he was a road dog of this Lebanese kid, Billy, who worked there as a bouncer. I believed I could trust Alby for one reason—when I needed his help once for something serious, he was there.

One afternoon the previous summer, I left my condo to grab something to eat. I hadn't gone far when I passed two black men sitting on the steps of a large brownstone, both of them drinking from paper bags. When one of them called me a faggot—my South End neighborhood had a large number of gays—I thought I'd been mistaken for someone else.

I turned around, faced him. "What?"

The larger of the two stood up and said, "You heard me, fucking *faggot*."

I wasn't a "faggot", just an angry guy down on his luck, divorced, and on the verge of losing his home. I grinned at him and returned to my condo.

A few minutes later I came out the front door carrying a pair of black, leather zap gloves, the knuckles packed with powdered lead. The two black guys, at the same spot down the street, now were passing a joint back and forth. I jogged down West Dedham to the Santo's apartment and knocked on the door.

When it opened I said, "Alby I got a problem give me a hand?"

Now, Alby might've given me ten reasons why he couldn't get involved, but didn't. All he said before running upstairs was, "Do I need a gun or brass knuckles."

See, that's how I judged who my friends were then. Anyone could lend you money, their apartment, vacation home or, if they're crazy enough, even their girlfriend but someone willing to put his skin on the line, for me? He's my friend. There were half a dozen men I could count on for that then, and vice versa, and Santos was one of them.

As we jogged side-by-side up to Tremont I explained what had happened but when we got to the corner and looked down the street, the men were gone. Alby looked at me, puzzled.

"What the fuck you think I'm crazy? They were right *there*," I said, pointing.

Suddenly I heard a voice. A little Latino kid, on a bike across the street, waved at us and shouted, "Hey mister, the big one's in the drugstore behind you."

I waved thanks back and walked through the door of Tremont Drug. The kid was right, the big guy was in front of me at the counter buying a pack of smokes. Without breaking stride I closed on him and said, "Hey, asshole," and he turned into my overhead right. The first shot knocked him cold, the follow-up hook just dressing as he crashed back into, and took down, a display case of Advil. Like a panther Alby was on him and, straddling his chest, pounding his solar plexus while the pharmacist behind the counter screamed, "You're *killing* him."

"Don't worry, he'll be fine," I said and rammed a box of Advil into the guy's open mouth.

The kid on the bike outside had watched the whole thing through the window. He clapped as we exited. He said, "Man, you boys *done* that motherfucker, other dude's across the street," pointing at a package store on the opposite corner. We let that guy go but the bottom line? Alby was someone I thought I could trust.

We talked in Alby's living room while his wife, a real sweet kid, remained in the kitchen. I hoisted the bag and said, "I got forty-six grand here. Sit on it for three, maybe four days you get two."

Santos agreed on the spot, and I used his phone to call my father.

When I was a kid he was rarely around but for the past five years when I needed a lawyer, bail, or just someone to talk to my father had been. Sure it was selfish, even childish, to expect him to be but at the time I figured he owed me.

Dad picked me up in his black Caddy Seville. He looked really scared but who could blame him? His son was now wanted for masked armed robbery, and someone was dead as a result of the crime. I stayed at his house for a week.

By the time I got back to Southie, the bad news concerning the Tank had gone viral, and my entire former crew had turned their backs on me, avoiding me like I was running for sheriff. Word on the street was I had talked Tank, who months before had pulled out of the heist, back into it and had gotten him killed as a result.

Then things got worse.

When "leads" brought police investigators to South Boston in an effort to get someone to snitch, they started a rumor—Tank's partners had bailed and left him to die, which was total bullshit. Only two men were actually there, and both of us knew he was dead.

Weeks passed and when the investigation ran into a brick wall, the cops started a new rumor: Tank's partners didn't leave him to die, no, they had *killed* him to prevent him from talking, which was even more ridiculous than the previous lie. If the situation wasn't so tragic, it would have been laughable, but there was good news too. No one in Southie, with the possible exception of a few members of Tank's immediate family, believed the cop's bullshit.

Heat from law enforcement relentless, a few of my remaining underworld friends warned me that I would be picked up soon for questioning, which never happened. Years would pass before I ended up in a courtroom charged with the robbery.

From a law enforcement standpoint, I was hot as a struck match, and my former associates, heavily involved in drug sales and loan sharking, could no longer afford to have me around. It didn't matter that the guy that shot Tank had tried to kill me too; the criminal investigation put anyone connected with me under a spotlight, and it had to be shut off. Concerned that someone might try to shut me off, permanently, I carried a gun everywhere.

I also had concerns that Jim Bulger himself might get involved, and either order me to deliver a cut of the money to him, or hand it over to Tank's mother. But Bulger, known for doing his homework, had researched the hold-up and come to the correct conclusion that Tank had died from a gunshot wound. To his credit, he remained completely out of our business, but others were willing to step into his place.

My former friend, Jack 'Pole Cat' Ferris suggested that I give the Tank's mother his share of the loot. I refused but offered to pay for the funeral. After thinking it over I told Ferris the next day, "I'll give her the money but *you* have to deliver it."

Pole Cat's faced flushed. "I can't do that," he said.

"Yeah?" I said, "then neither can I. I hand her the dough, and time passes and she decides that I'm to blame for the death of her son, then what? She runs to the cops and starts talking about the money she got."

Pole Cat passed on the offer.

Next, Polecat grabbed Sean, the driver, and convinced the kid to give Tank's mother, through a third party, ten grand. Following that transaction, one of Tank's brothers tossed what he referred to as "blood money" into the harbor. It was rumored, the same night, a local Southie player went diving off Kelly's Landing with a scuba mask and flippers and retrieved it.

The Tank's wake at O'Brien's funeral home was a mob scene, but I wasn't there. There was too much heat and people were angry. But the following day, with nothing to hide, I put on a suit and attended his funeral Mass at St. Augustine's on Dorchester Street, as well as the burial after. The way I saw it, if someone had something to say, then say it to my face, but no one said anything.

At the gravesite in West Roxbury undercover FBI agents that had infiltrated the funeral, acting as pallbearers, took photographs of the crowd. Everyone knew they were there, and a hush fell over the hundreds of mourners as I approached Mrs. MacDonald as she stood beside the coffin. I had known "Ma" for years and we always had a great relationship.

All I could say was, "I'm sorry, Mrs. MacDonald."

Through tears she responded, "It's not your fault, Rick."

Her exact words.

Next I apologized to John, a former friend and Tank's Navy SEAL lieutenant brother. He didn't respond but I detected no hatred, suspicion, or even anger in his eyes, only sadness.

Although few at the cemetery wanted to be seen anywhere near me, I still had a few friends. One of them, John L. Sullivan, a sibling of a notorious South Boston family, stepped up and offered me a ride home. As we left the cemetery, he gave me some solid and what turned out to be prophetic advice.

Sully said, "Let it go, Rick. You did nothing wrong. Let the assholes who turned on you stew in their own shit, and they will, brother, believe me. Move on with your life."

It was good advice and I wanted to take it but being heavily addicted to coke made it impossible.

Bottoming Out

I had to split from the city but first I needed my money from Alby. I was taken back a little when we met at his apartment and he said, "It didn't feel safe with all that dough around here, Rick, so I split it up and gave some to my brother. You know, just in case they raided the house."

He handed me nineteen grand and, struggling to remain cool, I said, "Yeah, I guess that makes sense." Thinking he wouldn't have the balls to steal from me, would he?"

I said, "I'll see you tomorrow to pick up the rest."

The next day we met in Quincy at the same Howard Johnson's where I used to wash dishes. Alby passed another six grand under the table to me as two state cops came walking in, one a classmate from the academy, and sat down at a table not thirty feet from us. My bad luck was on steroids.

That night I went to a bar, Nicely Nicely's, in Boston's Quincy Market district. I had learned that my old friend, Tommy Matook, formerly the manager of TJ's Lounge, managed the place. I hadn't seen Matook in over eight years but when I walked in he was thrilled to see me. We went down to his basement office to and he sat behind his desk and took an envelope from a draw filled with coke. He poured some on a small mirror and bragged he'd been selling it for years.

Matook did a fat line then passed me the mirror. "So, what's up?" he said, pinching his nostrils and grinning like a Cheshire cat.

I sucked up my line and told him that I had recently made money and asked him if he could hold some in the office safe. I said, "You do there's a grand in it for you."

When Mattook agreed, I handed him five grand plus another for his pocket. At least now I had a bank from which I could make withdrawals.

The following day I returned to Alby's apartment accompanied by the Greek. I had told Alby that I would be there at six but showed up at five, ringing the doorbell. When no one responded, we went around back. I peeked in through the kitchen window and my stomach sunk, the place had been cleaned out.

I was kicking in the back door when a neighbor rushed outside and confronted me. "What the fuck you doin'?" he yelled.

"I'm looking for Alby, where the fuck is he?"

"He's gone man. Packed up a U-Haul late last night and headed back to the Bronx."

I remember the look on the Greeks face, like it was his fault, since I had also asked him to sit on the money, but he refused because of the heat. I didn't blame him, it wasn't his fault it was mine for trusting Alby. The slimy prick, formerly a stand-up guy, had beaten me for almost twenty grand.

Initially I wanted to track down Alby and kill him, but that kind of work isn't like in the movies. Clocking someone takes time, skill, and I'd have to travel to the Bronx, unknown territory, and ask around about him. Then he gets dumped?

Twenty grand wasn't worth a charge of first-degree murder.

Nothing seemed to work for me, and without a driver's license or credit card I couldn't rent a hotel room or even a car. I talked Matook into booking a room at the Marriot Longwharf, and that's where I crashed for the next two weeks.

Days were spent drinking, alone, at Nicely Nicely's and snorting coke. Even the damn bartender, whom I tipped like a king, refused to give me the right time of day. His attitude reminded me of another fucked up time in my life when for two consecutive summers, after pulling off large scores, I had hid out on Nantucket at my friend Nancy's Winslow's house. While Nancy worked her day job, I drank in a bar called the Rose and Crown. The bar's motto, "The local bar where everyone is local," but apparently, I wasn't local enough. I would drink all day, tipping the bartender a goddamn month's rent, and neither he nor anyone else would even give me a glance. The message I was getting was loud and clear—the way I was living wasn't working—but I was a stubborn addict.

Looking back I think that was the point where I started to believe that a higher power, call it God or whatever, was forcing me to realize that no matter how much I robbed, or how violent I was, nothing without His presence would work in my life, the robbery in Medford a prime example. The score that I thought would fulfill all my dreams had delivered nothing but nightmares.

Even Matook was acting weird now. The armored car hold-up remained in the news and with me booked in a hotel under his name he put two and two together, became spooked, and I was on the streets again.

My life was hell. A small fortune at my disposal, I couldn't even find a safe place to sleep and, always high, couldn't sleep anyway. Years later, while I did time in state prison, an old con taught me a valuable lesson. He said he believed the way that God saves you is that he allows you to get beaten to the point where you're helpless and no longer able to fight him off.

I was almost there and only had a little bit further to go.

Less than three weeks later I was back in the Combat Zone, touring my old haunts. Whacked out of my mind on coke I was convinced that two cops followed me everywhere.

The Caribe, on the fringe of the Zone, was a small strip club near the corner of Stuart. When you walked in the bar was on the right and behind it a small stage where the girls danced.

The place just about half-filled I picked an empty table across from the men's room and sat in a seat my back to the wall. Soon, a stripper by the name of Sunny approached. We had been friends for years and, as she snugged up the belt of her silk ,Chinese bathrobe, she stared into my eyes. "Ricky?" she said, leaning closer. "Whatsa *matter* honey?"

I said, "Sunny, I got cops following me, everywhere."

"You high?"

"As the Goodyear blimp, here," I said, reaching into my pocket. Cocaine was sold in half-gram packets then and I pulled out about five and grabbed her hand, tried stuffing them into it but she yanked it back.

"No thanks, I'm all done with that."

"Whadaya mean, done? You get high."

"Haven't for two weeks, it was killing me, makin' my gums bleed, hair fall out. Jesus, look at *you*."

I looked at the entrance. The two cops had just walked in. I said, "There they are the fucking maggots."

Sunny looked at them. Her eyes were glued to them she sat down beside me. "Those two?"

"Ya, probably better you get away from me." I said and stood up.

"Ricky."

"Get away," I said and entered the men's room.

Certain that I was about to be arrested I threw the coke into the trash bin, and rammed it down to the very bottom. I came out of the men's room breathing fire and went straight for the cops, seated side by side at the bar.

I said to the nearest one, "You want me you fuck? Turn around I'm right here."

I felt like I was in the Twilight Zone. I'm screaming into the guy's ear and neither one so much as looks at me. I screamed, "You piece of shit, " and tried to left hook him off the seat but all I got was his hat. Now the other guy's off the stool and trying to tackle me but my own drunken momentum was making me fall and he tripped over my legs, and we both hit the floor. I got up and took off running.

Expecting to be shot in the back any second I dove under a van that was parked out in front. Cars were going by on Tremont Street, and I could see people's feet moving along the sidewalk, but the "cops" never came out of the bar.

I crawled partially out from beneath the van and looked up. In a second story window of the building next door there was a guy with a rifle —and he was aiming it right at me. I shouted to a passing cabby, "The fucking cops are trying to kill me." I mean I *saw* the guy and the rifle— and he *was* trying to kill me

Then another cab stopped and the driver got this look on his face when he saw me under the van. He said, "Man, you *alright*, need an ambulance or somethin'?"

I pointed up. "You crazy? There's a guy with a rifle up there and he's trying to kill me, motherfucker's trying to kill me."

The cabby's eyebrows floated up. He said, "Man *you* crazy, I'm calling the cops."

By this time I actually *wanted* the cops thinking, really believing, that some kind of federal SWAT team had tracked me down and was planning to assassinate me in the street. I wasn't carrying a weapon that night and somehow *they knew*.

When the BPD arrived it was on, again. The cops dragged me out and I began fighting and, right off, was nailed with a flashlight or billy-club, and it was like someone hit the "on" switch. I punched and kicked like a madman and was holding my own against two of Boston's finest until back up arrived and then I was swarmed, Maced, and cuffed on the street.

At the hospital, following the arraignment the next day, I was treated for fractured ribs, bruised kidneys, a partially deflated lung, and cuts.

Edgehill Newport

Sur-ren-der: To relinquish possession or control to another because of demand or compulsion.

Up to that point my father had been in denial when it came to my addiction, probably thinking, No son of mine's a drug addict, damn it. He would say things like, straighten out, Rick, get some exercise, sleep more and you'll be fine. I admit it shocked me, considering the stigma still attached to counseling then, when he suggested that I check in for treatment.

But my response was, "What are you nuts?" Then I went for the jugular, my mother's addiction problems. I said, "Growing up the way I did, you think I'd allow myself to end up like her?" I even hinted he had a problem with booze. Then I thought more about it. Beaten and broke I did have a problem, and if it continued I'd be dead either by my own hand or someone else's.

My father found a place in Rhode Island, Edgehill, in the business of rehabbing losers like me. An Edgehill flyer described it this way: "A private, for profit, freestanding facility on 65 acres for adults only. Treats a broad range of addiction, but not heroin addiction per se. Of all patients at Edgehill, 50 to 60 percent are pure alcoholic. Others are cross-addicted. Seventy percent male consensus. Average age 36."

I was evaluated at Edgehill then, two days later, admitted. After being detoxed for forty-eight hours I was placed in general population.

When I arrived, I was like a wild animal, and looked it. They took photos on the first day, and again on the last, and the difference between them was startling. I remained there thirty-one days. Edgehill saved my life.

The first week I was only there in body and not yet ready to surrender. Edgehill seemed to have too many rules, and for the past six years, there hadn't been a rule made that applied to me. I thought: Okay, I'll do your program and pick up a few tricks to keep me off coke, but that's it.

I was assigned to a counselor named Becky, a little waif of a woman who was both articulate and gentle, and who had a kind of energy that seemed to absorb pain. There was also a big guy, a former Massachusetts State trooper named, Pat. Pat had served ten years in prison for allegedly killing his wife in an alcoholic blackout. With almost fifteen years of sobriety under his belt, Pat was a valued member of the Edgehill team, and someone I believed I could relate to.

Group sessions were held daily. Twelve guys in a circle talking about addiction and/or the lack of it, because there were some that refused to admit they were addicts. To hear them tell it, they worked full time and only got drunk or high weekends.

And I had my own problems. When I first began group sessions, I refused to talk and believed I had legitimate reasons. A big redheaded guy sitting opposite me in the circle was a cop, I *knew* it even though everything was supposed to remain anonymous, first names only, no background information, no personal stuff ever. So, how did I know the guy was a cop?

He *looked* like one. Hey, I'd been around them enough and as a veteran of the Southie trenches where my freedom and, at times, my life depended on my ability to recognize them, I was good at it. I refused to talk in front of the guy.

Following a group at the end of the first week At the end of the first week Pat, the former trooper, pulled me aside in the hallway.

He said, "What's your problem, Rick, why won't you talk? Don't you want to get better?"

I told him I wasn't talking in front of a cop.

He gave me a suspicious look. "Who told—who do you mean?" he said.

"Fat boy, the red headed prick across from me."

Pat's shock turned to anger and he guided me into an empty room. "This is a breach of security. Where'd you get the information?" he said.

When I explained how he seemed to accept it.

Early the next morning, he brought me into the day room and introduced me to the cop. The two of us sat at a table and talked for an hour, mostly about him and his dual addiction to cocaine and gambling; he was up to his eyeballs in debt to the shylocks. He showed me pictures of his wife and kids and complained that he was as low as he'd ever been in his life. With my own self-esteem in negative digits, we got along fine after that.

That was a huge step, shelving my differences with others and putting aside my hatred, anger, and considerable ego in the interest of healing myself. I had no idea then but Edgehill was boot camp for what was to come.

For the next three weeks, I immersed myself in the program. I was elected group leader, ate well, put on weight, and began to exercise daily again.

Perhaps even more than physical exercise, Edgehill stressed the value of a strong spiritual base as an aid in fighting addiction. My spirituality grew only in whispers at first, but as days passed the voices grew stronger.

I believe there were other voices around me as well. Clear-headed and sober now, I thought a lot more about Frank "The Tank" MacDonald. It may sound crazy, but whenever I chose I could "talk" with Tank, and it always occurred the same way. I would visualize him coming out of a room that looked like a celestial gym filled with blazing light, and from inside it came the sound of heavy and speed bags being hit. It didn't matter whether our "conversations" were real or not, afterwards I always felt better.

The Edgehill groups stressed total surrender to a Higher Power, which most at the facility preferred to call God. I was raised Catholic so I knew about Jesus, the Virgin Mary, the saints, but for years I had chosen to ignore them.

Encouraged to try new things, one morning I got down on my knees and asked my Higher Power for help and, as sunlight streamed through the window and warmed my back, prayed to Jesus, the Blessed Virgin, God, *anyone* to give me strength. At Edgehill they called it "turning it over." I didn't know it then but I was on a path, albeit a winding one, that would eventually change my life.

But God could only carry me so far because no matter how many groups I attended or how much I prayed, the botched Medford hold-up continued to haunt me. I had only known my counselor, Becky, a short time but trusted her enough to talk with her about what happened. With a huge investigation still going on back home it was a risk, but I was willing to take it.

Later that day, Pat, the former state trooper, called me into his office. He had spoken with Becky and wanted to hear the story from me. When he was certain that I hadn't killed anyone that was the end of it. He said, "You're here to be treated."

At Edgehill I got what I needed to deal with my addiction to coke but another, potentially more deadly, addiction to adrenalin remained.

In an attempt to confront the problem, I developed a solid working relationship with in-house psychiatrist, Dr. Lee Goldstein and continued treatment with him on the street, traveling from Boston to Goldstein's Providence office once a week for sessions.

When my insurance ran out he continued to see me, on his dime, for weeks. At the conclusion of our final meeting, Goldstein said, "Richard, it's sad but I think you've got another armored car in you, and I don't think I can help you."

It was sad. But both of us knew he was right.

Re-entry

1985

After Edgehill I returned to South Boston and my O Street apartment. Just about everything: clothes, TV, boxes I had never opened following the move from the South End were still there.

In the bedroom my little wooden jewelry box remained under the bed. Two small gold chains and a knock-off Rolex remained, but the state police ring that Cara had given me as a graduation present from the academy was missing. I think it bothered me more than it should have.

Grateful to be healthy and drug free again, I made a half-assed attempt to apply the things I had learned at Edgehill. I remained humble, worked menial jobs that paid shit, and regularly attended Narcotics Anonymous meetings at the Waltham Hospital, but I couldn't relax there. I would watch people get up and tell their story and know damn well that I could never tell mine. I was an addict like them, but beyond our addiction it seemed we had nothing in common.

My first "civilian" job involved selling magazines door to door. Talk about humbling. It was crazy pushing *Field and Stream, Newsweek, Time, Ladies Home Journal, Architectural Weekly,* and twenty other magazines in package deals to people who had a tough time finding their own front door. It lasted less than two months.

Next I was hired as a termite exterminator. A Newton-based company called Certified Pest Control gave me a uniform, a can of bug spray, then sent me to school to learn how to kill them, with Chlordane, a chemical so toxic that the feds later banned it. At $7.50 an hour I was gone in less than four months.

A friend got me a job as a non-union laborer on a Quincy construction site. A so-called "composite job," the employees were a mixture of union and non-union labor. I stuck with it because my mother, father, and the Edgehill staff believed in me; the only one who didn't was me.

The months flew by, and as the building neared completion, heat from the Medford hold-up diminished to the point where some of my former South Boston associates, driving new Cadillacs and Pontiac Trans Ams, began to stop by the job site to visit.

It was funny watching these young gangsters tip-toeing through the muck and dust in their designer running suits and hundred dollar sneakers. They said I was nuts doing that kind of work and encouraged me to return to the fold, and I folded.

I took a lay-off from the job and contacted the Greek. The timing was perfect because the man with the connections just happened to have one, a friend in the western part of the state who was a hotshot at robbing banks. Within a week I had stolen a car and we were driving to Pittsfield to meet him.

Berkshire County

After serving seven years for armed bank robbery, Bernie Kiley had been recently released from federal custody, and was still on parole when I met him. Short, slightly built with thinning, greasy hair, he met us at a Friendly's restaurant in Stockbridge. Physically Kiley didn't impress me much but what did impress me was his knowledge of banks.

As I drank my chocolate Fribble, Kiley went on about a litany of scores that he had already scouted out. Armored car drops, when area banks were bloated with payroll cash, the number of employees in each, as well as the various routes of escape. He talked about target towns that I had never heard of: Becket, Savoy, Windsor, Dalton, Chester mentioning at the end that he had a nice fat bank in Pittsfield.

That first day with Kiley we checked out five banks, in as many different towns, with Kiley going on about the general lack of security in each. The crime rate in Berkshire County was less than half of what it was in Boston, so law enforcement there was much more relaxed. Pittsfield is the largest city in Berkshire County, and in 2005, it was ranked in the top twenty of the most secure places to live in the nation.

But probably not in '85.

The target bank in Pittsfield had a Berkshire County Armored Car Service pick-up scheduled for Wednesdays at ten in the morning. A guard went into the manager's office and picked up a large satchel of money.

For three weeks we watched the "play" attempting to determine the best way to hit them. After the pick-up, we could take the guard down easy inside the bank, but as we left, there was always a chance of a shootout with the driver. If it happened again, I planned to be ready.

A few weeks after leaving Edgehill I was contacted by a drug dealer named Aaron, a guy I had bought a hand grenade from. Aaron said that he had something he wanted to show me.

The weapon, a rifle, came complete with a twenty round clip and Aaron was asking fifteen hundred dollars for it, a lot of money for a gun at the time. A shotgun had always been my weapon of choice. They were inexpensive and ammunition was easy to come by.

I met Aaron at night in the parking lot of the Cleveland Circle Cinema, not far from Boston College, and from the moment he popped his Mercedes trunk I knew I had to have it.

The Heckler & Koch Model 91 rifle, on top of a plastic trash bag, had a look of pure menace. Powerful and accurate, with a seventeen-inch barrel, it was also compact and relatively light. When Aaron assured me that a round from it could easily pierce an armored truck's steel plate I handed him cash and drove home with the weapon.

It would turn out that the rifle wasn't necessary because we came up with a plan that excluded heavy weapons. We would be in and out of the bank in just under a minute, but first we had to verify the money was there. This was tricky because the manager's office, where the satchel was stored, was located in a blind spot impossible to see into from the main floor.

That's when I learned why Kiley had the reputation of being the "Jesse James of Berkshire County." The day of the robbery he would have a friend, a member of an outlaw motorcycle gang, pull up to the drive-thru window and request change for hundred-dollar bill. From that position the biker had a clear view behind the teller's cage and directly into the manager's office. Come game day, he would verify the bag was there just before we entered, minutes before the armored truck arrived. The timing had to be perfect.

Westward Ho

The Pittsfield bank was on a main drag. Across from it was a street that ran up a small hill. We were parked at the top with Watson behind the wheel of the stolen Chevy, the Greek and I in back. From our position, the bank's drive-thru clearly visible; we waited for the signal from Watson's biker friend. When he spotted the money, he would signal by flashing his hi-beam twice.

Kiley had on jeans that day and a Yankees cap while I wore jeans, a red windbreaker, and a Bruins cap. My disguise was simple: a week old beard, store bought human hair eyebrows, and handlebar mustache. I also wore my favorite gloves, Isotoner, for bank jobs. The company advertised that you could pick up a dime with them. I planned to pick up a hellava lot more.

For the Pittsfield job the Greek had gone all out. Along with his dungaree jacket and jeans, his face and neck were covered completely with dark stage make-up, and a short Afro-style wig that completed the look.

Watson spoke into the rearview. "Remember," he said, "just the money bag, you take nothin' off the teller's counter. Leave them fucking tellers alone, we don't need no dye packs stinkin' up the car."

"Relax," the Greek said, "the kid knows." He shoved me. "Nothing behind the counter, or I be kickin' yo ass."

The Greek suddenly pointed and said, "Look." Less than a hundred yards away, in the bank's drive-thru area, a motorcycle headlamp flashed.

The biker began to move then turned left into traffic and Kiley dropped the car into gear. Rolling slowly down the hill we crossed the street and pulled up in front of the bank. I opened the door and said, "Let's get these motherfuckers."

Once inside the Greek took up his position on the floor and stood quietly dead center, the .45 automatic hanging loose by his side as I entered the teller's area through an unlocked door, walked into the manager's office.

The woman seated behind the desk looked up and said stiffly, "Can I help—"

I pointed the gun at her head. "This is a hold-up. No alarms, push away from the desk, now."

She gasped and slid the chair back into the wall. The moneybag was inside the door to my left and when I grabbed it her jaw dropped like she'd been nailed with a tranquilizing dart.

It was different with the tellers on the way out. When I went in, no one seemed to notice but now all of them, as well as four customers, were frozen in place and staring at the Greek waving the gun in front of his waist like he was hosing a lawn.

As I went by the teller, I couldn't resist grabbing two, thick stacks of twenty-dollar bills off the counter and saying, "Excuse me," and stuffing them into my pocket.

The Greek went out first with me close behind him, and that's when I heard it, a weird electric chattering. Someone had hit the alarm.

Outside the wind had picked up and a gust tore some of the bills out of my pocket. People on the sidewalk stopped and watched the Greek enter the back of the Chevy. I paused long enough to say, "Home James," to Kiley before getting in too.

The tough part over we crouched on the floor as the car drove away so any police en route to the scene would see only one driver and not three in the car. Watson was nervous and driving too fast, and I had to bark to slow down. A mile down the road, we pulled behind a commercial building and made the switch into a Mercury Marquis. I never once heard a siren.

On the drive to the safe house Kiley was more relaxed, and so was the Greek. The house belonged to a cop friend of Watson's out of town on vacation that week.

By now the city had to be crawling with police. There was a good chance there were roadblocks and even helicopters hovering on the lookout for culprits; but as I sat in that house I couldn't feel safer. As Watson and the Greek counted the cash I cleaned up in the bathroom. I'll tell you it was weird shaving in the same mirror that a cop did every morning.

Once again the score was a bust though. The satchel was large and heavy and, as we drove away from the bank, I figured that the take had to be well over a hundred grand, but all we got was forty-three thousand, the rest of it cancelled checks and food stamps. It was better than nothing but considering the risk not by much.

The next day I was back in the unemployment line waiting to pick up my check. Two weeks earlier, in the same Quincy office while waiting in the same line, I had banged into my brother Scot. He said, "The civilian life's kind of tough, huh? Ever think of getting back into the old?"

"I just robbed a bank."

Scot's face twisted up. "I thought you were all done with that," he said.

"Was. Watch me, I'm just getting started."

Berkshire Follies

The armored car drop that Bernie Kiley had found in Williamstown was unusual for one, big reason, both the guard and the driver got out to make the delivery. Usually only one guard would get out, unless there were three, the driver always remaining inside.

All three of us watched the play, the armored drop, at the Williamstown Bank of New England on Main Street, a dozen times over the next three months. First the Greek, realizing his limitations, pulled out and, shortly after, Watson violated his parole and was sent back to prison.

Alone now with a heist too good to give up, I needed a crew, but had to be careful. After the Medford debacle, I was well aware of what happens when you talk to the wrong guys.

I gave Sean (not his real name), a guy that I had worked with in the past, a call. Only nineteen, the kid was fearless and tough, and most importantly, he followed orders. Sean introduced me to an associate named, Danny. Built like a brick wall, Danny had a sturdy reputation around Southie and plenty of experience when it came to heavy lifting.

With two good men now we still needed a driver. For an average score three men were plenty, but since I planned to take the entire truck I would need the extra body. Mutual friends introduced me to a guy that I'll call "Johnny Boy".

JB, a Southie hoodlum, was supposed to be this big time bank robber. When I met him for lunch, over a cheeseburger, he claimed that he had been robbing banks for years but had never done an armored truck. As I outlined the basic score he seemed hesitant and that should have been a warning, a big red flag but, desperate for a driver, I allowed this dirt bag into the crew.

Two days later, JB and I took the four-hour drive to Williamstown to watch the play and on the trip back our new driver gave every indication that he was psyched to be part of it. I dropped him off at his Dorchester Street apartment and said I would call the next day—and that was the last time I saw him. I thought, here we go again.

Sean, Danny, and I searched high and low for the bum but JB had gone underground. After deciding as a crew to deal with him later, we got down to the business of replacing him.

Brian Bean, was a big, tough kid that I had known for years. Bean loved guns and actually possessed a firearm license. We had both worked as bouncers at the Rat, fought side by side, drank, and got high together. Bean, a wannabe, was dying to be known as an action guy. He had told me, on many occasions, if I thought I could ever use him to give him a call.

But physical toughness had little to do with the world I inhabited. We were involved in serious crimes with potentially deadly consequences. We might be killed, might have to kill, or if caught, go to prison for a very long time. Though physically tough, Bean didn't have the mental toughness required to be part of the gang. I knew this and should have trusted my gut still, against my better judgment, I called him.

The Rat from the Rat

By the spring of 1985, Brian Bean had hung up his bouncer's black leather zap gloves and now worked as a bartender in the Rat's upstairs lounge. Working in the Rat wasn't easy but, speaking from experience, almost impossible if you battled a coke habit. I had received information that Bean, in an attempt to pay off his considerable drug debts, had been making some dangerous moves on the side.

Seated at the end of the bar one night I was approached by Quinn, a former Rat bouncer. Quinn was employed as a strong-arm enforcer now for the Irish mob in Southie. Bean served Quinn a beer and he walked away, Quinn aimed a thick finger at his back and said, "The kid's got balls."

Then Quinn related a story about how, the previous week, he and Bean had driven to the coastal community of Scituate to collect on a drug debt. A cocaine dealer had hired Quinn to collect a large sum owed by a construction contractor that he had fronted coke to. Quinn had brought Bean along for back up.

Quinn told me that once they found the guy and he threatened him, Bean had lifted his shirt to and exposed the gun tucked into his belt. Quinn said, "I was shocked when I saw it, fucking kid also wore a bullet-proof vest, had a gun on his leg too. Man, he was ready." It made me think, maybe there was more to the kid than I thought.

The next day I called Bean and told him I had something I wanted to discuss. We agreed to meet at seven p.m. in the parking lot of a Chinese restaurant, Weylu's in Saugus, off Route 1. We sat in his car and I explained, without going into detail, how I had something big coming up and needed a driver. Was he interested? When I told him his end would be at least two hundred grand, Bean was in, at least for a minute.

Then the exuberance drained from his face, and he said, "That's a lot of money, Rick, but I'm concerned about your partners. For that type of dough, they might kill me after." He shook his head. "Naw, I can't do it, don't want to," he said.

I understood, and Bean was right to be concerned. He knew nothing about my associates, but I told him, "Brian, they're my friends, and you're my friend. You do your job, nothing's going to happen to you." It wasn't an attempt to convince him, he either wanted in or not. I only wanted to make it clear that he wouldn't be hurt.

That night Brian Bean listened to his gut and recognized his limitations; I respected him for his honesty. And that was the end of it, or so I thought.

A week passed, and I had just finished an aerobics workout at the Joy of Movement gym in Kenmore Square when, as I passed the front desk, the clerk said, "Hey, Rick, some guy dropped this off for you" and handed me a sealed envelope.

I opened it in my car. The note inside read: Rick, please, please, I've reconsidered what we talked about last week. Give me a call. Brian.

When I did Bean agreed to meet me again, at the same place. Bean said that he planned to use proceeds from the heist to open a seafood joint in Marblehead. The current manager of the Rat, a guy named Robbie, was supposedly going in as his partner.

Before he left that car that night, I asked Bean one more time, "Are you sure you want in?"

"I'm positive," he responded.

A few days later, Bean and I drove out to Williamstown to watch the play. After he saw it, I made it very clear that he was in now, and couldn't back out. For his part Bean appeared upbeat and eager to get it done, and agreed to stay in touch by phone until the score the following week.

The next day Bean followed up with a call, but after that I heard nothing. Immediately we began searching for Bean, but this time I actually got lucky.

Bean had been screwing a girl named Ali, the stripper ex-wife of his best friend, Tom. Ali danced under the name of Princess Sativa at the Combat Zone's Naked Eye Lounge. Years before I had hired her then boyfriend, Tom, to work at the Rat as a bouncer, Ali became a regular at the club, and she and I became friends.

When I met her at her Lynn apartment, she told me that Bean had been in the hospital, but that he was home now. When I inquired what happened, she said, "Brian told me that he was supposed to pull a big job with you and your friends, but decided he couldn't go through with it."

She went on to say that Bean, a motorcycle enthusiast, had been so terrified of becoming involved that he had intentionally driven his bike off the road, and into the woods, hoping to break something, anything, to get out of it. He failed in his mission but was banged up enough to spend a night in the hospital. Ali gave me a number where I could reach him.

As Bean and I talked, I casually inquired about the accident, demonstrating concern about his health but never alluding to anything Ali had told me. To hear Bean tell it, he was simply driving too fast. Healthy again, he agreed to meet my partners and me the following day. What

Bean did was detestable, a coward's move but, desperate for a driver, I was stupidly willing to overlook it.

To get Bean to further relax, I scheduled the meeting with Sean and Danny at high noon in Southie's M Street Park. Bean showed up on time, appearing almost carefree now, and the meeting went smoothly. Once again the score was on.

Similar to the botched heist in Medford, once again I was getting a real bad feeling about Williamstown. In the planning for months it should have been the perfect score, but I couldn't shake the about to touch a third rail feeling boring its way into my gut.

As this memoir began, Williamstown was the ironic beginning of my new life, a good thing. The bad thing? It took a decade in prison to learn all the lessons.

13.

Babbling Bean

1987

It was early afternoon and I had just returned the rider-mower to Bridgewater's Walks and Grounds shed. On my way back to B-2 a cop stopped me in the yard and said that someone wanted to see me in the Ad Building. I knew the cop, so I asked him what's up? He shrugged and said, "I dunno, just told that someone wants to see you is all."

Right off it smelled bad.

My first thought it was probably Feld, but when I entered the building I was directed to an unfamiliar office. I knocked and went in and was surprised to see an old friend, Steve Long seated at a table. Steve was a classmate from the state police academy whom I hadn't seen in years.

This wasn't good.

I said, "Hey, Stevie, what's up?"

Steve was dressed in street clothes. He said, "Hey, Rick, how're ya doin'?" He shook my hand then pointed to the chair across the table.

He asked about Bridgewater, how they were treating me. Then he told me that he'd been working undercover narcotics for years, but that he was back in uniform these days. He said the job was treating him well.

I respected Steve, and I knew he was trying to be friendly, but this wasn't a friendly visit. Finally, I said to him, "So, Stevie, what's up? What're you doing here?"

He stared into my eyes a moment before he answered. "The armored car hold-up in Medford where Frank MacDonald was killed? They know you did it, Rick."

I settled back in the chair. I said, "Sorry, Steve but I don't know what you're talking about."

"Knowing we're friends, they sent me in to talk to you."

"They? Who?"

"The Bank Robbery Task Force, they're outside in the hall."

The task force had been formed in 1979 with teams comprised of a state police detective and an FBI agent. Its job was to investigate armed bank hold-ups. While I was still on the street, an associate had warned me that the Task Force had been investigating my activities for years. I figured they had sent Steve in to soften me up.

I said, "I got nothing to say to them."

Steve said, "Rick, they've got witnesses and ballistics that will put you away for life."

Witnesses? What witnesses? And the ballistics part was bullshit. At that very moment the only gun fired by me, the shotgun was under a foot of mud at the bottom of the Charles River.

"Rick, for me, will you listen to them? At least hear what they've got to say?" Steve said.

Deadpan, I said to him, "Look around us Stevie, where we are. It's a nuthouse, and I'm committed, insane. Whatever they say won't make any sense."

Steve grinned. "Yeah, okay, Rick. But, far as I can see, that's all the more reason to listen to them, right?"

Steve was in the chair next to me when the other two came in, one carrying a thick, manila file, which he slapped down on the table.

"Know who we are?" the taller one said.

I said, "Batman and Robin?"

"Well, we know you," he said. He pushed the file with my name in the corner toward me. "And this is your life, what you've been up the past five years."

I reached for the file and he tugged it back to the edge of the table.

"No, no, ohh, no" he said. "You're going to learn everything later."

The same guy did the talking, basically repeating what Steve had already told me. Ballistics and eyewitness reports had put me at the center of the Medford heist. And I was also being targeted for a couple of banks. The shorter cop smirked as the taller one said, "The witnesses, want to know who they are?

"Brian Bean, remember him, your co-defendant in the Williamstown score? Well, he's been talking, *a lot*, and will testify that you mentioned the Medford score to him years ago. The other witness—you'll love this—is the mother of the deceased, Frank MacDonald. She'll testify that she overheard the two of you planning the score in her very own living room."

I wasn't surprised about Bean but Frank's mother? I knew that Bean, the phony tough guy, would say anything to get out from under the time he faced. But the allegation that Frank's Mum had overheard us plotting the score in her house was ridiculous. That never happened. And now suddenly, three years later, she remembers we did?

The fed continued, "Look Marinick, you're doing an 18-20 year bid, you're off the streets. You cop to this, we're not looking to hang you. The DA, Scott Harshberger, plans to run for Attorney General next year, and he wants to wrap up outstanding cold cases. Convicting you would be a real feather in his cap."

So I was to be a feather in Scott Harshberger's cap?

I said, "I don't know what you guys are talking about. We're done here."

I stood up. The cops looked at Steve and shook their heads. They left the room. Once again it was just me and my old friend. I could see the strain in his face.

He said, "What are you going to do?"

"It's alright, Stevie. I didn't do it, they can go fuck themselves."

"They convict you, you're done, Rick, you know that."

He wasn't acting. The guy was genuinely concerned. He was a Southie guy, and we had gone through the academy together, twenty-two weeks of hell. A lot of recruits had fallen by the wayside, but the two of us had hung in there and graduated. No matter which side we were on now, there was still a bond between us.

I said, "Listen, it's going to work out. Someday we'll be sitting around having a beer somewhere talking about this. No hard feelings, Steve, you're just doing your job." We shook hands. "You gotta leave," I said "It doesn't look good me talking to cops."

Steve said, "Think about what I said, okay?"

"Yeah."

"How's your canteen, need any money?"

I told him I was good and thanked him.

I had a lot to think about on the walk back to the unit. Before this happened, my lawyer had explained the worst-case scenario if the 18-20 year sentence was upheld. After I had served six years, I would be eligible to apply for a "one-third consideration" which meant, if I kept my nose clean, there was a possibility of parole. But if I got nailed with the Medford heist, any hope for that was off the table. I would have to do the entire bid, the "wrap-up" on the sentence, with the deduction of statutory good time, eleven years eight months. With "earned" good time I could knock it down to ten years.

If I copped to the Medford score, I would receive a concurrent sentence to run parallel with the one I was serving. But if I took it to trial and lost, the DA would ask for life. For me there wasn't much of a choice.

During my eleven-month stay, there were seven unexplained deaths in Bridgewater State Hospital. One victim, about my size but older, wore glasses, and I'd always see him on a bench with a book in his hand. Then one day he allegedly assaulted a cop.

I watched them haul him through the yard to F Ward, where he was tied down in four-point restraints. A few days later in his underwear unable to move, with ankles and wrists bound to the bed, he was found dead.

A *New York Times* article, dated July 19, 1987, stated that a patient in Bridgewater, placed in solitary confinement with his arms and legs in restraints, had somehow managed to choke on an eyeglass lens and a piece of material, a sock, stuffed down his throat. When the death was officially ruled another Bridgewater suicide, I knew it was time to get out.

The day of my Appellate Court hearing, I entered the tiny courtroom in which, according to my lawyer, should have contained just him, the prosecutor, Doctor Feld, the three-judge panel, and me. Unfortunately, there were additional guests. Batman and Robin, the dynamic duo from the Bank Robbery Task Force, were seated at the back of the courtroom. Both grinned and waved when I was brought in.

After a presentation by the DA, my lawyer, and then Doctor Feld, I knew it was over when, just before the hearing concluded, the lead judge addressed me over the top of his glasses. He said, "We want you to know, Mr. Marinick, that the fact you're currently under investigation for another armored car hold-up, as well as some bank robberies, will in no way effect our decision today."

Put the fork in, I was done.

The 18-20 year sentence upheld I used my connection to get out of Bridgewater.

14.

Concord Prison

1988

MCI Concord was a DOC classification center, the place you were sent to learn where you were going. My goal was Norfolk State Prison. Not only did it have the reputation of being the best stop, it offered college courses to qualified men. I had tried college once but it didn't work out. I figured at Norfolk perhaps I'd try it again.

Concord was a tough stop. Prisons are rarely the way they are depicted on TV. I almost busted a gut laughing watching *The Shawshank Redemption* because it would be like heaven doing time in a place like that.

The correctional system had yet to change over to the system of colored, jumpsuit uniforms common today. We wore street clothes: color-coded jeans, t-shirts, and sweatshirts, but in Concord you could only wear what you came in with, even if you were going to be there for months. Sure, the state issued things like boxer underwear, socks, flip-flops and a t-shirt, but you were shit out of luck for anything else.

A jail-wise con would go into Concord looking like the Michelin Man, wearing three sets of everything: underwear, sox, jeans, *and* sweatshirts. If you weren't smart, or like me, still learning to jail, all you had were the clothes on your back, and that's pretty much what I wore for the next six months.

Like every joint, Concord was grossly overcrowded. For the first two weeks, in mid-ninety degree July heat, I slept on a stinking mattress that was lined, end-to-end, with thirty others along the corridor of an old administration building. There were no showers, and only one toilet, which constantly ran.

Daylight hours were spent walking the yard, hundreds of men wearing nothing but boxer shorts circling a dirt track. The guards in the towers would site their rifles us. I'd look up and see some asshole pointing a carbine me at me, and it gave me dark thoughts. I imagined lining up the iron sites of my old carbine on them.

After weeks, I worked my way into a two-man cell in the "New Man Line". From there, I was assigned to an eight-man cell, then to a tiny, windowless room containing six bunk beds and two huge stand-up fans that blew hot, foul smelling air day and night. Just the noise from the fans almost drove me insane. I was resigned to the fact that I would probably remain there for months when suddenly, less than a week later, I once again was saved.

Early one morning a screw ordered me to pack my gear up and follow him. After traveling a maze of corridors, I ended up in a cellblock known as East Down. After what I'd been through it was like I had moved into Beverly Hills. I had no idea how it happened, but somehow I had jumped a sizable queue to get there. I was about to get my first lesson in jailhouse recruitment.

My new home, a rare two-man cell, I had just tossed my gear on the top bunk when there was a rap on the door, and a face I didn't recognize appeared. "Hi, Rick, I'm Frank," he said. "Chuckie wants to see you."

Chuckie?

Frank Stewart, built like a Jersey Barrier, had these unblinking killer eyes, and it wasn't the practiced put-on look that some guys use to intimidate others. I knew nothing about Stewart but sensed mayhem pulsing just beneath the surface like the throb of low bass.

Stewart and I followed the corridor down the tier to a room at the end equipped with a slop sink and a rack on the wall that held brooms and mops. Chuckie Flynn, the same build as me but with a full head of white hair, wielded a spatula and carefully moved eggs around an electric frying pan. He looked up and grinned, "Rick, Chuck Flynn. Eggs?"

I politely waved them away. "Thanks, but don't like them."

Chucky looked at Stewart amazed, and shrugged. "He don't like eggs?" An egg popped and crackled loudly in the grease. Chucky turned his attention back to the pan. "That's okay, Rick. A lot here think I'm an oddball too."

Charles "Chucky" Flynn had a solid reputation as a gangster and stone killer from Lowell, Massachusetts. He also robbed armored cars.

He flipped some eggs onto a plate and started to eat. Between bites he said that he had heard good things about me, what I was in for. "You're just startin' your bid," he said "so learn this, prison is loaded with maggots, but there are good guys like us too, and they take care of each other. There are a lot in this block and you'll be with us until you go." He said, "Where you looking?"

"Norfolk," I answered, then mentioned the college program.

"A good guy and smart too, I like that," he said.

Over the next four months I walked the yard with Chucky Flynn every day and learned a lot about him and his crew. One thing was certain: the guy was a hard-core criminal, but also tough and very smart. Chucky also had a vicious temper and didn't tolerate fools. A former New England Golden Glove boxing champion, in his forties now, he had remained in tremendous shape, power walking daily before it was popular, his pace as quick as a jog.

Chuckie became my mentor. He gave me tips on how to a good "bid," like the importance of developing a good routine that would help make the time pass not just quickly, but constructively. He'd say to me, "Don't worry about the time, Rick. It's going to pass, and once you're out, I'll put you to work." He had armored car scores already lined up he said, just needed the muscle to do them. He'd say, "Don't worry about a thing because down the line you're gonna be rich." And Chucky Flynn didn't talk out his ass.

A busy man on the streets, he had already served 13 years in a Rhode Island prison for an infamous caper called the Bonded Vault Job, a heist worth upwards of thirty million dollars in jewels, cash, and gold.

While on parole for the crime, his reputation as a killer firm and tied in with Providence Mafia figures, Flynn had taken over all gambling, loan sharking, and protection rackets in the Merrimack Valley. He was exactly the type that I wanted to meet. Finally, I was making solid contacts with successful career criminals who recognized my skills. When it came to criminal pedigrees, Chucky Flynn had it all, and that was my problem. Guys like him still looked like winners to me.

I still considered attending college once I got to Norfolk and believed it might even change my life, but deep down I had doubts. Could I handle the curriculum? And even if I could and graduated what good would it do me? With my record, classified now as a career armed offender, who the hell would hire me? I decided to pursue two courses of action. I would hedge my bets and attend school while, at the same time, continuing to associate with guys like Chucky Flynn. In time I would decide on the direction my future would take.

While I was in Concord, for the first time, I was challenged for being an ex-cop. In the tiny basement gym one day, after finishing a light sparring session with a tough kid, from Fall River, as he left the ring and headed down the wooden steps I saw a guy approach and heard him say to him, "Hey Dom, why you training with him? He's a cop."

Right off, Dom started to defend me. "Hey, he's a good guy."

I jumped from the last step to the floor and approached the heavy-set Hispanic dude, *beach ball*, running his mouth. I said, "I'm no cop."

"Yeah?" he said, turning to face me. "In my eyes, once a cop—"

I stepped in and hit him with a hand grenade right hand high on the cheek, then savagely hooked him. It was lightning quick, bang, bang, and he hit the floor and rolled like a Weeble. I was glad I had kept my wraps on because after a fight the first thing the screws do is look for cuts and bruises on hands.

There was an investigation, there's always an investigation, but neither the beach ball nor anyone else ratted. The kid suffered a fractured Zygomatic bone (I learned a new word) and that was the last time anyone in Concord looked at me cross-eyed.

Five months later, the classification board approved my request for Norfolk. I was ecstatic and glad to be leaving. In Concord I had met some good men, but I had also seen some real assholes.

Inmates housed in the PC (protective custody) block were fed separately, so three times each day they were paraded to the chow hall along the walkway outside of East Down. The cons in my block, as well as in others along the route, would line up at the windows to curse and jeer at these *skinners* (rapists), *diddlers* (child molesters), and jailhouse rats.

Shortly before I left for Norfolk, Chucky Flynn and, Ricky B. a big-time Cuban coke dealer were lugged for attempting to bribe a DOC official, over the phone, with $25,000.00 to facilitate a move to minimum security. I never saw Chucky again.

A few years later he was released and made the mistake of climbing back into bed with the Providence Rhode Island arm of La Cosa Nostra, then retaking control of the rackets in the Merrimack Valley. In the process of setting up yet another armored car heist, he was ratted-out by a member of the gang, arrested, convicted, and sent to federal prison for forty-five years, where eventually he died of cancer. My take? God Bless him, Chucky Flynn was a good man.

MCI Norfolk

1988

According to the state website, "MCI Norfolk is a medium security facility located just south of Boston, with an average daily population of 1524 inmates. Rated medium security, Norfolk has a maximum-security perimeter with a wall five thousand feet long and nineteen feet high, (topped with electrified wire) enclosing an area of thirty-five acres."

The reality? Norfolk Prison Colony was just that, a colony where red ants, black ants, army ants, and termites were forced to co-exist at gunpoint.

A week before I was shipped from Concord, Chucky Flynn had introduced me to a Revere Mafioso named Frank Oreto, Sr. A hardened ex-con, Oreto had been recently been returned to the system on a parole violation. Prior to that he had served sixteen years for a gangland hit. Flynn was highly respected, especially by wise guys from Providence and Boston, so an introduction from him was the gold standard.

On the bus ride to Norfolk, Oreto and I got to talking, and he introduced me to a friend nicknamed, The Greaser. From Boston's North End, the Greaser was a skinny, likable guy about my age who'd been in and out of the system for most of his life. The Greaser told me, "Rick, you're gonna love Norfolk. You can cook your own food, work out, and land a half-assed job to earn good-time off your sentence. We'll sponsor you, right, Frankie, for the Italian club too, as an *honorary* member. You'll dig it, they have pizza nights, Christmas dinner with your family, a cook-out in summer, there's all sorts of shit happening."

Who wouldn't be impressed, all this along with a *college* program?

But like every other prison, Norfolk was overcrowded. For the first two weeks, everyone who came down on the Concord bus slept in the basement of the hospital unit. From there we went to the "Mods", the Modular Unit whose twin, side-by-side, buildings housed one hundred and twenty inmates. In the Mods the bunks were packed so tightly together that if you stretched out your arm you would hit the guy in the next rack.

In the Mods, I continued a familiar routine that I had begun back in Berkshire County. I prayed before I went to sleep, actually got on my knees, on the top mattress, and thanked God for getting me through another day. As I prayed, guys walked below me and looked up at me curiously, dominoes slammed on tables, and music blasted from ten different radios.

Why did I pray? Simple. In prison you lose just about everything: women, money, weapons, friends, connections, everything that bolstered your confidence on the street, gone. Serving time can force a man into serious soul searching, drive him insane, or into the tentacles of readily available drugs. Prayer helped me. It still does.

But prayer was one stitch for a deep wound, and it couldn't take me over the walls. There was no escaping the fact that my new environment was a college for crime, a place where I could learn a better way of doing the things that had put me behind bars in the first place—and someone was always willing to offer advice.

My former partners Sean and Danny, already in Norfolk for a year, were thrilled when I arrived. Our small crew complete again, we met the first day and walked the Quad, the oval-shaped road in the center of camp.

On either side the Quad was bordered by cellblocks. At one end the Administration Building, housing the school and library, on the other the CSD, Community Services Building, with its auditorium and meeting rooms for groups like the Veterans, Lifers, Italian and Irish Clubs. It also contained a small chapel and mosque. Off the center of the Quad, two alleys led to the east and west yards, or "fields" as they were called. Cadillac Alley to the east and a nameless alley to the west. Over the years both, out of sight of the gun towers, both had had their fair share of inmate on inmate violence.

The first time together in almost a year, the three of us walked in the lesser-used east field, catching up on jailhouse gossip and news from the street. I learned that my former Southie crew, run by Jack "Polecat" Ferris, was doing extremely well through loan sharking and cocaine sales. Ferris now worked directly for mob boss, Jim Bulger, and raked in thousands of dollars a week.

Even my old crew's former mascot John "Red" Shea, all grown up now, was in on the act with a thriving drug business moving kilos of coke to a growing list of smaller dealers. Southie had become a boomtown where everyone was making money while our only boom was dropped on us in Berkshire County.

While I was in Bridgewater and later in Concord, Danny, ever the businessman had been busy networking. First in Walpole Prison and now behind the walls of Norfolk, he had connected with a group of hungry, young Charlestown hoods. On a first name basis with every Mafioso in the camp, Danny had even made inroads within the growing Asian population, particularly with a diminutive Chinese gang leader and alleged killer, Chay Chiang, who went by the nickname of "Wing". According to Danny, once we were on the streets again, there was an excellent chance that South Boston and Chinese gangs would form an alliance. Danny's news was exciting.

The Boston University Prison Program was more of a dream than a goal. What Danny presented was tangible. Right in the camp, all around us, were Irish, Chinese, and Italian gangsters, and soon I would meet them too and make my own connections.

I was looking at a lot of time and I didn't want to waste it. The BU Prison Program seemed interesting and, if I could get a degree from it, worthwhile. In 1989 I took my first college class and for the next four years attended school year round. When doing well academically I felt as if the old life was over. Then, a few days later, Frank Oreto, Danny, Sean, or someone else would give me news from the streets about someone we knew who had recently left the system, and was already making a fortune out there.

I reasoned if they could do it so could I. So what I'd been caught? Part of the game, right? I had balls, brains, and after getting sober was stronger than ever. Why not stay a criminal?

But the fact I was an ex-cop kept getting in the way

During my first few months at Norfolk it became obvious that a lot of the "old guard" convicts, men who had been in the system for years, decades in some cases, wanted nothing to do with me. It was uncomfortable, sure, but I wasn't in prison to get comfortable. I was there to do time. Sean and Danny remained loyal to a fault, as did the rest of the Southie crew. At the time, South Boston men were a formidable presence in every Massachusetts State prison.

When you're incarcerated you meet lots of people, usually like this: Good guys introduce other good guys to each other. You don't just walk up to someone and start chatting. For me though, inevitably, within a few days of meeting someone new, the guy would cautiously approach and say something like, "Excuse me, Rick, someone told me, uh, that you were a cop once. That true?"

I always gave the same response. I'd ask if he had a problem with it. The answer was always no. Then I'd say, "Now go tell that fucking maggot that told you if he's got a problem to come and see me, and I'll beat him into a fucking coma. Go tell him now, exactly." It didn't matter who was behind it. In the ten years I was down, no one ever stepped up to the plate.

Then I viewed my police background as a curse. In hindsight it was more of a blessing. In any case it marked me as being very different from the average con.

I had only been in the camp a short time when Oreto sent someone into the block to get me. I met him in the Quad. "C'mon, take a walk," he said, and we went to the West field and followed the track.

It didn't surprise me a bit when he said, "We got problems with the Italian Club."

True to their word, both he and The Greaser had sponsored me for membership, but they had a by-law, that said no ex-cops.

I said, "Hey, Frank, fuck it I--"

He signaled me to shut up. "Naw, naw, you're a good guy, serious, you held your fucking water. That was all years ago, I argued this."

I had only known this big shot Mafioso a matter of weeks, but he had stuck out his chin for me. "Some of the guys saw it my way," he said, "but others didn't."

In particular he said the president, Stevie Rossetti, wouldn't let it go, and a lot of the guys looked up to him. Oreto shrugged.

Rossetti was my age and was also doing time for armored cars. He was a big shot in the camp and a rising star in the Italian underworld. The rumor was when he hit the street, "they" were going to "make him." Rossetti would get his "button" and become a full-fledged member of the mob.

Oreto said, "Stevie's a good man and he runs the group. His viewpoint, I don't agree, but it is what it is. Sorry."

I guess deep down inside I knew, because of the police background, that I wouldn't be allowed into the club. It wasn't the first cold shoulder that I would have to deal but it didn't matter because I'd taken the advice of an old Berkshire County con. "Remember you're not in prison to make friends, you're here to do time."

Then the same thing happened with the Irish Club—no ex-cops. Sean and Danny wanted to quit both clubs in protest, but I persuaded them not to. I didn't take the snub personally, so why should they? Rules were rules and I wasn't there to be popular. Oreto put it nicely when he said to me once, "If you're popular in prison something's wrong with you." The funny thing was, in a relatively short time, I had dozens of friends that were members of both clubs.

But even the popular guys had their detractors. One day a Southie killer by the name of Freddy Dunca, who had been down for sixteen years, came up beside me as I walked in the yard. He said, "Gotta ask you a question."

Now "the Dunk," as Freddy was known, was a real "old-school" convict who would never talk to an ex-cop. Caught a little off guard, I was even more surprised when he said, "Rick, is Buck O'Connell (not his real name) a rat?" O'Connell was a younger, very popular South Boston convict. Years before I had learned that, when facing a long stretch for a crime he committed, he had given up information concerning my involvement in the Medford armored car heist, but later recanted.

I stopped walking and looked into the Dunk's eyes, "Gee, I wouldn't know about that," I said.

Not, 'No I never heard that', just I wouldn't *know*. The Dunk got the message. He thanked me and turned off. Somehow, even in here, the word had gotten out about O'Connell. The Dunk and I were friends after that.

After six hellish months in the Mods, I landed a single cell in a block off the Quad, and it was like I hit the Lottery. My new home, a second floor cell in the 2-1 block, faced the rear of the building. I dumped my gear on the filthy mattress and looked out the window at the empty handball court below. I relished the silence, something that I hadn't experienced in months.

Within minutes Steve Rossetti, the president of the Italian Club, stood at my door with a tray of cut fruit: cantaloupe, watermelon, and honey melon. "Welcome to the unit," he said.

I was totally confused. Was this the same guy who since I'd arrived hadn't said a word to me, the guy who had barred me from the Italian club? The hell with it, I accepted the overture because that's prison. Sometimes it's smarter to let shit go.

Over the months that followed, I would occasionally stop by Rosetti's cell, filled floor to ceiling with stacks of meticulously organized legal paperwork, just to kibitz. He was intelligent and articulate and seemed more like a college professor than a gangster. Six months later Rossetti was shipped to the feds where he began to serve another sentence. That's how the msystem works. If you violate both state and federal laws you can actually end up serving two sentences, state first and then the federal. I never saw Steve Rossetti again.

Years later, when I was back on the streets, I heard that Rossetti was doing well and running a legitimate business somewhere on the North Shore. But unable, or unwilling, to get out of the rackets, he was arrested and charged with conspiracy, when he and another Norfolk alumnus, Carmine Merlino, along with two others, plotted to rob an armored car depository. One member of the crew was a government informant, the entire charade a concoction to trap them. It was a tragic waste of what could have been a prosperous life when Rossetti was sentenced to forty-five years.

BU Prison School

In September of 1989 I took my first Boston University college course, creative writing. The instructor, Mike Koran, had a quirky teaching style that allowed his students to relax and just write. Soon any doubt I had concerning whether or not I could handle the curriculum faded. I received an A for the course, but writing was something I knew I could do. Could I handle the more difficult courses like Western European History, oceanography, or math?

Over the next five years, including one for graduate studies, I attended classes every week taking such courses as: Urban Communications, Oceanography, Journalism, Modern Middle Eastern History, Comparative Economics, and Philosophy of Religion. I was hungry, like a bear waking from a long hibernation, for knowledge, and the more that I learned the more I wanted.

One of the best parts of the day was mornings when I would leave the block and walk up the Quad to the Ad Building and school. As we passed the screws they would mean mug us for attending. They hated us for getting a "free" education. BU offered the guard's union the same deal, but cops had to attend on their own time.

There were a lot of great things about the BU program. One was I realized that I was a pretty good student. But good grades didn't come without stress. A college student on the street faces stress from federal student loans, peers, or making the monthly rent. In prison stress is strictly people related.

Every day I was forced to share a classroom with some of the system's most despicable inmates, sex offenders, men who had raped, or in some cases killed women and children. Worse, I had to sit quietly and listen to their opinions. A good example of one of these scumbags was "Bob," who showed up on the first day of the History of Western Civilization course. He sat in the row next to me. A big guy, Bob had sturdy features and wore glasses. He was articulate and smart enough to be one of the instructors. I had no idea what Bob was in for and didn't ask.

Following class one day, as Bob and I descended the steps of the Ad Building to the Quad, a couple of Townie (Charlestown) pals of mine were walking by. A giant by the name of John Fidler yelled out, "Hey Rick, why you talking to that fucking skinner?" (prison term for rapist).

I turned to Bob and said, "You a fucking skinner?" and he took off like a deer down the steps. I changed my seat in class after that and never spoke to the low-life again.

But I still had to listen to him.

I learned later from a screw that Bob might have been a serial rapist. He was doing a twenty-five year bid for aggravated rape, which meant he had beaten the hell out of his victims before, during, or after the act, and this was his second bid for the same offense. The screw went on about Bob being a prime suspect in the rape and murder of four women in two southern states, so there was a good chance that he was also a serial killer. In Norfolk I'd like to think that most of BU students were solid cons, but the "Bobs" made the classroom uncomfortable at times.

On the subject of rapists, the average citizen likes to believe that once a rapist is in prison "someone" will get him. But the truth is that rapists are highly prized by corrections officers as informants. Skinners (rapists) and diddlers (child molesters) are fiercely protected.

But sharing a classroom with people like Bob did have one positive effect on me. It helped me with my people skills and taught me to get along, something that for years I rarely had to do. My world on the street was filled with familiars, men and women that I trusted and liked. People I didn't or who didn't like me kept their distance, because if they got close I'd bite.

I had dreamt of someday becoming a writer since the age of twenty-two. I took every creative writing course they offered and I was fortunate to have excellent writing instructors such as: Michael Koran, Munroe Engel, and former TV news anchor Christopher Lydon constantly critiquing my work and offering encouragement.

In the summer months, retired Harvard professor and novelist, Munroe Engel came into the camp and ran a writing seminar. It was through Engel's efforts that a short story I wrote, "Dying to See a Movie," became my first published work. Encouraged by this I began to believe that maybe I really would be a writer someday.

Then reality would settle in because this was prison and not everything revolved around school.

Bad Moon Rising

In June of 1987 my friend, Frank Oreto, was indicted by the feds for alleged violations of the RICO (Racketeering Corrupt Organizations Act) statute. He faced a minimum twenty-year sentence on top of the life sentence that he was already serving.

While Oreto went to trial things weren't rosy on my end either. The Medford armored car heist was coming back, full throttle, at me. Not only was my former friend and Williamstown co-conspirator, Brian Bean, testifying against me in exchange for a lighter sentence, but Tank's mother, three years after the crime, planned to testify under oath that she heard us plan the score in her living room.

On the day of the Probable Cause hearing in Somerville District Court, I was transported in an old DOC station wagon, along with another Norfolk inmate with a case in Quincy Court. When we pulled up to the side the courthouse, the same building where I had worked for years, I prayed that no one would come out and recognize me. But, once more, if God laughs while men make plans, he must have been on the floor that day.

After a court officer came out helped one of the screws take the other guy inside, the driver got out, went to the rear of the car, and then he started to curse. We had gotten a flat tire. When the other screw returned panic set in, especially when they realized the car had no spare. They contacted the prison and requested alternate transportation, but nothing was available. Now I'm sitting there thinking this is funny as hell, but still wanting to leave before somebody saw me.

Then someone did.

Linton Ellsmore, a Southie guy and a long-time probation officer, happened to walk past the car then he stopped and backed up. Bending at the waist, looking in he said, "Ricky?"

A screw barked at him, "Hey you, get away from him you can't--"

Lynton flashed his badge and told him that he worked in the courthouse and had known me for years. The screw grudgingly backed off and allowed him to reach through the half-opened rear window to shake my hand. Though handcuffed and shackled, with chains around my waist, it was good to see a friendly face again.

Lynton's joyful expression quickly turned serious. "Hey, you okay, Rick? They treating you okay?" I told him that everything was fine because at that exact moment, it was. I had often wondered what would occur when someone from the past saw me, and naturally I had imagined the worst. I was truly amazed when this strait-laced officer of the court was genuinely happy to see me.

Linton said, "Hey, mind if I tell some of the guys you're out here?"

For the next fifteen minutes, to the screw's disgust, a parade of employees: court officers, the janitor, an assistant clerk, as well as a prosecutor from the DA's office, came out of the courthouse to shake my hand and offer encouragement. There wasn't a negative vibe in the lot. The only thing close was sadness at my plight.

Finally the screws had enough and shooed everyone away, bellowing that the state police were enroute to transport me to Somerville District Court. Still, I had gotten a helluva lift. The compassion of my friends reinforced the notion that it wasn't too late for me, that I still had time to accomplish something and to be productive with my life.

But first I had to deal with the state police.

Fifteen minutes later, out the corner of my eye, I saw a MSP cruiser pass by on the street in front of the courthouse. The familiar squawk of the dispatcher's voice emanated from its radio as the cruiser stopped behind us, and one of the screws lowered his face until it was level with mine. He smirked and said, "Statey's here, one of your former *buddies*."

The cruiser's door opened and I heard the trooper say to the screws. "Alright, let's get this bad motherfucker."

Footsteps approached the side of the car, and the next thing I heard was, "Ricky? Jesus, that you?"

I looked up and saw Eddie Burke, a classmate from the academy. He said, "Holy shit, brother, you okay?"

I was elated. Eddie, a Dorchester kid, was someone who understood that we didn't live in a perfect world. He reached in through the window and when he shook my manacled hand, the screws went berserk. One screamed at Eddie, "What the fuck is this? He's a criminal and half the courthouse comes out, and you're his pal too? He's a goddamn gangster."

Eddie said, "Maybe, but he's also a classmate and friend of mine."

The screw's face, he looked like he was sucking kitty cat butt.

We followed the expressway north into Boston, one screw up front with Eddie and the other in back in back with me. Eddie and I talked about the academy, the hell we'd gone through there, and the career paths taken by some of our classmates. It was amazing how good it felt to talk with someone in uniform who wasn't a flaming asshole.

We were going through Dorchester, passing the brightly painted Boston Gas tanks, when Eddie looked up at the rear mirror and grinned. "Rick, I probably shouldn't be telling you this, but, ah, fuck it. They got word, with the flat tire and all, that someone might be tryin' to break you out."

"Eddie, that's fucking insane, ridiculous," I said.

Eddie chuckled. "Yeah, I know, I know," he said, "but that's DOC *intelligence*."

The screws grumbled as he winked at the mirror. "Anyways, to cover their ass, they put a chase car behind us."

He mentioned the name of one of the troopers in it, also a classmate of ours.

I said, "You're shittin' me, he's behind us?" I twisted in the seat as best I could and sure enough, right behind us was an unmarked cruiser with two state troopers in it. I got my hands up far as I could and waved. The cruiser's siren went, whoop-whoop and the lights flashed as a pair of hands waved back at me through the windshield. Eddie and I laughed out loud as the two screws swore a blue streak.

After we took the Somerville exit, Eddie suggested that we stop for coffee and donuts. The screws were dead-set against it, but Eddie said, "Well, I'm in charge of the prisoner, and I say coffee and donuts. What do you say, Rick?"

Never had a better chocolate cruller.

At the Somerville courthouse, Eddie and I shook hands again, and he wished me good luck. I told him not to worry. Someday I said we'd be sitting around having a beer somewhere and talking about this. I had no idea then how true this would be.

During the Probable Cause hearing, my former friend, Brian Bean, took the stand against me. I'll never forget the anger and indignation on this pussy's face as he jabbed his finger in my direction and testified that he heard me say this, and I had told him that. Here was a former trusted friend ratting me out for no other reason other than to save his own sorry skin. Because of Bean's testimony, Probable Cause was found and I was indicted for the Wells Fargo hold-up in Medford.

For his efforts on behalf of the state, I was told later that Bean would allegedly serve eleven months in a county jail PC unit somewhere in New Hampshire.

When people ask me about him today how I feel, I tell them this. When I get up in the morning and look in the mirror I see a man. Bean never will.

In 1990, after pleading guilty to the Medford heist, I received a ten to fifteen year sentence to run concurrent with the eighteen to twenty I was already serving. I would serve no extra time, but any chance I had of receiving a one-third consideration for parole after six years was gone.

For me 1992 was a good year, but for New England Mafia figure Frank Oreto it was the opposite. I graduated from the BU Prison Education Program and received my Bachelor degree, Magna Cum Laude, in Liberal Studies. My proud father and mother attended the graduation ceremony.

The same year, after a sixteen month trial, Oreto was convicted of loan sharking and racketeering and sentenced to twenty years in federal prison, to be served on and after his prior conviction for second degree murder. His attorney, Barry Wilson, immediately filed an appeal, but for most in the camp the message was clear. Oreto would die in prison.

Big House Bug House

I'd been hard-wired for years with anger and addiction problems. College had helped me get back on track but I knew that needed more, so I made the decision to seek psychological counseling. I drove the prison administration crazy until they gave in and I finally got what I wanted. For the next five years, once a week, I met with a social worker named Marcia Carey,

During the sessions, unbeknownst to me, Carey utilized something called Cognitive Behavioral Therapy, which over time enabled me to commit to positive change. When she finally left Norfolk, I was reassigned and continued working with another LISW (licensed social worker) named Jean Fain. For the first time in decades I was healing.

Prison can make a man crazy. When the monotony, violence, boredom, stress, and concern about family or a girlfriend boils over, for some, the easiest path out is insanity. I saw it all around me, even in my former partners at times.

On a Spring day in 1992 I was walking the yard with Sean and discussing a familiar topic, how sometimes he didn't trust Danny. Years before, according to Sean, the two of them were involved in a crime, and Sean believed that Danny may have hidden some of the swag from him.

I had heard this particular story before. That's another downside to prison, stories get rehashed, forever, but finally I had heard enough and said, "Hey, if you think he ripped you off either let it go, confront the guy, or kill him, because I don't want to hear it again."

Sean and Danny were childhood friends. They were tight and had done a lot of work together, so basically what I said to Sean was shut up and forget about it. We changed the subject, continued walking, and I forgot about the conversation.

A month passed and I'm in my cell one day when Sean called from the Quad up to my window. I yelled down, "What's up?"

"Gotta talk to you," he said.

"Be down later, gotta finish this paper."

"We gotta talk, now."

We met in the yard and, as we followed the track, Sean made a startling confession. He had told Danny that I had said to kill him. I stared at him. "You're kidding me, right?" Sean could be a little crazy, but to tell the other guy something like that?

"He's going to have you clipped," Sean said.

"Are you out of your mind? I never meant to actually *kill* him. What the fuck's wrong with you?"

Sean got this look on his face like he knew he fucked up. "I know, I know, I'm sorry," he said. "Why I'm telling you this."

He went on to say that the year before, when Danny was lugged to MCI Gardner, he had hooked up with a real bad crew from Charlestown. Sean said, "Danny told me that once you get to (minimum security) Shirley, he's planning to have them clip you."

Talk about stress. And anger. I couldn't believe this was happening.

According to Sean, MCI Shirley was surrounded by woods. Danny's plan was to get me into the tree line somehow, where his pals would be laying in the shadows.

My head was spinning, but at least I'd been warned. I had another two years to go in Norfolk, plenty of time to plan a response. An old TV antiperspirant ad once suggested 'You don't ever let them see you sweat.'

Danny never would, not one fucking drop.

I told no one about it, not even Frank Cincotta. I walked around pretending that nothing had happened. Time passed then one day while I was walking the yard with Danny, he suddenly wrapped his arm around my shoulder. He pulled me in close and said, "Rick, it won't be too long before you're out of here, brother."

I told him that I was looking forward to leaving and right away he suggested MCI Shirley. Then what he said next raised the hairs on my neck. "Good choice," he said. "When you get down there you'll see the place's wide open, Rick, and surrounded by woods. In summer when it's hot, you can walk to the tree-line and lay down in the shade, chill out and relax."

Chill out? I was *flipping* out, but showed Danny nothing.

I said, "Yeah, really? It sounds great, thanks." And that was the end of it; there was never any mention of Shirley again.

Then, once more, God laughed while men made plans. A few months later, Danny's scheme unraveled when the Townie crew he depended on to take me out were taken out themselves. After pulling off an armored car heist in New Hampshire and killing two guards, the heat became so intense that a gang member's brother turned rat and put everyone else away for life. The threat from these men, if it ever existed in the first place, was gone.

So, what did I do about Danny's treachery?

To be honest, with the threat eliminated, I didn't plot revenge. The mindset that may have worked for me in the past was gone. Somewhere between strengthening my spiritual connection, the BU education, and the years of Cognitive Behavioral Therapy, I had changed.

I was a different man now, not weaker but *different*. Professor Elizabeth "Ma" Barker, one of the founders of the BU Prison Program, said once "When the mind's been expanded, it can never return to its former dimension."

Danny had made a serious and potentially deadly mistake, but I had no plans to compound his error by plotting against him. It wasn't worth it. But I vowed I would never work with Danny again.

While I did my time I was grateful not to have a wife, girlfriend, or kids to worry about. The only thing I had to focus on was me, rebuilding my own life, which I did by attending school, exercising, praying a lot, and making daily entries into the journal I kept.

I also attended Catholic Mass weekly, where I met some great people like Sisters Kathleen and Ruth, nuns from the Sisters of Bethany Prison Ministry. I met with Kathleen once a week in her little chapel office in the CSD building. We'd talk about everything: religion, politics, my past, future plans, etc., and Kathleen helped get me through some tough times, like when I learned that my father had cancer.

As the years passed in Norfolk, my former partners, Sean and Danny, occasionally "made the circuit". See, if you violated prison rules and committed a breach of security, which could be anything from selling drugs, strong-arming other inmates, fighting, or for a host of other offenses, you would get lugged and spend time in the hole (i.e., isolation). In Norfolk the hole was located in the RB (Receiving Building) aka "The Submarine". The final step in the process was Reclassification.

You might be reclassed (reclassified) back up to "The Hill," maximum security Walpole, or to medium security SECC (Southeast Correctional Center) in Bridgewater, or be sent to prisons in Gardner or Shirley. If you were smart and kept out of trouble, after a year or two you'd complete "the circuit" and be reclassified back to Norfolk State Prison.

With a lot of pissed off people in such a tiny area it took very little to set someone off. If you stepped out of line you'd get taken away quick.

I awoke one night to the sound of footsteps and keys jangling as a dozen screws rushed past the block below my window. In the 2-3 block a few buildings down a man had been murdered for farting. Bunked in a cell with three others, the victim had his brains splattered all over the walls by a cellmate who had attacked him with a table leg.

While the assailant waited for the screws to arrive, he broke open a box of cookies and offered them to his remaining cellmates. "I will not have time to eat them," he said.

It wasn't just lunatic inmates, but also the DOC's lunatic rules. The windows in the cells could only be opened so far, but the whack-job Director of Security decided that they shouldn't be opened at all and ordered them all to be welded shut.

In my seven and a half years in Norfolk, a lot of men died there, at least six from asthma attacks, suffocating in the dead of night. Others were murdered, while some died from more natural causes. After 25 years behind the walls, my South Boston pal, Ronnie Mac (Ron MacDonald) suffered a fatal heart attack in his cell.

"Maca," as we called him, spent every minute of his life sentence for murder behind the walls of medium and maximum-security prisons. He didn't believe in God but told me once he did believe something might be out there, but that he couldn't put a finger on what.

On rare occasions though, beneath Maca's brutal exterior, I saw something flicker. It was like when I was a kid in church seeing the little votive candles on either side of the altar. I'd put my dime in the box, grab a wick, and light the candle in the little glass cup. Back in my seat again I would look for *my* candle, and for an instant my heart would stop because I was unable to see the flame. But then I'd see a flicker of light. It was faint, almost imperceptible, but there it was a glimpse through the dark glass. That's how I saw Ronnie Mac.

On a fall morning in 1991 the head "count" had just cleared and "movement" was in progress. Almost immediately my Mafia friend, Cincotta, was in the Quad outside calling up to my window. This wasn't Cincotta's style, if he wanted to see me he would send someone else over. Something was up.

When I left the block he said, "Let's take a walk," and we went up and turned left into Cadillac Alley toward the East Field. Up to that point everything appeared normal. When the count cleared, half the camp had emptied into the Quad. Hundreds of men on their way to work, school, the gym, programs, or to the east and west fields to walk the track.

We stopped at the edge of a small embankment overlooking the East field. Directly in front was a softball field and to the right the new gym. A tall security fence, topped with Concertina wire bordered the field, and between it and the wall was a thirty-foot space known as the Dead Zone. Get caught in it good chance you'd be shot.

Cincotta tapped the back of his hand against my leg, said in a hushed tone, "You see it?"

"See what?"

And then I did. From the top of the wall, mere inches below the electrified wire, a length of white-knotted sheet hung almost to the ground. It rippled in the breeze like a tired anaconda.

Someone had escaped.

I said, "Holy shit," and Cincotta whacked my leg harder.

"Shut the fuck up and watch," he hissed.

Trying to be nonchalant, I looked around. Did anyone else see it? Then a couple of guys winked as they walked by.

On the other side of the field a screw followed the fence line checking for cuts in the wire, a routine done every morning. He stopped at a spot thirty feet from the sheet and prodded the fence with his toe, without seeing it. He must have been blind.

It was time to get out of there.

Frank and I had just about finished a lap in the west field when the escape siren went off, making the same sound that you hear in movies when the convict escapes. The prison was locked down for most of the day.

We later learned that in the wee hours of the previous rainy night a con, from the 3-2 block, was able to creep out of it and cross the field in the mud on his belly. Using a wire-cutter on the fence, he had crawled to the wall then tossed a sheet, with some kind of hook on the end, over it.

Unfortunately the con wasn't in good physical shape and after pulling himself halfway up his strength had given out and he fell. He remained on is back in the rain and mud until his strength returned then made another attempt, which ended the same way. Exhausted, he returned to the block where, a few hours later, tracking dogs followed his scent to his cell.

In late winter the same year, I was in my cell watching *America's Most Wanted* one night when the host, John Walsh, announced: "Coming up next a dangerous fugitive from Massachusetts, John Bianchi, wanted for kidnapping, robbery, and posing as a US Marshal."

What? My old nemesis on *America's Most Wanted*?

I ran up and down the block telling everyone to put on the show. When it came back on, sure enough it was him. Wanted in two states, in deep shit, Bianchi was arrested a couple of weeks later due to viewer tips.

Future Tense

When I thought about the future it made me nervous. Once I was out where would I live? Who would give me a job with a record like mine? Could I stay away from old friends and associates? Make new ones? And what about a woman? I knew that I'd need a good one to help keep me grounded, but where would I find her?

I had been down seven years, with at least three more to go, when I thought about those things, especially about women. To simplify it I compiled a list of what I desired. Call me superficial, but the woman had to be beautiful, and she had to have inner beauty too. She should be focused, intelligent, unafraid of hard work, and willing to stand up for herself. She also had to be spiritual. The spirituality part was important to me, and there was one other thing. It wasn't a deal breaker, but it would be nice if we shared some kind of former connection so she'd *know*, have no questions concerning, what she was getting into.

Then, like I was nailed by a bucket of water, it came to me. For years there had been a woman like that in my life, my friend Elaine Cunniff, I just never saw it. She was everything that I needed, and more, but it was too late because Elaine was married now.

During the first four or five years of the bid I rarely thought about women, especially as far as a relationship went. In the middle of a long stretch I was too busy trying to survive.

In the past when Elaine would visit I'd pretty much act the same around her as I had on the street. Sure I was thrilled to see her, but my reaction was always controlled. It would be "Hey, Elaine, how're doing, pal?" Of course she would always look and smell great, but she was just an old friend, a *married* friend now.

Now seven years had passed, and things had changed. Now when Elaine visited, usually twice a year, my head would spin for days after. But because she was married I never, not once, let on how I felt.

In general visits were something that I could take or leave. It sounds strange but my reality was prison and beyond those walls, to me, was another planet.

There were some though that had to have visits. Even tough guys, and in some cases gangsters, who insisted that their wives or girlfriends visit them every week. To me it was selfish and weak because they were making someone else do their time with them.

I was lucky enough to have people, loyal friends, who would periodically come up to see me. My father came like clockwork every two weeks, and my mother every three. There were ladies too, like my friends Michelle Haber and Kim Ernst, members of an all-girl rock band, The Bristols, and Nancy Winslow, a former Rat waitress that had become a high-powered New York fashion executive. My old pals Eric Joseph, Rich Torsney, and Jim Costello, confined to a wheelchair, and his wife Jerry and Southie men: Tony Attardo and Joe Curran always found the time to visit.

There were times when I believed that my life was changing; then others when going to school and praying seemed like a big waste of time. Back and forth it went like that for years because, at its core, prison is a college for crime and I was constantly exposed to new opportunities—like the one offered by Bernie the chemist.

Bernie had a degree from the prestigious Worcester Polytechnic Institute and was doing his second bid for the manufacture of methamphetamine. On the street Bernie had made a fortune selling pounds of crystal meth to biker gangs. He was also proficient in the manufacture of PCP (Phencyclidine) a.k.a. Wet, Dooby, or Angel Dust and when I asked him which drug was more profitable, without blinking he said the latter.

In two days he could whip up a quart of pharmaceutical grade Phencyclidine and earn ten thousand dollars, over eighteen grand today. If he was feeling particularly industrious he could pump out two quarts in a week, and sell them in hours.

Angel Dust, except for users in the housing projects, was never big in Southie. Charlestown, by far, was the county seat for the drug. Nowadays people say that it was a myth that Jim Bulger kept drugs out of Southie. But to a certain degree he did.

When Jim ran the town I never once heard of a heroin dealer. Sell it and you were dead, period. The same thing went for Angel Dust. Dust was a mainstay in C-Town but so were stabbings, and most of them dust related. People stabbing each other brought heat from the cops and Bulger didn't like heat.

Here's how he handled dust dealers. In 1983, when I lived on O Street, a kid down the street sold dust, and Bulger grabbed him and warned him to stop. The kid did for a short time then he started back up—and disappeared shortly after.

It didn't take long to get the word from the "Bishop" as Bulger was known, that anyone who sold dust had a hole waiting for them too, across the border in New Hampshire.

Angel Dust sales in Southie plummeted.

In the past I had moved small packages of coke at the door of the Rat, and made larger deliveries for George Pappas, but that was mostly to feed my own habit. I never made a profit selling any kind of drug. But that was then and now one thing was certain. Sell Phencyclidine, and I would make a ton of money, something I hadn't seen in years.

As Bernie and I walked the yard, he would explain in detail the thirty-four steps involved in the manufacture of PCP. I learned everything about its ingredients and where to find them, even the federally banned Piperidine integral to the process.

He wrote down the steps on a yellow, legal pad, and I memorized every one. As we walked, he would question me. You add this ingredient when? What happens if you add too soon? The proper temperature to cook at this particular stage is what? For how long, and then you turn it down to what degree? If this occurs, what should you do? What if it starts steaming? On and on it went until both of us were certain I had the process down pat.

I hid Bernie's directions in the guts of old notebook and mailed it home as insurance, just in case things didn't work out for me the way I planned. I remember a screw grabbing me in the yard once and telling me that he *knew* that I was up to something, but couldn't catch me. He was only partially right. Actually I was up to nothing in *there* but—if was abandoned by God, didn't find that good woman, my writing never took off—was preparing myself for the street.

Shortly before I was reclassified to minimum security MCI Shirley, Oreto introduced me to a new arrival in the camp, Steve, from Revere, Oreto's hometown. Revere, located on Boston's North Shore, was a bastion of the Mafia at the time.

Serving a short sentence, Steve was just twenty-two, big, and athletic. Due for release soon, the kid was ballsy too. Oreto was eager for me to answer any questions he had in regards to criminal activities familiar to me, especially armed robbery.

Steve was a fast learner and demonstrated a particular interest in armored cars. I happened to be friendly with a former Wells Fargo driver serving time in the camp on a drug beef, so I introduced him to Steve. The three of us walked the yard together and Steve picked his brain clean.

Oreto had a friend with a connection to a large armored carrier company. The plan called for us, once Steve and I were free again, to find someone we trusted to apply for a job there. Oreto's connection would ensure that he got it. The new guy would become our mole, our eyes and ears, and hand us a score worth millions.

MCI Shithole

In the spring of 1995, after nine years behind the walls, I was re-classified to minimum security MCI Shirley. It had taken years of me doing the right thing to get there, and now that I was from the first day the place was a nightmare.

You could be lugged for almost anything. In my "cottage" a guy named Troy was lugged for daring to ask for extra fries as he went through the chow line. They shipped him to "the Valley" as MCI Shirley medium was known, another hellhole, for having the audacity to be hungry.

Now you might say, Hey, its prison, you put yourself in there. True but, by their own rules, the DOC wasn't supposed to function that way. DOC rules required you work (as in *earn*) your way down from maximum to medium security, then to minimum, and finally pre-release. As an incentive, at every level, there was supposed to be more freedom, and certainly fewer restrictions. MCI Shithole didn't work that way.

After five months of walking on eggshells, I requested reclassification to pre-release. I figured at least there I would be able to get an outside job and sock money away for when I got out. In mid-May 1995 I went before the classification board.

The board, especially one guy, grilled me hard. What about drugs and alcohol, did I still have a problem with them? What happened to me between 1977 and 1986? Why did I leave the state police? It should have been nerve wracking, answering all of those personal questions, but I found I was calm once I began talking. I enunciated my words and explained my position on a variety of questions comfortably and accurately. I told the truth and truth did the trick.

The hearing concluded with Derek, the unit manager, saying that the board's only concern was I had only been in minimum security a few months. That was true, but in the previous nine *years* I had earned two college degrees, participated in every program requested of me, remained out of trouble, and voluntarily participated in psychological counseling. I believed that I was a perfect candidate and qualified to be in pre-release for the last eight months of my sentence.

I remember leaving the room and waiting outside in the corridor for a decision. When they called me back in, I was pleased to learn that the board had unanimously voted to send me to a Boston area pre-release. I called my father and gave him the good news.

Then, six weeks later in the middle of a brutally hot summer, Derek, the unit manager, gave me bad news. The superintendent, a guy named Corcini, had refused to sign off on my transfer saying that his decision was based on the "serious nature of the offense." In Corsini's opinion, I needed more "positive adjustment" time in Shirley, a facility that made me want to kill someone daily.

As I had in the past, I settled down, moved on, and fortunately landed a job where I could earn good time—at the prison wastewater treatment plant.

Mornings I'd be picked up by a fat screw named Huck and taken to the treatment plant that was located in the woods behind the facility. Huck, a two-faced con-hater, was always on the lookout for ways to duck work. One day I asked Billy, one of the bosses, about the difference between Huck's vacation and his regular duties, and Billy responded, "Not much."

The best thing about the shit plant was the lab that contained a treasure trove of state-of-the-art equipment used to test wastewater after treatment. As I swept and mopped the floor every day, I thought about Bernie, the Meth King of Norfolk, and how someday I might have a lab like this of my own. I familiarized myself with the purpose of every piece of equipment by asking casual questions.

Bernie had said the equipment used to make Phencyclidine was expensive, but in the Shirley lab there was everything I needed. Along with the necessary flasks and beakers, it contained fancy, high-priced stuff too. I made a list:

1. Nopco Model 9000D-AutoClave Sterilizer

2. Coliform Incubator

3. Mettler AJ100 Scal (box-type with glass walls)

4. Electro Mantel 10 Setting Heating Apparatus

5. Thermolyne Type 48000 Furnace (Sybron)

6. VWR 1305U Drying Oven (approx. two foot square)

I fantasized about returning to Shirley someday and taking everything. It wouldn't be hard. The plant was located deep in the woods, out of sight of the gun towers of the prison next door. The building that housed the lab had no electronic security. There were no cameras, motion detectors, or even window alarms. A dirt road led from the highway to the rear of the building. All I had to do was park a half mile away, backpack in and walk out with twenty grand worth of equipment.

While I was in Shirley, the environment in South Boston was rapidly changing. In 1990, following years of state and federal investigation, fifty of Jim Bulger's cocaine dealers were rounded up in a sweep.

As a result of the raid, my former associate Paul "Polecat" Ferris, after spending a few years in federal prison, was hit with a superseding indictment for racketeering. Looking at real time now, Ferris flipped, after serving five years of a nine-year sentence, and became a cooperating witness against his former mentor and boss, James Whitey Bulger.

I wasn't surprised when articles began to appear in *The Boston Globe* painting Bulger as a Top Echelon informant for the FBI. The startling revelation sent shock waves through the city, as well as throughout the correctional system.

In late fall, I resubmitted a request to move to pre-release, and received it. My new destination, the South Middlesex Correctional Center in Framingham, was next to a women's prison.

Second Thoughts

After three months in pre-release, I received my first PRA (Program Related Activity), allowing me to travel outside the prison, on my own, for the first time in almost ten years. The trip took me to a local bank where I was supposed to open a checking account.

My favorite part of that first day on the street was walking past the women's prison. It had no walls, just a fence, and the ladies were lined up behind it waving, hooting, and whistling at me. Though initially I was taken aback, it was exquisite to receive all that female attention. I didn't care that that among them were killers, drug dealers, and prostitutes. They were *women* and I loved every one.

The First Shawmut Bank was a mile down the road, but even walking the short distance to it distance was eerie. And I had to be careful. On the first PRA you're given a prescribed route to follow, and if you're supposed to turn right or left somewhere, you'd better. The DOC had people watching, hiding in some cases, or driving by in cars hoping to catch you doing the wrong thing.

As I got close to the bank, a thought popped into my head. What if, when I arrived, an armored car was making a delivery? Should I take it as some kind of sign? I caught myself whoa, slow down man, what's the chance of it happening?

But when I turned the final corner, out in front of the First Shawmut Bank, was a huge, gray Brinks truck with a guard loading moneybags onto a dolly.

For a moment I was excited—then I felt cursed. For almost ten years I had had to budget money just to be able to buy an ice cream on a hot summer day. Now, less than thirty feet from me, was at least three hundred grand.

My heart racing, I entered the bank. I'm not saying that I had thoughts about hitting it later; it was just the rush I got thinking about it. Out of old habits, I scanned the bank's interior. The building was long and narrow, and its huge windows were filled it with natural light. I was willing to bet that the back door led to a parking lot.

I joined a queue waiting to see a woman at a desk, and then turned to watch the front entrance. The guard wheeled the dolly in nonchalantly, like he was delivering pizza, and barely turned his head as he pushed the treasure past me. Near the rear of the building, through an unlocked door, he entered the teller's area.

I watched him through the glass divider; the manager met him and he followed her through another door that I was certain led to the vault. I asked the guy behind to watch my place and went out the back door into the parking lot. The layout was perfect; the bank could be taken.

All I had to do was have a man parked out front with a walky-talky give the two, sitting in the car out back, the head's up when the guard wheeled the dolly in. Wait thirty-seconds then burst in and grab him, take his gun, tie-wrap his legs, and wheel the money out.

I went back inside and opened my new checking account.

Hadn't I learned my lesson? I was still thinking about crime? But I *had* learned my lesson. Treated like garbage, like a wild animal, for a decade, I was white-hot angry and continued to doubt that I could change my life. I had busted my ass, for years, to make those changes, but also believed in hedging my bets. No real convict ever walks out the door of a prison believing, one hundred per cent, that he's all done with crime. It doesn't matter what he says.

I knew for a fact there were guys out there, men I had done time with, that had gone back to the old ways and were kicking ass and making big money. A good example was Steve, the guy I had schooled about armored cars. In Shirley watching the news one day a story came on about an armored car heist in Revere. Just the way it went down, I knew it was Steve.

Still in pre-release, on the way to my supermarket job one day, I called Steve from a pay phone. It was against the rules so I kept the conversation brief.

"That thing I saw on TV, you?" I said.

"Ya," Steve said, "I got something for you when you get out."

"Thanks," I said. "Talk to you then." And that was it.

In February 1996, I was released from the Massachusetts Department of Corrections. My mother pulled up in front of the building in her old, blue Dodge Spirit, and I walked out of the South Middlesex Correctional Center carrying a small plastic bag containing a few articles of clothing.

I tossed the bag in the trunk, jumped in and said, "Drive, Ma."

Like any mother, the first thing she asked was if I was hungry. "I'll take you anywhere that you want," she said. I asked her to take me to McDonald's. I stayed with my mother for the next two months.

The day after my release she took me clothes shopping at Braintree's South Shore Plaza, and I was almost overwhelmed by the chrome, glass, piped in music, crowds, and aromas, things that I hadn't experienced in years. For the entire two hours that we spent there I remained glued to the side of my one hundred pound mother.

I had left the system with basically nothing but was fortunate in that my mother had squirreled away a portion of the funds that my older brother, Bob, had sent me over the years. I took some of it and purchased an old wreck of a car, but I still needed a job.

That's where Walter Collins came in.

While I was in prison my former brother-in-law and good friend, Walter, had been busy opening a string of successful sports bars he named TKO' Malley's. I called him about a job a few months before my release and, without hesitating, he told me that one would be waiting.

A few weeks after my release Walter picked me up at my Mum's house in a hotrod Firebird, and we toured of each of his facilities. He told me to pick any one I wanted. I chose TK's on Scituate Harbor. Soon any doubts I had about whether or not I could work again in the bar scene disappeared because everyone at TK's, unaware of my past, worked as a team. It took some getting used being accepted again as a normal person, and not some dirty convict, and I was just beginning to relax when a blast from the past walked into my life.

On a busy Sunday afternoon, Billy, a friend from prison, stopped by TK's with two pals, one a Somerville bank robber recently released from federal prison. For the next two hours, they sat at the bar, ate, drank, and watched football. At one point Rich, TK's general manager, called me into the kitchen. Physically huge and imposing, Rich was a great guy, but concern etched his face. "Rick, I think we've a problem with your buddies," he said.

Problem? What kind of problem? Far as I could see they were behaving like good customers, spending money, and minding their own business.

Rich said, "A customer overheard them talking about holding up the bar. Walter's on his way down now."

I couldn't believe it and I told Rich, "No way, no fucking way, man."

In the first place the men would never disrespect me like that. They were professionals, bank robbers for chrissakes, not amateurs that would stick up a bar. I told Rich that.

Fired up now I wanted to confront the asshole, or assholes, which had relayed the bad "tip", but Rich refused to point him/them out.

I returned to the bar and gave my friends the bad news. The picture became clearer when Bill explained that he had once been a resident of Scituate and was well known to the cops there. More than likely some jerk at the bar, with a grudge against him, had made up the story to have him tossed out.

When Walter arrived and I explained my thoughts to him, I think he believed me but said the cops wouldn't. We walked to the front of the building and he pointed out the window. Three Scituate police cruisers circled slowly between the restaurant and the parking lot across the street. The fiasco ended when a convoy of cops escorted Bill and his buddies from town, arresting one in the process. I had learned a hard lesson; the stench of prison *never* leaves you.

I'd been home three months, and though I liked the bartender job and was grateful to have it, I knew it held no future. I had my own apartment now, a little studio, and could afford the rent, but beyond that, I was barely getting by. I pondered my next move and knew that if I made the wrong one, I'd be right back in prison. In an attempt to shine some light on my future I visited the Tea Room in Quincy.

Regina Russell's Tea Room, located in a house just outside Quincy center, was a psychic salon offering services that included: spiritual readings, a crystal ball, palm readings, astrology, tea leaf and Tarot card reading. Russell even advertised a toll-free number for psychic phone readings, "Just ask for the ten minute special when you call!"

I paid the twenty-dollar fee at the tiny front desk, and the hostess guided me into the living room and sat me down at a table. A few minutes passed and a woman in her late twenties pushed through a beaded curtain in the wall to my left. Busy talking to the hostess as she crossed the room, she sat down across from me. When she faced me she stared a few seconds and then her eyes became huge. She *shrieked*, jumped up, and ran from the room.

Freaked out myself, I jumped up almost knocking the table over.

When the hostess scurried back into the room, I said, my voice rising, "I want my money back, *now*."

She said, "Calm down, sir. Please calm down. I've no idea what's wrong with that girl—but I've got someone else."

I was really spooked, wanted out of there but then another woman, very cute, glided into the room and sat down at the table. She motioned for me to join her.

Okay, I thought, one more time. She put a deck of Tarot cards in front of me and asked me to shuffle. I handed the deck back, and as the woman turned the cards over in front of me she told me what she saw. It was pretty much the usual stuff: You'll be getting a good job, money's coming your way soon, you've got great taste in clothes, blah-blah-blah. But nothing was mentioned about prison, and I had to know if I was going back?

She was almost to the end of the deck, and I'm thinking this is a big mistake, then she turned over another card and a gentle smile curled her lips. Her large eyes rose and locked onto mine. She said softly, "It's your guardian angel."

Maybe I said something like, 'I could really use one', but then she turned the next card over and stared at it.

"This is really interesting," she said and looked at me again. "You have *two* guardian angels."

Immediately, I knew what she meant. For years I believed that Tank had never left me, that he was still around.

She focused on the card and spoke slowly. "He was a young man, a friend of yours." She looked up. "He died violently, near you."

My throat constricted, my eyes burned and welled up with tears.

"It's my friend Frank MacDonald," I said.

She put her hand on mine, "It's okay, he's okay," she said. "He's still around, he never left you."

I took a few minutes to settle down and then she continued the reading. She never mentioned anything about prison. When she was done I explained the real reason that I was there.

She went hmmm, and re-checked the cards still spread across the table. "There's nothing here indicates prison," she said then dragged a card toward her. On it was the figure of a man, a knight or something, and in his hands, or maybe laying at his feet, I don't recall which, was a broken chain.

"I missed this chain, its broken," she said, tapping the card. "You will not return to prison."

15.

Old World

I'd been on the streets a few months when, on an early weekday morning, I decided I'd swing into the South End to visit two of my old haunts, the Franklin Café and Waltham Tavern. It was a little after nine when I walked into the Franklin and found that the place looked pretty much the same. A stranger tended the bar, where two other strangers sat, and I asked him if my old friend Al still worked there?

His eyebrows went up. "Al? He's been dead five years now."

It was difficult to hear. The knowledge you really can't go back added weight to my legs as I walked up Shawmut Ave toward the Waltham Tavern.

The Waltham was almost empty too but, like the Franklin, looked pretty much the same. The old bumper pool table, when you came in on the right, was gone, and an old, stooped-shouldered, black man, wet-mopped the space where it had been once.

When he noticed me standing there, he stopped and leaned on the handle. "Can I help you?" he said.

I explained how I had been a regular there once and nodded at the bar. I said, "Drank a lot of beer over there, and had a million laughs."

He looked back over his shoulder like he could see me sitting there, and maybe he saw something, because when he turned and faced me again he was grinning. "Yeah," he said, "them was some good days."

I mentioned a few names of the people I knew, Franklin and Waltham regulars, and his head bobbed as I went down the list, but his grin quickly melted.

"They, most of them's, dead," he said. He winced as if he'd been stuck in the side. "Or right now dyin' in prison," He shook his head, slowly pulled the mop from the bucket and dropped it into the wringer.

I asked him, "Do you happen to remember a guy named Bobby Sullivan?"

"Know him? Damn, me and Bobby's frens for years," he said.

"He used to come around the Franklin a lot with his crew," I said. "A black man used to run with them, Pepper. Know him? He was said to've been a serious dude."

In the process of wringing the mop the old man suddenly released the spring-loaded handle, and it returned with a crack. He came to a kind of shaky attention, his fingers pinching the crease in his pants, said, "I'm Pepper."

I almost fell over.

We talked a bit more, finishing the little that was left to say, and I left the Waltham and never went back. Years later I heard talk about how the place had changed, really changed, and how yuppies and drag queens had become its main clientele. Then one day I read in the newspaper that the Waltham's formerly Mafia connected owner, in his eighties at the time, had been busted for selling drugs in the place, and the bar shuttered forever.

When I finally reached out to Steve, my pal from Norfolk Prison, we met at Kelly's Roast Beef, a popular take out joint across from Revere Beach. Steve was in good spirits and had remained in great shape, something a lot of guys let slip after they hit the streets. We sat on the seawall noshing on cheeseburgers and clams and talked about what he'd been up to.

One of the first orders of discussion was the armored car robbery in Shirley I had seen on the news. The take was only forty-five grand, but Steve had invested the money in twenty-five pounds of high-grade weed from some mutual friends—young Mafia associates, and then had spent the rest on "tools."

As he had promised, Steve pulled a small wad of cash from his pocket and handed it to me. I thanked him and as I tucked it away he said, "I got a few guns back at the apartment," he said. "Take your pick. There's some other stuff there that I'd like you to see." I was grateful for the money but passed on the gun, something I viewed as a one-way ticket back to the can.

In the bedroom of Steve's apartment, he pulled two canvas bags from under the bed. In one were two automatic rifles, a tactical shotgun, seven handguns, and some Kevlar vests with trauma plates and neck guards. The other held a treasure trove of the latest electronic police scanning and communication equipment, similar to the stuff that was used by the feds, maybe even better. No more highly visible bulky radios, these had a range of a quarter mile, plugged into your ear, and had wrap-around wires for mikes. When Steve saw how impressed I was he put on the pressure.

"Rick, back in Norfolk Frank said when I got some dough to get the best equipment money can buy. Well, here it is, pal. My partner and I have been waiting for you to get out so the three of us can whack out the next one. It's all lined up. You want in, right?"

That was the signal for me, and a strong one, to take a big step back. I had been out on the streets less than two months and already I was in room with machine guns.

I said, "Hey, Stevie, I just got out. I appreciate the offer. I do, but remember what I told you back in the can. When I'm out, I'll need at least six months to get my street legs back. I have to see if I can make it legit. Gotta give myself a chance, pal."

Steve was disappointed, but understood. "Ya, okay," he said. "But how about taking a peek at the score and giving me some feedback?" He grinned and said, "You can earn the dough I just gave ya."

The same afternoon we drove to a bank in a nearby town, and Steve showed me the play. "The armored car shows up at this time of the day, it parks over there. We hit the guard at this spot before he goes inside, get out of here this way."

Right off I saw flaws in the plan and I reviewed them with Steve. He listened intently and nodded in agreement. "Yeah know, I think you're right," he said, "Jesus, why didn't I see that?"

I said, "That's the thing kid, you've got to see everything. You give them a chance and they'll kill you."

Then I strongly suggested that he stick with moving weed. There's no violence involved, and he already had his start-up money. If he turned the product over, he'd double his dough. Buy more and double that and he'd be on his way. The problem with Steve was his age, and, like me, he was an adrenalin junkie.

I said, "Think about what you're doing."

"You too," Steve said. "If you change your mind, call me."

That was the last time I saw him. In the end Steve passed on the score he showed me, opting instead to get involved in something bigger, much bigger, a multi-million dollar hit. Steve had put the plan, concocted in Norfolk with Frank Cincotta, into action and had placed a man inside an armored car service. The strategy called for the mole to work there for six months gathering information, especially regarding delivery times and payloads. He then would deliver a three to five million dollar score to the rest of the team, receiving twenty percent for his efforts.

Just to touch base I'd call Steve once a month, and through our limited conversations, I learned that his pot business was thriving, but he was experiencing problems with the young Mafia associates, who Steve claimed owed him money. I knew the crew, they were hungry and violent, and I suggested he stay clear of them.

And for a while I think he did. He was living the good life. He had moved into an expensive new apartment complex across from Revere Beach and was dating a beautiful, young stripper who danced at The Squire, an upscale gentlemen's club.

I hadn't seen Steve in over three months when I called him one day. When his girlfriend picked up, I asked her to put Steve on. I was met with silence. Growing impatient, thinking maybe she's high, I barked at her, "Put Steve on the phone."

I barely heard her say, "Stevie's dead. We buried him last week."

Standing in the kitchen of my studio apartment I asked her what happened. My first thought, wise-guys had killed him.

"I can't talk about it, can't talk anymore about it. I have to go," she said and hung up.

At that point my own life was good; the chance I'd given myself paying off. I had a steady girl, a decent job, and my future looked promising. From my perspective Steve's death was a warning. God was saying, no shouting at me as he had in North Adams over a decade before, that it was *over* for me. Any thought I might have had that I could always fall back into the old way of life, if things didn't work out the way I had planned was gone, forever.

The night Steve died he had been out with friends drinking, snorting coke, and at the end of the night some asshole had offered him heroin. For me it was hard to accept that a kid who was always in shape would mess with that shit. He inhaled the narcotic and went to sleep, vomited, aspirated, and choked to death.

Dead at 23.

Job Fair

As my release date from prison neared friends, well-meaning men, warned me that the streets were a minefield. There would be opportunities they'd said, lots of them for a guy like me with a solid reputation, but pick the wrong one and bang; I was dead or back in the can.

My friends were right. The offers kept coming.

It was 1996 an old friend from Southie, Sal Grassi, reached out to me through a mutual connection. Sal asked me to meet him at his bar, the Sports Connection in Southie. When I arrived the bartender directed me to Sal's basement office, where I found him seated behind his desk.

A diminutive ex- amateur boxing champion, Sal, never an overly talkative guy, launched right into it. "Rick, I got a problem," he said. "It's the fucking Dominicans. They're pushing their product in Southie now,"

Sal had been moving blow in the town for years, allegedly the entire time I was in prison. He had done well for himself, but with Jim Bulger gone and Southie's demographics changing, Dominicans had moved in.

When I asked Sal what he planned to do about it he said, matter-of-factly, "Shake 'em down. I can't fucking stop 'em dealing but, if they're selling in Southie, they'll pay for the privilege. Jesus, Jim would've made 'em."

Sal was right; Bulger wouldn't have tolerated Dominicans, or anybody else, on his turf, but Jim had been gone since late 1994, on the run from multiple federal racketeering indictments.

"I'm going to need help, some muscle," Sal said. "You and your friends can put 'em in line quick. They kick in an envelope every month, everyone's happy."

Immediately, warning bells went off in my head. It was tough enough trusting people I knew, never mind Dominican drug dealers. I asked myself if these Dominicans get busted would they stand up? From my experience drug dealers were usually the first to flip. Not only that, the police didn't seem to care much about Dominican drug dealers, but would foam at the prospect of taking down a crew of Southie hoodlums.

I explained this to Sal and said, "Thanks, but I'll pass and if you're smart you will too."

But as sharp as Sal was, he was also stubborn. "Listen," he said. "I understand how you're thinking, but I've got a friend who knows these Dominicans. He's the guy who turned me onto them in the first place. He's worked for them, vouches for them, swears they're solid. He said they would be more than willing to pay, Rick."

To me the whole thing stunk, so I asked Sal, "Who's this guy, your *friend*? Where'd he come from, how long you known him?"

"He's a local kid, been hanging around the bar for years. You'll like him."

I didn't *like* the whole thing, but I told Sal if you insist on going through with it here's a suggestion. "No pay-off every month. Make it a one-time thing to reduce your exposure."

Sal wasn't stupid, but sure as hell wasn't thinking this through. He said, "Oh, Donnie, my friend, he's got that part covered too. He's got a buddy, supposed to be an ex Hell's Angel. For a double C-note a month Donnie says the guy will make the collections for me." And Sal gave me a grin like we got this.

An ex-Hell's Angel? I knew a little about the Hell's Angels, had met a few in the can. It was a tight knit brotherhood, hard to get into and, once accepted, even harder to leave. If this guy really was a *former* Hell's Angel, how come he left?

More than ever I wanted nothing to do with it and doubled-down on my effort to convince Sal to do the same, but, as I said, the guy was hardheaded.

A few months go by and it's a Saturday night. I'm in Sal's bar having a beer with Eric, my old pal from the Rat days. I'm watching the bar, and the length of its packed with plain-clothes police. From my years on streets, and a decade in prison, I could pick out a cop easily. I said to Eric, "This whole place is cops."

"Yeah?" he said, looking around.

"Yeah, those guys," I said, pointing out individuals at the bar. "He's a cop, and he's a cop." Then one of them turned and looked directly at me. I stabbed my finger at him. "That guy, right there, he's fucking cop," I said. The guy turned back to his beer and lowered his head. "Jesus Christ, Eric, this whole place is cops."

I let Sal know too, but he swore that I was being paranoid. Paranoid? It was obvious. Why the hell didn't he see it?

Six months into the "Dominican shakedown," Sal's telling me one night how everything's going smoothly and that I'd missed out on a wonderful thing. I laughed because I was certain I'd missed out on nothing. Then I asked about his buddy Donnie and the HA who worked for him.

"Oh, they're both fine," Sal said, "and doing a great job."

I was certain they were.

I said, "Do yourself a favor. The next time you see your biker collector take his license plate number down and have one of your cop friends run it. More than likely he's a cop too."

A week later Sal reported that he had done what I suggested. He ran the biker's plate and came up with an address in Chelsea. But when he went to Chelsea to check the place out, a two-family home, the biker didn't live there. Sal said, "I confronted him about it later, and he explained it by saying that he lived there with his girlfriend. It was her house."

I said, "Oh, so his girlfriend's name's on the mailbox box, and not his?"

Sal nodded and grinned.

I said, "Sal, the broad don't exist. He's a cop and you're fucked."

The following Saturday, following an early morning run around Columbia Park, I stopped by The Sports Center Pub to see Sal. Richie, the clean-up guy, had just finished up mopping the floor. The odor of Lysol and stale beer filled the air. Sal sat on a barstool reading *The Herald*. He lowered it and glanced at his watch. "Hey, Rick, little early for you ain't it?"

Before I could answer, he said, "And early for them too." He nodded toward the large, side windows.

In the street next to the bar was an obvious police surveillance van, its windows tinted coal black. Tiny antennas sprouted from the roof like thorns from a prickly pear.

"They were there when I opened up," Sal said, looking around the room and commenting that the bar was probably wired too. He shrugged. "So what, I'm doing nothing but reading the paper. Let 'em sit there."

Then he took off his glasses, and his eyebrows went up. "But maybe not for long, Rick"

Pulling a roll from his pocket, he called Richie over and peeled off two twenties. He grabbed the janitor's hand and pressed the bills into it. "Richie here, make yourself a fast forty; go over that van and see who's inside."

Richie ambled out the door and, within a few seconds, we almost pissed ourselves laughing

Richie, all a hundred and thirty pounds of him, first went up to the driver's side window and, cupping his hands over his eyes, pressed his face to the glass and peered in, then turned, shook his head and shrugged. Sal signaled to keep going.

Richie climbed up on the bumper and grasping the wipers, peeked inside. He jumped off and shrugged again. Sal vigorously knocked with his fist now and Richie got real excited. He made little circles next to his head and mouthed that the engine was running. He ran around back and knocked on the windows. Sal signaled do it harder and Richie did. Then belted the sides for good measure. When he came back into to the bar, exhausted, the van drove away.

Less than a month later, Salvatore Grassi was busted as he attempted to purchase thirty-thousand Percocets from an undercover agent at Farragut Park in South Boston. I was right about Sal's friend, Donnie, who was a paid federal informant. And Donnie's friend, the ex-Hell's Angel? He was actually an undercover state trooper.

Oh, and the Dominican coke dealers that Sal was shaking down? Actually they were undercover DEA agents. Bad judgment cost Sal a long stretch in the feds.

The bartending gig was a good start but to remain on the street I needed to earn more money. That's where Eddie Cochran came in.

Eddie had been married to Cara's sister Grace and was divorced now like me. He was a "sandhog" a member of the Tunnel Workers Union, Local 88, with its hall in South Boston. When Eddie, a TK's regular, told me one night how much he made every week—fifteen hundred to my five—I wanted to join the union too and asked him, as a 'family member" if he could help me to get a book in Local 88.

16.

Sandhog

My first night on the job I was seven miles from Deer Island's wave-battered shores, and four hundred, fifty feet below the surface of Boston Harbor. The huge topside electrical generator dead, in a darkness that mirrored deep space, I had been ordered by the crew chief, to get off the train tracks and climb onto the slimy discharge pipe that ran the length of the tunnel. Prior to that we had been laying sections of twenty foot steel rails in a "switch" area that allowed trains, on the single access rail system, to get out of each other's way.

Officially sworn in as a member of Local 88 Tunnel-workers Union, I was assigned to work as a "shaper," someone who shows up on a job-site hoping to get picked for work, on the Deer Island Effluent Outfall Tunnel. At that time the project was grinding into the fifth year of its estimated nine-year completion date. Once completed the Outfall would be the longest underwater sewerage tunnel in the world.

The giant pumps silent and water level rising, I was still happy to be there when I recalled the other dark places I'd been in my life. Employed now in a respected profession, I'd rather be sightless hundreds of feet down inside the black earth than sitting in a DOC cell.

Wikipedia describes tunnel-workers as, "urban miners and burly construction workers." When I worked at TK O'Malley's and dealt with the public, I was always concerned about presenting the correct image. That wasn't the case with the Sandhogs, as Local 88 members are called.

The union membership consisted of rough men, and no one cared how you dressed, what you looked like, or what you might have done in the past, as long as you did your job. When I joined, I would estimate that half the membership had criminal records. Maybe a quarter of us were ex-convicts.

Like a prison environment, Local 88 was a man's world where just about every kind of problem was handled in house. If you had a beef with someone, you didn't run to your shop steward to complain. You either talked or fought it out.

That said, there wasn't much fighting, and most sandhogs got along fine, probably due to the fact that out of all trades: carpenters, laborers, electricians, heavy equipment operators, and even iron workers, tunnel work is perhaps the most deadly.

In my first five years as a sandhog, I was almost killed on two separate occasions. I suffered from cuts that required stitches, contusions, a chipped elbow, a broken nose, and second degree burns from welding and cutting steel. I broke my right kneecap, then later my left ankle. Sandhogs got along because their very lives depended on it.

The job was tough but I loved it, as most Sandhogs do. But like most organizations, a union is only as strong as its leadership, and we were lucky to have a great one in Scott Boidi, Local 88's Business Manager.

Boidi was smart, tough, and ambitious. He always had the memberships back. Boidi's star was also on the rise in the International. Our union was just one cog in the huge Laborer's International Union of North America, and our business agent had big, and very achievable, aspirations. Only one person could stop him, Scott Boidi.

In almost every construction trade members have drug and alcohol problems. The sandhogs were no exception. What was exceptional was the amount of drugs used. Alcohol, mostly beer by the case, would be smuggled down into the tunnel, concealed usually in huge lunch boxes. The drugs, mostly marijuana, but some crack and powdered cocaine, Benzos, and

Angel Dust as well, were also present. I couldn't care less what a man did on his own time, hell I partied myself on weekends, but when you're working underground it's different. As I said, our lives depended on each other and it was hard to depend on someone stoned.

At the time, the Outfall Tunnel had the longest underground single access rail system in the world, nine and a half miles from the shaft to the end of the line. On the "man-trip", the German-made trains that hauled sandhogs to worksites, it wasn't unusual for cars to derail and flip over onto their sides. One minute you were riding along smoothly, the next the car was on its side and being dragged down the tunnel.

Less common, though I saw it occur, would be a locomotive traveling between fifteen and twenty-five miles an hour passing by us the engineer, head bobbing up and down sound asleep behind the throttle and the Brakey, the Local 88 brakeman in back, curled up and sleeping as well. The fact that no was killed as a result was proof that God did shifts in tunnels too.

Soon after their release from prison, almost a year after my own, my former partners Sean and Danny were inducted into the union. Now all of us now had good paying jobs, but the scent of the old life was everywhere. Like an unsolicited aging whore, the streets continued to beckon. It seemed like every week there were offers from friends to re-involve myself in hardcore criminal activities: drug rip-offs and sales, armored car heists, loan shark activities, shakedowns, large scale credit card fraud operations, which promised to make me rich.

I'll admit that in a strange way it was nice to be asked, but I was done with that life; I had changed and so had the world. When I was young, rats, informants, snitches, whatever you want to call them, were almost non-existent. Now they were everywhere and hardly a month passed without me hearing about some formerly solid guy who had flipped on his co-defendants. If I could see it was OVER, why couldn't my friends?

In the union, I had found steady work, and envisioned a future there. I saw myself moving up in the ranks. I would become a shift boss and then eventually a shop steward. I even entertained thoughts about running for union office someday.

In 1999, Scott Boidi's star was still on the rise, and the big bosses from Rhode Island groomed him for the national stage. Our headquarters had moved from the decrepit building it had occupied for decades on the South Boston waterfront to a brand new million dollar building in Quincy, Boidi's hometown—the mortgage paid off in cash with Local 88 funds.

I couldn't believe my luck or how, in just a few years, how dramatically my life had changed. I believed now that all I had to do was work hard, keep away from criminal activity, and everything would fall into place. That's how it went for most people, right? But just when I thought that the worst was over, like snow in early spring, a blizzard hit and buried me again.

While I had been behind the walls, Elaine Carter would come up to visit twice a year. Midway through my eighth year she came by and, over the course of the visit, told me that she was experiencing trouble in her marriage. All I could do was offer advice and hope for Elaine's sake that things worked out, but they didn't.

I had been on the streets for about five weeks when I called Elaine and asked her if she would meet me for lunch. I wanted to catch up and, naturally, was curious about the status of her marriage. We met in a coffee shop in downtown Boston. She told me that because the problems in her marriage had accelerated, she was leaving her husband.

When next I saw her, a month or so later, Elaine had just graduated from nursing school. She said that her marriage was over and though she still lived with her husband was preparing to move on.

Although totally in love with Elaine, I refused to tell how I felt for two reasons. First, she was still with her husband, and second, she was emotionally frail at the time. Besides, I had nothing to bring to the table. Elaine was at the beginning of a brilliant new career while I was an ex-con/bartender recently spit from prison. I could offer my love, but it could not be called a tangible asset.

Still, we began to see each other and after Elaine finally left her husband the lunch dates became dinner dates, and late nights. In 1998, both of us working hard and committed to each other, we moved into a tiny third floor flat in a Victorian home in Dorchester's Pope's Hill section.

The new arrangement wasn't all roses. Elaine's divorce had taken a nasty turn, so she was fragile and edgy at times while I dealt with my own demons, deep-seated anger related to my years in prison. At her insistence, I participated in weekly anger management counseling sessions, and every few years went in for a "tune-up," which helped me to better deal with my problem. I realize today, more than ever, that Elaine *always* knew what was best for me.

Tunnel Nuts

On the union front things were really starting to look up for me. In 2001, while assigned to my new job as a "top man's helper" on The Braintree-Weymouth Tunnel Project, I was summoned to the union hall by Business Manager Scott Boidi. In his office he told me that on the next big job he planned to promote me to the position of steward. Again it happened that I *envisioned* myself a leader, and Boidi would put me in a position to lead. Unfortunately as we talked I noticed that Boidi was high, whacked out of his gourd high.

Drug use, particularly the use of cocaine and Percocet, was wide spread in the union, but this was a weekday, one o'clock in the afternoon, and Boidi, a guy who I thought had the world by the balls, was higher than the Hancock Tower.

I had heard rumors concerning his escalating drug use, and how certain union members had been feeding him coke in exchange for good jobs. In his office that day I had the first of many conversations with him about addiction. I hit him with every argument. "Can't you see they're using you, Scotty? You're throwing your career away" (And mine too). "You're better than this. You're going to lose everything. Think of your family."

None of it worked. All Boidi did, paranoid as a hoot owl, was wire the union hall up with thousands of dollars of electronic surveillance equipment, hunker down, and wait for the law enforcement tsunami.

My motives weren't entirely selfless, but I genuinely liked and respected the guy. He had done a wonderful job of rebuilding the Local and was poised to move up the ladder himself. Soon Boidi would legitimately earn a salary of close to two hundred thousand dollars a year, not bad for a guy with just a high school diploma.

Soon the rot at the top sunk into the ranks. Drug dealing on Local 88 job-sites, clandestine before, was out in the open. There were other rumors of DEA investigations and undercover cops infiltrating the union, and talk of a federal racketeering probe.

For me it was a catastrophic turn of events. In my early union years, everything was great. There was unity and a real sense of being part of a hard-working, hard-partying brotherhood. It was almost like being in a gang, except gangs are involved in criminal activities and unions aren't supposed to be.

By 2001 Boidi was totally out of control, and more and more it seemed that ex-cons were being inducted into the union, directly from prison. Hey, I was an ex-con and all for giving someone a chance—if he was solid—but some coming into the union now were snitches, known goddamn rats.

My ship was going down fast. There were more rumors concerning Local 88 members who, allegedly, had involved themselves in hardcore criminal activity. Sandhogs punched into work, left the jobsite to commit serious crimes then used the job as an alibi. I admit it was hearsay, but one was thing was certain; the heat was on and state police helicopters hovered over the job site for days.

Mornings, when I'd report for work the Hoghouse, the union building containing the lockers, showers, and toilets, was an open drug bazaar: Cocaine, Percocet, grass, and benzo transactions taking place everywhere. I worried that the cops would throw a net over the place and arrest everyone inside.

Here's how crazy it got. On a graveyard shift in 2002, a drug-addicted sandhog was cutting locks off lockers searching for drugs. But one locker he should have left alone. When the lock hit the floor and the door swung back, an avalanche of weapons piled up at his feet: semi-auto rifles, handguns with silencers, loose ammunition, and thirty round clips.

When I came in the next morning the Hoghouse was still in an uproar, not because of the guns though. No, everyone was pissed at the thief, and the low-down actions of a union brother.

Even a blind man could read the writing on the wall.

Just reporting to work became a cause for concern. Rank and file members were forced to choose sides as talk of an open revolt against Boidi gained momentum. Then, early one morning before the workday began, a take-over faction led by an Irish maniac stormed the Braintree-Weymouth jobsite. He stalked the yard wearing a black, Che Guevara-style beret and waving a .50 caliber Desert Eagle pistol, ranting about how all of us were now in a state of "DEFCON TWO" until cops came and hauled him away.

Bridgewater State Hospital had nothing on Local 88.

Within a short time, federal agents raided the union hall and arrested Boidi. When some of his closest union confidants testified against him, he was convicted of federal racketeering charges, and embezzlement of union funds, among other crimes, and sentenced to seven years in prison.

Along with Boidi went my future in the union.

17.

All Lies

In the middle of 1999 just after supper one night, the kitchen telephone rang. My brother Ronnie was all pumped up and shouting into the phone. "Rick, Frank's brother, Michael MacDonald, wrote a book. He's on the radio right now, and he's saying that you murdered his brother."

My head was spinning. "What? He said *what*?"

"He just got off the radio. He was talking about this book he wrote, *All Souls*, and in it he says that you murdered his brother, strangled him or something."

The little son-of-a bitch. Frank "The Tank" MacDonald had been dead, what, fifteen years? And his brother writes about it now, something he personally knows nothing about?

In the days following the 1984 hold-up police, in an effort to make an arrest, had spread the lie around Southie that the Tank had been left to die. When that hadn't gotten the result they hoped for—someone to snitch on me—they'd started a new rumor, Tank had been murdered. But no one believed them.

Now Tank's younger brother, Michael MacDonald, implied on a radio show that I had murdered my friend, possibly strangled him, although an autopsy had proved conclusively that Tank had died from a gunshot wound.

Infuriated, I reached out to an associate who thought he knew where MacDonald lived. I drove into town like a maniac, picked up my pal then raced to MacDonald's house, but no one was there. At least no one responded to the pounding on the door. It was probably a good thing I didn't find him that night.

MacDonald's book, *All Souls: A Family Story from Southie*, quickly became a best seller, and for a time every week it seemed like there was another article concerning it in the newspapers. MacDonald went on a whirlwind book tour and spoke at dozens of readings. But there were others from Southie, besides me, were just as unhappy with what he had written.

One article in *The Boston Herald* described an episode where MacDonald had just taken to the stage to do a reading in some hall when hecklers from South Boston stood up and screamed and shouted at him. The article stated that, "he fled (the stage) in terror."

From my perspective it was sad because MacDonald did have an amazing tale to tell, and he was a good writer. But he had woven into the story a series of incorrect claims and other disingenuous information. His brother, Frank "The Tank" MacDonald, wasn't strangled. The autopsy had proved that conclusively. Nor did the Greek, who had nothing to do with the Medford heist, buy himself a small restaurant with "blood money" from it as was stated in *All Souls*. I wanted to confront MacDonald and have him explain, in a courtroom, where he got all the *mis*information.

When, during an interview on the popular local TV show *Chronicle,* MacDonald said that Tank had been murdered by his cohorts; I began to contact attorneys, but each one I spoke with said the same thing, you may have a case of libel here, even though MacDonald had never used my real name, referring to me instead as Ricky Marino, an ex-state trooper and former bouncer at the Rat, and a rising South Boston gangster who became Tank's best friend.

But no matter how promising the case might have been for an attorney, no one would take it. I didn't have any money and no attorney was willing to take the case on a "contingency" basis. The reason was simple. A monetary settlement tied to a proven libelous statement would be based on how the statement affected my ability to earn a living and/or my reputation. Well, a long as there were tunnels, I'd work. Reputation? I was ex-con and as far as the lawyers were concerned, I had no reputation.

It took years for me to find an attorney. Boston lawyer Michelle Grenier agreed to look into the situation, and in 2002 filed a multi-count libel and defamation claim in Suffolk Superior Court against MacDonald, and WCVB-TV (Channel 5), which broadcasts the newsmagazine *Chronicle*. I caught a bit of luck because all of this happened just a week before the statute of limitations to file against MacDonald was due to expire. Grenier would not actually represent me on the matter but she felt I'd been wronged. By filing the action, Suffolk Superior Court NO. SUCV2002-03934, she hoped that it would allow me more time to find an attorney to litigate the case. I never did.

Neither MacDonald nor Channel 5 ever filed a response to the claim and the case was eventually dismissed, without prejudice, in 2003. Then in February, 2005, *Boston Globe* columnist, Alex Beam, wrote an article, *Tangled Tales from Southie* which detailed the problem between Michael Patrick MacDonald and me. The article's opening line said it all: "It's fair to say that the events of July 17th, 1984 remain in dispute."

But not for me or Medford Police Captain, John Keating who, when interviewed in the same *Globe* article said, "an autopsy was performed on the dead man and showed he died from a single bullet wound to the upper back."

Beam went on to say, in regards to MacDonald's book *All Souls*, "MacDonald writes that his mother learned from the coroner that Frankie had been strangled, presumably so he wouldn't squeal to the cops."

Near the conclusion of the same article Beam went on to say, "Reached by telephone, MacDonald said he knew of no lawsuit. He alternately claimed to be too busy to discuss Marinick's story and pled ignorance about the facts of the armored car heist described in his book. 'Ricky was there? I didn't know that,' he said. Switching gears, he said, *All Souls* is a memoir. I'm not talking about Ricky. I don't engage in the whole blame thing. He's on his journey; I'm on mine.'

Well, during his *journey*, in an attempt to inject some cheap *National Enquirer*-type sensationalism, and while making the rounds of his book tour, MacDonald implied that I had killed his brother, a close friend.

It is a false accusation that continues plague me.

In the end though the people that mattered the most, the police, in particular the Massachusetts State Police, put no stock in MacDonald's claim.

Reunion

In late fall 2003, my mother called my apartment. "Ricky, the state police are looking for you."

I was surprised but this was my mother so I kept my voice calm. I said, "State police? What do you mean, Ma, what for?" I wasn't a bit nervous and it actually felt good knowing that I hadn't broken a law in years.

"They want you to call them," she said. Then gave me a number, and a name."

I'm thinking they won't be getting a call back from me, until I recognized the name, Bob Murphy, Captain Bob Murphy. I remembered Murphy as a classmate from the academy. Still I was hesitant.

"I don't know, Ma," I said, "about talking to cops. I haven't done anything."

"Call him, Ricky, he really wants to talk to you," she said.

Great.

I waited an hour then dialed the number. Captain Murphy picked up. "Rick, how're you doing," he said, sounding pleased.

"Murph, how you doin' man? Made captain, you bum?"

Murph chuckled. "Ya, I'm doing alright, you?"

I told him that I was doing great, then quickly filled him in on what I'd been up to. I said, "So, what's this about, Murph?"

"It's 2003, Rick, and the 25th anniversary of our graduation from the academy's just around the corner. The class is planning a reunion at Lombardo's in Randolph, and I'd like to know if you could make it."

"Murph, you're kidding me, this some kind of ambush?"

Murphy laughed. "No, I'm dead serious," he said. "You graduated with the 60th RTT and, if only for a short time, were a great trooper. You never tarnished the badge. Hey, you screwed up, but you did your time. Bottom line, since you're doing the right thing now, we want you there with us."

"You said 'we'. "What about the classmate that gave me the speeding ticket last year? You heard about it? There's gotta be others who don't want me there."

"Ya, I heard about the speeding ticket," Murph said, "and what that guy did was lousy my opinion, but you're right he'll be there. As far as everyone else, we took a consensus and the majority of the class wants you there. What do you say, Rick, will you attend?"

"Gee, I don't know, Murph, it's still kind of …"

Murphy said, "Hold on a sec, I've got someone else here who wants to talk with you."

A deep voice came out of the phone, "Hello."

"Who's this?"

"It's Oscar, Rick. Oscar Langford. Actually it's Major Langford now."

I couldn't believe it. Oscar Langford III had been a hard charging recruit at the academy, one of only two black men in our class. We spoke briefly and I congratulated him on his career advancement.

Oscar said, "Are you coming, Rick? A lot of guys would like to see you."

The whole thing was surreal, but I couldn't say no. I thanked both men for their kindness and consideration and told them that I would attend.

On February 28th, 2003, the night of my 52nd birthday, the lovely Elaine and I entered the grand ballroom at Lombardo's where the 25th Class Reunion of the Massachusetts State Police 60th RTT was in full swing. In attendance that night were eighty-two police officers: majors, captains, lieutenants, sergeants, detectives, road troopers, and one convicted, South Boston, armored car bandit.

When I entered, I didn't know what to expect. Would the room suddenly fall silent? Would a few individuals try to kill me with stares? But nothing like that happened. The music continued to play, and a few men turned from their small circle conversations to lift their glass or bottle and smile.

Kathy Colletta, now a state police major and the sole woman graduate of our class, approached and gave me a warm hug. I introduced her to Elaine and, like that, one of the best nights of my life began.

Elaine and I were seated at a table that included retired academy commandant Captain John F. Kennedy along with my old friends: Sergeant Steve Long, Captain Brian Lilly, former trooper Paul Maher, Sergeant Bob Blazuk and their wives.

I mixed with the crowd and shook hands with many of my other classmates, guys like Al Manzi, Wayne Mackiewicz, Jim Grady. From each I felt a sense of genuine warmth and saw the joy in their eyes that I had made it back. Eddie Burke, the trooper who years before had transported me to Somerville District Court, with that side trip to Dunkin Donuts, and I tapped Heinekens and shared some laughs.

As I expected there were classmates that showed me their backs. I understood but didn't need them to like me; I had moved on. Those who refused to, including the trooper that had issued me a speeding citation the previous year, were seated together at a far corner table.

That night I received nothing less than a lot of support and offers of help from most of the troopers there. I assured my old friends that I was fine, and that my life couldn't possibly be better. I had to look no further than my new wife, Elaine—we had been recently married in Key West--sitting next to me to realize how lucky I was. Adrift for years, I had found my anchor. Elaine called me the prodigal son. After squandering what may have been a brilliant career with the state police, I had been welcomed back. It was the best birthday present ever.

Two years later after *Boyos*, my first novel, was published, I was asked to address a large audience of inmates at Boston's tough South Bay Correctional Center. At the conclusion, I fielded questions and big, black guy in the audience raised his hand. He said, "So, at one time you was a cop, then you was a gangster. What are you now? Cop or gangster?"

I said, "Neither, today I'm just me."

Boyos

In 1987, while sitting in a Bridgewater cell, I realized, for the first time, there was a treasure trove of stories waiting to be written about South Boston. By 2002 writers were just beginning to tap into the South Boston goldmine. It seemed like every time I opened a newspaper, there would be another story about Jim Bulger, who had been on the lam for seven years and was the target of an FBI manhunt.

In his columns for *The Boston Globe*, Mike Barnicle, had developed a penchant for describing members of Bulger's former gang as *boyos*, an Irish word that meant boys or lads. The first time I saw it I thought what a great title it would make for a movie on the Southie Irish mob. But movies are made from screenplays, and if I planned to write one I had better learn how.

So with a great title, *Boyos*, I signed up for an evening screenplay-writing course at Emerson College. After work, on my way to class early one night, I was pulled over for speeding by the state police. Only going forty in a thirty mile an hour zone I wasn't overly concerned. I relaxed even more when I recognized the trooper approaching the car as a former classmate of mine. Immediately it was obvious that Bill, now a sergeant, recognized me too. I knew I had a problem when, without changing expression, he requested my license and registration.

I handed him the documents and said, "Hi, Bill, sorry if I was going too fast, but I'm on my way to school. Any chance of a break, maybe getting a warning this time?"

Bill glared at me like I had just taken a dump on his spit-shined boots. He said, "After what you've done, *Mr. Marinick*, you get no breaks." He walked away then turned around, faced me and said, "And I'm writing you up for no seat belt too."

Steaming mad, I watched him in the side mirror return to the heavily manned speed trap and gesture back toward my car. I was certain that he was telling the other troopers about my background, the piece of shit he was writing up. Sgt. Bill had no a clue how far I had traveled to get to that place, and I wasn't going to allow him to ruin my day.

When he handed me the ticket, I said, "Thanks Bill, and you have a nice day, because I'm *still* going to have one."

The next day I paid the fine and over the next five years, due to insurance surcharges, I had to shell out over another grand.

I completed the screenplay course and decided to write a novel instead. I developed an idea for the plot then carried a notebook to the Braintree-Weymouth Tunnel Project job-site every day and began to write. As a "top-man's helper," between picks with the huge crane that sent equipment and supplies down the shaft, I utilized any down time to work on the novel.

At the end of the day, I went to the gym then on the way home, would stop at the Thomas Crane Public library in Quincy and force myself to sit and write for an hour. Slowly the story took shape. Like one of those old Polaroid photos that popped from the camera and you watched it develop, every day more of it came into view.

Boyos would be a brutal tale of two South Boston brothers, mid-level operatives in the local Irish mob, and their struggle to survive in a world where lions ruled. It would be authentic, told by an insider, and the first South Boston novel ever written on the topic.

People told me that one of the toughest things to write was good dialogue, but I had an excellent model to emulate in the George V. Higgins crime classic *The Friends of Eddie Coyle*, and it quickly became my Bible.

Writing in long hand it took two years to finish the project. Call it ego, confidence whatever, but I never stopped believing that I was creating something special and that it would be published.

I contacted my old friend and fellow writer, Jean Fain, and told her about *Boyos*. Jean was excited and said that she had a friend at *The Boston Globe*, a Pulitzer Prize winner, willing to look at a few chapters.

But when I spoke with him the following week, the news wasn't good. I am certain the writer meant well, but he believed the story was too dark and the characters too violent. I was disappointed but hardly deterred, and had no plans to tone down *Boyos*. It was an authentic story, and the Southie I knew was like the goddamn Wild West.

Then Elaine had an idea. She had a friend, John Rapinchuk, who lived in San Francisco and happened to be a Boston crime buff. I mailed Rapinchuk the manuscript, and he called me a week later to say that he had really enjoyed *Boyos*, and had a friend, Kate Mattes, who might also.

Mattes was the owner of the well-known mystery/crime emporium, Kate's Mystery Books in Cambridge. I sent her the manuscript, and she liked what she read and connected me with a small Boston publishing house, Justin Charles & Sons.

Justin Charles owner, Steve Hull, was initially impressed with the work, but he had some reservations. He wondered if anyone would buy a book written by an ex-con? After Mattes and I convinced him they would, Hull bought the publishing rights to *Boyos*, and then Mattes got her old friend, prolific Boston crime novelist, Robert B. Parker, to write a great blurb for the cover.

Boyos, a Kate's Mystery Books imprint, was released in September of 2004 to critical acclaim, and almost immediately there was a media frenzy. Soon lengthy articles on the author appeared in *The Boston Globe, Boston Magazine, The Baltimore Sun* and *The London Daily Telegraph*, among other publications. I was interviewed on TV, and NPR.

Then when it seemed like things couldn't get any better, they did. Renowned, Boston born crime novelist, Dennis Lehane, graciously agreed to introduce me at a reading for *Boyos* at the Boston University Barnes and Nobles bookstore. *Boyos* would remain on the Boston Globe top ten-bestseller list for thirteen straight weeks.

Even Hollywood came knocking. An old friend, Brian Goodman, a former Southie hoodlum turned successful actor, got a copy of the manuscript into the hands of a big-shot producer. Two weeks later, while I was vacationing Key West with Elaine, the producer called to say that not only did he want to option *Boyos* for a movie but asked if I could write the screenplay. I was ecstatic. On top of the world, Ma!

But not for long.

Steve Hull had the exclusive right to sign-off on film offers and turned the producer down flat—then he offered me an option for a second book.

Out of Work but Not Out of Luck

In 2004, with the Braintree/Weymouth tunnel project nearing completion, I was laid off. The guy who replaced Boidi as Business Agent had his own favorites, and I wasn't one of them, so it was the last time that I worked as a sand hog. For months I was unemployed with no money coming in. The only thing that saved me was the forty grand in my union annuity. For over a year, I used it to pay the mortgage on the South Boston home that Elaine and I had recently bought.

I worked hard on my second novel. After *Boyos'* success, my publisher had requested a sequel, but I was against it. Because I believed that sequels, in general, were just more of the same old thing. I pitched him a new tale, which would feature characters from *Boyos*, but have a brand protagonist, and this time one colorful enough for series potential.

The novel, *In For a Pound*, featured a Southie born and raised former state police detective recently released from prison. He returns to his hometown and finds work as a bartender. When a former friend, a Boston police captain, comes into the bar and requests his assistance on a mysterious case, the ex-con cop is pulled into a deadly web of treachery and deceit.

Thrilled with the new concept, I wrote every day disregarding the naysayers that said, as a writer, I was probably a "one trick pony," but I intended to prove them wrong.

For a long time, I attempted to find steady work as a laborer. At one point I was desperate enough to approach an old Mafia associate rumored to have union connections, but all I got were empty promises.

Eventually I got a "book" in Local 82, the South Boston Teamsters. I didn't come into the union with pie in the sky dreams that I would always be working. As usual, the local's business manager, John Perry, had his own favorites, and I wasn't one. I had to take whatever I got, and I hustled for it.

Work for the Teamsters involved setting up booths at the big trade shows at the new Boston Convention and Exhibition Center, as well at some of the smaller venues like the Prudential Center located downtown. Desperate to work I made it a point to show up at the job early, tools in hand, hoping to get picked. But like a scene from the movie *On the Waterfront*, generally the hiring boss would approach the crowd of hopefuls, usually fifteen or twenty men, and point over my head to some stoned-out friend of his without any tools.

It was frustrating as hell. If I thought the Teamsters held the key to my future, I would have done what I had to do to guarantee that I worked, and slept well after. But I had proven there was more to me than just rolling carpet, climbing ladders, and slapping together a booth for Proctor and Gamble or Chevrolet. With the success of *Boyos*, I knew I could write.

The passage of time demonstrated how lucky I was *not* to have been part of Perry's crew. In 2012 he and several of his cronies, following a multi-year federal investigation, were hit with a 30-count indictment that included, among other charges: racketeering, extortion, mail fraud, and theft of government money. In November of 2014 Perry was convicted of various counts of racketeering and conspiracy related to extortion at Boston trade shows and sentenced to federal prison.

In For a Pound

Writing my second novel, *In for a Pound*, proved tougher than writing *Boyos* because I had been part of that world. The new novel brought me into uncharted territory. How the hell do you write a mystery? I decided the best way to learn was to go with the masters.

I read novels by Elmore Leonard, Robert B. Parker, Raymond Chandler, and Dennis Lehane, but it only confused me. When I handed my publisher the first thirty pages of the new manuscript, he said it seemed like four different authors wrote it. It was obvious to me too, so I backed off, settled down and began to rewrite it. Slowly the story, loosely based on events in my life, began to take shape. And this time it was in my own voice.

With the release of *Boyos*, doors had opened for me. I received calls from literary agents and organizations requested my services as a motivational speaker. So it came as no surprise when John Dolan, Senior Supervisor of Program Services at the Suffolk County House of Correction asked if I would come to the jail and speak to the men.

When I visited South Bay, as it's known, I spoke from the heart. The thing I stressed most was to believe in yourself and in your ability to change, and everything else will fall into place.

That first speaking engagement quickly led to another when Mark C., an old bouncer friend from the Rat days, invited me to come to the jail where he worked, the Billerica House of Correction, and do the same thing.

The following week, for the second time in two months, I walked into a correctional facility neatly dressed in khakis, a pressed shirt and loafers looking every bit the professional.

When Mark and I met in the jail's lobby, the crazy bastard from the rock and roll Rat days, now a substance abuse counselor, looked more like a college professor.

Mark and I briefly caught up and then a corrections officer led us to the SAM, the substance abuse module, where fifty men were waiting to hear me. I took my place at an improvised podium, surveyed the crowd and saw, along with men who couldn't care less that I was there, many expectant faces. I realized that I had been just like them once, incarcerated and sitting in a room hoping to hear something from a speaker that might change my life.

I wasn't nervous because I already knew what my message would be: I'd done time and changed as a result. If I could do it, so could anyone. That first talk at the Billerica House, followed later by questions, went well enough that the administration asked me to return the following week, and then the week after.

After my third speaking engagement at the Billerica House, I was eager to do the same thing in other jails, so I drafted a resume and made a request of the captain in charge of the SAM unit. Could she get me a simple document from the Sheriff's office stating that I had spoken there?

The captain assured me that it wouldn't be a problem, but when weeks passed and no letter materialized, she told me, off the record, that the Director of Security had a problem with giving an ex-offender a letter of acknowledgement.

The praise from the staff that I had received didn't matter. Nor did the fact that I had been asked to return there twice. I have nothing against the jail's rank and file, who couldn't have been nicer. It was just the decision of one jerk-off in a suit. As I did everything else now, I turned it over and moved on.

In 2007, with assistance from Congressman Bill Delahunt, I was employed by the human services agency SMOC (South Middlesex Opportunity Council) and Sheriff Michael Bellotti hired me as a re-entry instructor at the Norfolk County House of Correction. In 2008 my second novel, *In For A Pound* was released. The book was the first of a planned series utilizing the same protagonist, a hard-nosed ex-cop named Delray McCauley, and his beautiful, private eye, sometime assistant, Macky Wainwright.

Local and national reviewers loved the book, as they had *Boyos*, but this time it wasn't enough. Unbeknownst to me, my publisher, in his personal life, was drag racing down a dead end street, and within weeks of the new novel's release, Justin Charles filed for bankruptcy. With zero dollars to publicize *In For a Pound*, sales were slow. It was discouraging, sure, but I had been there before.

19.

NCSO

I decided to take a break from writing and, instead, immersed myself in creating interesting courses for the men at the Dedham jail. For the next six years, my office a converted cell in the block, hardly a day passed when I wasn't reminded of where I had come from, and how easy it was to return. Everything I had dreamed of while serving my own time, I had now: a beautiful wife, a nice home, respect in the community, and a job that I loved.

But around me remained the stench from the past.

When I first began work at the jail I was encouraged by co-workers to leave its restrictive atmosphere at lunchtime. What they said made sense so at noon everyday I would drive a mile down the road to Needham's DiFazio Park, park at the edge of the ball field, and eat my lunch.

Halfway through a sandwich one day, I looked up at the rearview and noticed that a police cruiser had pulled up behind me. A few minutes passed and two more pulled into the lot forming, at the same distance, a semi-circle around me. My first thought was the cops knew who I was, and were curious as to why I was there. Then they rolled in closer. A cop got out and slowly approached. I got out too.

The visibly nervous cop said, "Excuse me, sir. Uh, can I ask what you're doing here?"

I held up my half eaten sandwich. "Eating lunch, what's the problem?"

The cop looked at his buddies outside now too. He said, "It's just that, well, I noticed your plate and ran it."

The vanity plate on my car said BOYOS, as advertisement for my first novel.

I was standing there in a shirt, tie, and dress pants, just an average citizen. To get the cops to relax, I said, "I work up at the jail as an instructor." Then showed him the jailhouse ID attached to my belt.

"Wow," he said. "That's pretty interesting." He came closer to me and grinned. "And I, uh, well I read your book."

We talked a little more about my new job at the jail, what I did at there and about my first novel, but the whole thing still stunk. This guy with the badge wasn't a fan, but a cop who only minutes before had concerns that I still might be dangerous. I never went back to DiFazio Park and ate lunch at the jail from then on.

In 2008 my mother was dying. Sick and in terrible pain, but stubborn as ever, for months she had refused to go to the doctor, and when she finally did, she was promptly diagnosed with Stage Four cancer in both lungs and her liver. My mother had been a smoker her entire life.

Our often-contentious relationship had mellowed over the years, especially following my release from prison. I had forgiven her for all the negatives that had been so much a part of my early life and focused instead on all the good she had done.

While I was in prison, whatever I needed, whether it was clothes, school supplies, books or money, Mum would send in. She never once complained about the hassle or cost. There were the visits too. Every three weeks, for a decade, she would be waiting for me in the visiting room of a half dozen different prisons, often after driving for hours to get there.

Did we still argue at times? Sure, but the problems were always resolved when I'd put my ego aside and call her, or she'd write me a letter. Years after she died, I was going through a bureau draw containing treasured memorabilia. Inside was a note my mother had sent me shortly before she passed. I guess I had forgotten about it but, boy, was I glad I kept it. This is what it said.

To My Ricky,

All that has been done for me in the past couple of months more than makes up for any differences we have had before. You are a true and caring son proved countless times in the past but reinforced these weeks.

I am a hot head. You are a hot head—so what—that is surface stuff. The 'Real' stuff has come blazingly to the fore and I know you Love me as I do you.

Have an easy conscience Ricky and do not FRET. All is well and I love you dearly.

Your Mom
Xxxooxxx

Since my brothers were living out of state when my mother was dying, I was the one who cared for her in her final days. I considered it a privilege to do the things that needed to be done: housework, food shopping for her and her kitties, trips to the pharmacy for her medication, or transportation to and from the doctor's office or hospital.

I always had a knack for making her laugh so right up to the end, I never let up in the humor department. At the time, I drove a little hot rod, a 2008 Mazda Speed 3, and when I took her to the hospital, just before a traffic light changed I'd say, "Buckle up, Ma, we're about to hit warp speed." Then I'd blast through a couple of gears as she squealed and pleaded for me to stop. "Pll-ease," she would say, "Ricky, you divil."

As her life slipped away, I was fortunate to have her admitted to South Boston's Marion Manor which was located just a few blocks from our home. Mum, always a huge fan of the Virgin Mother, was exactly where she was supposed to be.

I spent hours with her daily, usually in two shifts writing her eulogy in a chair beside her bed, even reading small parts of it to her. As hard as it was, I was happy to be there and to share this peaceful time with her.

On March 11, 2009, with her family around her, my mother died but I don't believe ever left me.

Jail Do

While I worked at the jail, SMOC partnered me up with another employee, James Bynum, a street kid from Roxbury, a great guy totally committed to helping the men.

What had begun as a part-time job became full-time within a few months, and my curriculum expanded proportionately. I ran eighteen groups a week at the jail, with Bynum doing the same amount. The classes were varied: substance abuse and recovery (including weekly AA and NA groups with outsiders brought in), Slow Burn Anger Management, computer training, English as a second language, screen-play and memoir writing, Men's Work, Alternate View, Life Skills, Current Events, creative writing, and poetry.

Boredom's a huge part of doing time, so to break up the boredom of jail life, I threw in a class that I created called *Alternate View*. In AV we examined paranormal events, conspiracy theories, ufo's and the like. The group was unconventional sure, but the men loved it, and the classroom was usually packed.

I took a little bit of heat from the administration for running such an unconventional class, but the funny thing the contents could be found any day of the week on the Discovery, Science, or History channels. It is my belief that any learning's good if it keeps inmates off their backsides, away from TV, and requires them to use their minds.

Unfortunately in any jail or prison, there are always inmates who believe that being a "convict" is what defines them. As a re-entry instructor I tried to get the men to think outside that box, beyond what they believed to be "true." I'd remind them of what the Spanish painter Pablo Picasso once said, "Anything you can imagine is real." Picasso meant it literally, and for me that included change. If a train wreck like me could, so could they.

From experience there are generally three types of inmates: the mentally ill, the ones just confused, and the real hard cases. Try as you might you can't reach everyone. The problem lies mostly with inmates whom you can never reach, the losers who refuse to make positive changes. They already know everything, and will do and say anything to prevent someone else from participating in a program that might save their life.

That's where South Boston author Michael Patrick MacDonald and his incorrect claims continued to haunt me, and had a deleterious effect on my work at the jail.

On at least a dozen occasions an inmate would approach with a strange, but familiar, look on his face. As soon as I'd see it I'd know what was coming. It would usually be someone who, maybe after a rocky start, was just beginning to come around and do well in groups, and it always began the same way.

He'd say, "Uh, Rick, 'cuse me. Uh, I was talkin' to one of the guys and he told me, in this book, *All Souls*, it says you murdered your best friend. Did you? I mean if it's written in a book don't it have to be true?"

I would become angry. I'd want to find MacDonald and confront him, really straighten his ass out. Instead, I would quietly explain the inaccuracy of his claims.

While I was at the Dedham House the "pigeons came home to roost" on more than a few occasions. While eating lunch in my office one day there was a knock at the door and an unfamiliar face filled the small window. I signaled him in and the door opened and a tall, good-looking kid, about twenty-five was standing there.

"Mr. Marinick? My name is Bill Connelly (not his real name). My father told me to look you up."

It was a good thing I wasn't in the process of swallowing because I would have choked. Yeah, he even looked like him. I said to the kid calmly, "Is your father a state trooper, a former classmate of mine?"

He broke into a wide grin. "Yes, he is sir. I mean *was*, he's retired now."

Man, what goes around comes around. The kid's father, Bill senior, was the same state cop that six years earlier had given me a speeding ticket. I said, "Your old man gave me the only a speeding ticket that I ever got in my life."

The kid blanched, his jaw almost bounced off the floor. I quickly added, "But you didn't," and directed him to the opposite chair. I said, "Sit down, we'll talk," and gave him half my sandwich.

From the conversation that followed, I learned that Bill Jr. had a substance use disorder, with a preference for narcotics. At one point a police cadet, he had been caught with drugs and fired from the post and the problems didn't stop there. He had stolen a safe from his parent's home then, allegedly, did the same to a neighbor, the crime for which he was jailed.

No one has to tell me that people screw up their lives and make mistakes, but no one's got a license to punish them forever. I worked with Bill Jr. the same way I would with any other guy that expressed a desire to get back on track. The kid needed a break and got one. I'd like to think that, maybe in a small way, it changed the way that his Dad saw things too.

A darker example of pigeons coming home to roost involved a former associate. I had exited one of the large housing blocks of the main jail and was approaching the Control module and the exit outside when I noticed an inmate approaching from the opposite end of the corridor. Dressed in an orange "pretrial" jumpsuit he was escorted by an officer and carrying a large box. A common sight I thought little about it until the inmate shouted, "Hey, Ricky."

My eyesight lousy at distance I had no idea who it was until we got closer. The inmate, Dennis, was a Townie, a Charlestown kid that I had known for years. We had done time together in Norfolk Prison, his cell next to mine at one point.

Like me, Dennis was a Teamster who set up trade shows at large Boston venues. Unlike me he was fortunate to be a "list" guy for one of the major trade show contractors, which meant it was rare when Dennis didn't work.

I had heard that, monetarily at least, life for Dennis had been pretty good, certainly much better than it had been for me. But I had also heard rumors, since they were none of my business I never looked into them, concerning activities that he may have been part of.

We paused in the corridor long enough to shake hands and briefly catch up. Dennis had been charged in two armored car hold-ups, one in which a guard was almost fatally shot. He faced twenty-five years *if* he pleaded guilty. He didn't the prosecutors would ask for life.

I can't say that Dennis and I were ever close, but we shook hands again and I wished him well knowing, more than likely, I'd never see him again. That morning I walked out of the building and, blasted by crisp spring sunlight, was never more grateful for my own freedom. I recalled my time prison and realized, again, if I hadn't built a foundation utilizing the building blocks of education, spiritual awareness, and deeper personal insight through counseling, there was a very good chance I would have ended up like him.

My former partner Danny, part of the gang, was also sentenced to twenty-five years in a federal penitentiary. Since I've hit the streets again, over twenty years ago, many former friends and associates have been re-convicted of serious crimes. Some serve sentences today in excess of forty years.

I was lucky and to a degree smart enough to remain on the streets but elements of the old life, even years after my release, continued to haunt me.

While I worked for SMOC at the Dedham House I was fortunate to be invited to attend various seminars, the focus of which usually involved one of four topics: drugs, gangs, prison education, or recidivism. While attending an education seminar at the University of Massachusetts in Boston, I met a woman named Ann. Ann was employed as a teacher by the Vermont Department of Corrections. We talked awhile and at the end of the conversation Ann invited me to tour her prison.

It just so happened that the following month I was scheduled to attend a *Habits of Mind* conference in Burlington, Vermont, which Ann had also planned to attend. I could make the side trip to her prison after.

Jump ahead a few weeks and I'm at the Habits of Mind conference where the majority of the one hundred or so attendees were employed by the Department of Corrections. During a break I was engaged in conversation with my new friend Ann and two other men; one the Director of Security for a large Vermont prison.

As we talked he said, "So Rick you're from Boston huh?" When I told him I was he said something that floored me. "You ever hear of a guy named John Bianchi?"

Bianchi? I'm thinking, you're kidding me, right? He wasn't. I told him what I knew about Bianchi, the main thing? Whatever came out of his mouth was a lie.

Both men agreed and said that Bianchi was a real smooth talker. Ever the conman he was serving time for a conviction related to posing as a state trooper, and kidnapping and robbing a Vermont couple. He was later convicted of posing as a US Marshall and robbing a convenience store in New Hampshire.

And it wasn't just guys like Bianchi popping up from my past. Even today, twenty years out of prison, they occasionally still do. For example, in the fall of 2012 I had just left a bookstore in Concord, MA, where a good friend, Jean Fain, was signing copies of her wonderful new book, *The Self-Compassion Diet*.

A nice, sunny day I decided to stay off the highway and take back roads on the return trip to Boston. At some point, stopped at a traffic light, I recognized a man panhandling in the middle of the street.

The last time I saw Connie Hughes I was in my cell at Norfolk State Prison. I was at the desk writing when Connie came in, grinding his teeth, eyes bulging, and waving a small bag of coke. Struggling to squeeze the words from his throat he said, "Rick, wanna do a line?"

A line? Clean for over eight years I got scared just *looking* at him. I said thanks, but no thanks. Now, here he was panhandling in the middle of the street. I put down the window and said, "Connie, what the fuck you doing man?"

Recognition lit his eyes and a grin crushed his cheeks. He said, "Rick, how're you doin'?" Then, after not seeing me for sixteen years he said, "Wanna to do a *stick-up*?" Whoa. I handed him eighteen bucks, everything I had in my pocket at the time, and got the hell out of there.

Less than six months later Connie was a resident of the Norfolk County House of Correction.

Bouncing Back and Back Bouncing

In 2012 my employer, SMOC, lost a competitive bid to renew their grant at the jail and, after almost six years, I was laid off. My friend Sheriff Michael Bellotti graciously offered me a position with the new contractor but my time at the jail was over. Other projects required my attention. I put aside the novel that I had been working on and decided to write this memoir instead.

While Elaine remained the main breadwinner and paid most of the bills I had landed a new part-time job to help with the mortgage.

Eric Joseph, my old friend from The Rat days, had been supplementing his income by doing security work at an Irish bar in South Boston. Eric asked if I wanted a job? At first I declined recalling the old days of working in some of Boston's toughest nightclubs, the fighting and getting arrested; I was done with it.

But Eric persisted; he said clubs aren't like that anymore. Broke, I took the risk and twenty-nine years after quitting Club Soda I began working as a doorman again, and continued to follow my dreams.

Today it's not the door of an armored car that's about to pop, but a brand new career. In February 2015 I enrolled in the Addictions Counselor Education Program at the University of Mass. in Boston. In December 2016, after passing the tough state exam, I received my LADC II (alcohol and drug counselor) license—me an addiction clinician, who would have thought?

I read an Internet posting one day that described my background this way, "Within the first three months of his incarceration, he says he had a spiritual awakening and vowed to change his life." I was caught by surprise because that wasn't the case, and it was hardly that simple.

It took years to fully realize that the old life was behind me. When I entered the prison system, physically, I was in the best shape of my life; but I needed a lot more than physical healing. Hence my participation in the Boston University Prison Education Program in the belief an education might make me complete. It helped but something still was missing.

As a kid I spent summers at my grandparent's West Island cottage. Once, on a late Sunday morning I was out in the piazza and spotted, through the screen, a large raccoon wandering aimlessly around the back yard. He had thick, shiny fur, and muscles that rippled beneath it. My grandfather joined me and explained that the raccoon was sick, most likely had rabies. He said that soon it would die a horrible death.

Thirty years ago, at the roadblock in North Adams, I was like that raccoon. After I left Edgehill I was healthy and strong physically, but continued to suffer from, what I call a sickness of the soul. Had I not gotten the help I did I would have died on the streets or in prison. I believe three main things were responsible for that healing: the BU Prison Education Program, psychological counseling, and strengthening my connection with God every day.

Today life is much better but it's certainly not easy; nothing falls in my lap. I am thankful for the good people that worked hard to persuade me to give myself a second chance, and sad that so many others from the past, Frank MacDonald and Frank Oreto among them, never got theirs.

I am grateful and take nothing for granted, especially the peace that comes from reconnecting with my higher power and the realization that each day all I have to do is remind myself to get out of the way, and allow Him to work through me.

I've had ups and downs, sure, but sometimes the further you fall the higher you rise. I shouldn't be here writing this. I should be just a memory in the minds of a few people. I was black and dead inside before but now I am green, the color of new life and growth, and from recycling my past something better has risen.

Made in the USA
Coppell, TX
07 May 2022